Frank Batten

FRANK BATTEN

WITH JEFFREY L. CRUIKSHANK

THE IMPROBABLE RISE
OF A MEDIA PHENOMENON

Harvard Business School Press

Boston, Massachusetts

06 05 04 03 02   5 4 3 2 1

Library of Congress Cataloging-in-Publication Data

Batten, Frank, 1927–
    The Weather Channel : the improbable rise of a media phenomenon / Frank Batten with Jeffrey L. Cruikshank.
      p. cm.
    Includes index.
    ISBN 1-57851-559-9 (alk. paper)
     1. Weather Channel (Television station : Atlanta, Ga.)—History—20th century. 2. Television weathercasting—Georgia—Atlanta—History—20th century. I. Cruikshank, Jeffrey L. II. Title.

QC877.5 .B38 2002
551.63'09—dc21

                                   2002000219

TO MY UNCLE, SAMUEL L. SLOVER,

BORN LEADER AND ENTREPRENEUR

CONTENTS

ACKNOWLEDGMENTS

I have used the word *I* a lot in this book. It's true that I was the responsible authority, and the largest owner, of The Weather Channel. But the word *we* better captures the experience of building The Weather Channel. It took the best efforts of many people to create and launch our network, to lead it through its battle for survival, and to develop it into a medium that benefits the lives of millions every day.

I wish this book had the space to mention the legions of people who worked with so much devotion to build both The Weather Channel and weather.com, but I can mention only a few. In the beginning, The Weather Channel was John Coleman's idea and his dream. His energy, drive, and determination to get it started were remarkable. And The Weather Channel could not have survived without Dubby Wynne's commitment and tenacity, shown over twenty years. He made wrenching personal sacrifices to guide The Weather Channel through its mortal crisis, and with exceptional skill and faith, he oversaw its development through good times and bad. Mike Eckert brought an expert's skill and instincts for building revenues during The Weather Channel's period of largest growth. How could I fail to mention Gordon Herring, Alan Galumbeck, Nick Worth, and Doyle Thompson, whose ingenuity in creating the WeatherSTAR gave The Weather Channel its most valuable asset?

Without the devotion of hundreds of people, The Weather Channel could not have become *the* icon for weather of millions of Americans. I am referring to the meteorologists, on camera and off, the producers, engineers, technicians, marketing and sales people, graphic designers, managers, and scores of others who bring The Weather Channel into our homes twenty-four hours a day, seven days a week. Watching these people at work, it's easy to feel their pride and share their conviction that they are making life safer and better for the millions of devotees who trust and depend on The Weather Channel.

I approached the writing of this book with a good bit of apprehension. Before I dug into the task, the longest pieces I had ever written were articles, speeches, and memorandums of a few thousand words. My anxieties quickly disappeared, though, as I realized how much help I could get from so many people who have been involved with The Weather Channel. A measure of their pride is how eager they were to tell of their work and speak so openly about their experiences.

Jeff Cruikshank, my partner, researcher, and editor, was invaluable. He guided me through the intricacies of book publishing and added zest to my writing, and he conducted scores of perceptive interviews that helped me bring The Weather Channel's story to life. In short, Jeff's contribution was indispensable. I'd also like to thank all the people who agreed to be interviewed, many of whom also shared letters, memos, storyboards, newsletters, notebooks, and other historical materials.

Decker Anstrom, the current CEO of The Weather Channel, has succeeded Dubby Wynne as president of Landmark upon Dubby's recent retirement. Both Dubby and Decker have been enthusiastic supporters of this book project. They have given me all the help I could ask for.

Melinda Merino, my editor at Harvard Business School Press, has been generous with her advice and has kept my spirits high with her encouragement. Steve Schiffman, marketing chief at The Weather Channel, has been project coordinator in Atlanta and has always given prompt and responsive support.

My assistant at Landmark, Carolyn Redmond, cheerfully kept track of piles of papers and documents I collected, and she bore the burden of tedious fact gathering for me. My wife, Jane, has been an interested and adept critic of my writing as the manuscript progressed.

I owe thanks to these people and more. Without their help, this book would not have taken shape.

INTRODUCTION

The date, as I will not soon forget, was July 30, 1981.

Not surprisingly, for this time of year, it was a hot day in midtown Manhattan. If anyone had bothered to check—and I'm sure no one did—he or she would have discovered that July 30 wasn't a particularly interesting weather day, historically speaking. Connecticut's all-time record high temperature (102 degrees) was recorded on July 30, 1949. Out on the other coast, Oregon hit an all-time high of 107 degrees on July 30, 1965. And on July 30, 1979—two years before the event I'm about to describe—a forty-minute hailstorm had bombed Fort Collins, Colorado, with baseball- to softball-sized hailstones. Two thousand homes and twenty-five hundred automobiles were damaged. More than two dozen people were injured, mainly from being hit on the head by the huge stones.

The place was the Park Lane Hotel, on New York's Central Park South. When you're hoping to make a media splash, it makes sense to go to the media capital of the world.

The event was a press conference, at which Landmark Communications—the company of which I was chairman—was about to reveal its plans for the satellite transponder that we had leased fewer than three weeks earlier.

In the preceding hour or so, several dozen journalists had crowded into the hotel's ballroom. They represented both the mainstream press and a number of specialized trade publications. Even among these seasoned pros, I thought I detected a fairly high level of expectant murmuring. It had been only five years since Home Box Office had cablecast "The Thrilla in Manila," the memorable heavyweight title bout between Muhammad Ali and Joe Frazier, to a nationwide cable audience, thereby launching the era of satellite-based cablecasting. But satellite space was already at a premium, the industry was evolving quickly, and cable operators and pundits alike were abuzz with plans, schemes, and rumors. What would be the Next Big Thing to hit cable programming?

To that question, many in the Park Lane ballroom might well have been tempted to add, And who in the world is Landmark to be answering that question? Our company—a privately held, Virginia-based business that operated local newspapers, TV stations, and cable systems here and there across the country—had never been known as a programmer. In fact, we had never put together a program for distribution much beyond a few local TV stations and cable outlets. So what were we planning to do with our new, hard-won, and expensive satellite resource, which had the wonderful capacity to transmit a signal nationwide? Was television history about to be made?

I approached the podium. Red lights winked on above several TV cameras around the room. "Good morning," I began. "I'm Frank Batten, chairman of Landmark Communications. I'm here today to announce the launch of an exciting new concept in cable television. By this time next year, we'll be offering the nation's first all-weather television programming. It will be all weather, twenty-four hours a day. We call it . . . The Weather Channel."

First, silence. Then a collective groan went up from the audience. And from the tone of the questions that followed, it became all too clear what those groans meant. Isn't this a waste of a scarce transponder? Isn't twenty-four hours a day of weather going to be, well, dull? Who will actually watch this stuff?

Not an auspicious beginning for our infant Weather Channel—which at that point was little more than a good idea, good intentions, and a *very expensive* transponder lease. Nevertheless, we plunged, and ten months later, The Weather Channel went on the air.

Our first year was full of crises, culminating in a full-fledged near-death experience. We had to sell ads before we had any clear evidence that anyone was watching The Weather Channel. This didn't work very well. Unexpectedly, we were forced to part company with the talented person who came up with the idea of The Weather Channel in the first place—an unhappy but fairly common story, in entrepreneurial ventures. We had to completely rethink our business model, and then we had to persuade our customers to rewrite all of our existing contracts in our favor.

Yes, this was a rocky start, and no one who saw our product in the early days would have said that our programming was sophisticated. But over the ensuing two decades, we have greatly improved our product. By doing so, we have built one of the strongest brands anywhere in the media business. We have won legions of loyal viewers—many of whom, by the way, learned to watch our programming episodically, when they needed it, just as we had hoped they would. With a strong push from The Weather

3

Channel and other new networks, "narrowcasting"—the long-delayed potential of cable television—has become a reality.

We also have contributed to an enormous surge of interest in the weather, which in turn has helped our business and that of companies in related industries.

Most important, working with the National Weather Service and our other partners, we have helped save lives and protect property.

And through all this, we have made good money, and had a great deal of fun.

This book is about The Weather Channel: how it started, how it almost failed, how it has grown, how it works today, and where it may be going tomorrow. It's a story that embraces both big wins and big losses. It's a story about fast-moving technologies and how we have mastered them mostly before they mastered us. Part of this story involves The Weather Channel's rapid expansion from one medium to many media, and a high-stakes race in the late 1990s to leverage our product across many platforms before our competitors got there first. It's a story about personal satisfactions and frustrations, about struggles among a small group of extremely bright and strong-willed people, and about the building of a remarkable business in an unforgiving field.

It's also a book about a resourceful growth strategy of a relatively small, private newspaper company that grew rapidly in a variety of new and early-stage media businesses. In the early 1960s, what is now Landmark Communications owned the daily newspapers, a radio station, and a television station in Norfolk, Virginia. We were not large enough then to rely on the same growth strategy of much larger media companies: acquiring other newspapers and broadcasting stations. In most cases, bigger companies were bidding the prices up beyond our financial capacity. So we started looking for opportunities to enter media businesses that were in their early stages of development and had not yet been "discovered."

Our first new venture was to enter the Community Antenna Television business, now known as cable TV, when it was in its pioneering stage. Our cable businesses grew far beyond our expectations, and by 1980 were generating enough cash flow to greatly enlarge our financing capacity. And being a cable operator enabled us to embark on our next major venture, The Weather Channel. After that, we developed and started up a large number of specialty publications, a business that grew larger than any of our other media businesses. Along the way, we also acquired a number of small to medium-sized newspapers.

Our strategy of concentrating on early-stage businesses, underdeveloped companies, and a few start-ups was riskier than a traditional growth-by-acquisition strategy. But it enabled Landmark to grow larger and more profitably than our available resources would suggest. In the process, we were also able to develop products that were themselves public services.

I decided to write this book about The Weather Channel to illustrate a range of problems, opportunities, and risks that start-up ventures often encounter. And, more generally, I wanted to tell a story about entrepreneurship: about placing large bets after you've done your best to manage your risks, and then working like crazy to make those bets pay off.

Even on dark days when it looks like you may have made a really bad bet. . . .

CHAPTER ONE

FOUNDATIONS

F ans of The Weather Channel may be expecting me to plunge right into tales of isobars, rogue storms, and the art of corporate branding. All in good time. But for reasons I'll make clear, my story of The Weather Channel has to start with its corporate parent, Landmark Communications, of which I was in charge from 1954 to 1998.

The story of Landmark, in turn, has to begin with the man who founded the company that became Landmark: my uncle, Samuel L. Slover. When my father died while I was an infant, my mother moved us to live with the Slovers. My uncle became my

7

surrogate father, and he was the key figure in my life. He instilled in me many of the values and beliefs I still hold today, including a chronic, relentless dissatisfaction with the status quo. So I feel that I need to present "the Colonel," as he was known to family and friends. (The title was honorary, acquired when a Virginia governor appointed him to the rank of colonel in the state militia.)

Sam Slover was a classic entrepreneur. He surely was a gambler, but he was a gambler who knew how to manage his bets successfully. Over the course of his lifetime, against long odds—he was forced to drop out of college after his freshman year, when his own father died—he assembled a small newspaper empire in Virginia.

Sam Slover got an early taste of entrepreneurship when he was seventeen. With the help of his father's name as the cosigner on a note, he acquired an option on 100,000 acres of Tennessee land. The site was one he had taken the measure of while hunting. Coal was lying in abundance on the surface, and it appeared to be an ideal site for mining. He took his option to New York, intending to sell it to J. P. Morgan. Despite numerous visits to the great financier's office, hat in hand, he was never able to get beyond Morgan's assistant. At last, seeing few other options, he disclosed his mission. No, the assistant said forcefully, Mr. Morgan was not interested.

Soon after Slover's option expired, one of Morgan's companies bought the entire tract and developed it as part of one of the legendary coalfields in east Tennessee. This time-honored lesson—hold your cards close to your chest—taught to the young would-be coal pioneer by one of America's true business titans was one that young Slover never forgot.

BUILDING A SMALL EMPIRE

Having left college after one year, my uncle got a job selling ads for the *Knoxville Journal,* which was then owned by Col. Alfred Sanford, a state senator who had been his father's close friend. The paper was fighting for its life against entrenched competition, and it carried a crushing burden of debt. Sanford was so impressed with young Slover's salesmanship that he made him business manager when my uncle was only twenty-one. My uncle was able to double the *Journal's* circulation, but the promotion costs were so high that he could not stop the bleeding. The bank foreclosed, and the owners lost their stakes.

When the dust settled, the paper owed the East Tennessee National Bank and its other creditors $36,400. Sam Slover's sense of failure and culpability was agonizing; he felt personally responsible for the paper's failure. Accordingly, he resolved to pay back the debt in full, even though in 1894 $36,400 was a staggering amount of debt for a nearly penniless young man to assume. Legally, he was under no obligation to do so. Some today might view his determination to take personal responsibility for the debt as quaint—a relic of long-forgotten Victorian business ethics. I don't see it that way. Instead, I see it as early evidence of his personal integrity. It took a number of years, but my uncle eventually paid off all the paper's debts, one hundred cents on the dollar.

The story of how my uncle acquired his first serious equity stake reveals much about his ingenuity and daring. In 1901, while traveling through Virginia selling ads for a New York trade publication, he thought he spotted an appealing opportunity in Norfolk, where four competing newspapers were locked in a deadly struggle for survival.

With no capital and lacking any sort of introduction, he walked into the Richmond office of Joseph Bryan—then Virginia's wealthiest publisher—and asked for a loan to buy a newspaper in Norfolk. Taken aback by this brazen proposal, Bryan declined on the spot. My uncle then asked for a job selling advertising for Bryan's Richmond paper. No salaried positions were available, said Bryan. My uncle then proposed to work for no salary, if Bryan would guarantee him a 25 percent commission on any ads he sold to businesses that had never before advertised in the paper. To this proposition, Bryan agreed readily. Where was the risk?

9

In less than a year, my uncle was earning as much as the paper's general manager. The story spread within the newspaper trade, creating new opportunities for him. The owner of a failing newspaper in Newport News offered him a half interest if he could put that paper in the black within a year. My uncle did, and within another year, he was able to buy the other half of the paper. That was the first of several stakes in newspapers that he was offered on roughly similar terms.

But he was still eyeing that opportunity in Norfolk. In 1905, he persuaded a bank to lend him enough to buy one of the struggling Norfolk dailies, the afternoon *Public-Ledger.* His goal, then as four years earlier, was to consolidate the four dailies in Norfolk, beginning with the afternoon papers and moving on to the morning papers.

Years later, James Thompson, owner of the *Dispatch,* the other afternoon paper, told me how and when he decided to capitulate to the Colonel. One evening, while seated in the orchestra section of a Norfolk theater, he saw my uncle arrive with his fiancée. Thompson was then in dire financial straits, and was anguishing that night over how he would meet his payroll the following week. What he didn't know was that Slover was in the same fix—having to go to the bank every week before payday to scrape together the payroll. Thompson couldn't keep his mind on the performance. Meanwhile, he found himself looking at Slover, who was laughing and enjoying the show, seemingly without a care in the world. "I decided then and there," Thompson told me, "that if he was that confident, I had better get out." The next morning, he walked into my uncle's office and offered to sell his paper, which after the purchase became known as the *Ledger-Dispatch.*

During his long life—he lived to be eighty-six—the Colonel bought and rebuilt newspapers in the largest cities in Virginia: the Norfolk *Ledger-Dispatch,* Newport News *Times Herald,* Richmond *Times Dispatch,* Portsmouth *Star,* and Petersburg *Progress Index.* Each of the papers was in financial trouble when he acquired it, and under his control, each became the leading paper in its market. Later, he sold his out-of-town papers, but he continued to focus on consolidating Norfolk's dailies. By 1933, he accomplished his goal, and the combined Norfolk papers became the foundation of what is today Landmark Communications.

Throughout this most active period of his professional life, Slover established a distinct profile as a businessman. He had an exceptional talent for sizing up people and developing their skills. He sold substantial interests in the papers to his key managers at generous prices and arranged for the company to finance these purchases. He gave his employees large responsibilities and helped them succeed. In return, he demanded and got from them superior performance. He was effusive in his praise for high achievers, but could also be an unforgiving taskmaster if he concluded his faith had been misplaced. I've already mentioned his high ethical standards. The one thing he demanded from all his people was integrity—without it, one would not last long in his company.

I have a vivid childhood memory of one of my uncle's most significant business moves. We were spending the summer of 1932 in his oceanfront cottage at Virginia Beach. A man so obese he would be hard to forget came by on a Sunday afternoon. He and my uncle sat and talked in the living room we rarely used. After a while, the corpulent man stood up, shook my uncle's hand, and shuffled out. The Colonel came out on the screened porch and said he had just bought a radio station. He had paid $15,000 for WTAR in Norfolk—the first radio station in Virginia.

Some of the Colonel's newspaper lieutenants were dismayed, feeling he had saddled them with a money-losing business in an economic depression that was already full-blown in Norfolk. But thinking that radio would eventually become a serious competitor with newspapers, my uncle thought they needed to have a foot in that business, and thus made this first venture into broadcasting. Also he guessed that the station might help his *Ledger-Dispatch* in its competition with *The Virginian-Pilot*.

The consolidation of the Norfolk newspapers represented the culmination of a longstanding dream. After achieving it in 1933, the Colonel went into semi-retirement, leaving the management of his papers in the hands of the people he had been training for years.

THE NEXT GENERATION ENTERS THE PICTURE

Growing up in my uncle's home was the most important educational experience of my life. I never tired of hearing his stories. They were fascinating in their own right, and they also illuminated and defined his character and values. He never preached at me, and I don't recall him ever punishing me—at least in traditional ways—but when I disappointed him, he would just say, "I'm through with you," and then refuse to talk to me for a day or two. Being shunned by the Colonel was by far the most painful punishment I've ever experienced.

My uncle had high expectations of me, so high that I often felt I came up short. From an early age, I knew that he wanted me to succeed him in the newspaper business. But I had serious doubts about going down that road. I worried about living in his shadow. I wondered if I could ever live up to his high standards. I lived with those doubts for more years than I care to admit.

In retrospect, I can see that the Colonel wrestled with his own insecurities. He never got the chance to finish his college education, and I know the lack of that particular credential bothered him. In a subtle way, though, this insecurity worked to my disadvantage. Because I received such a superb education—from prep school through graduate school—the Colonel probably thought things should come more easily to me.

My uncle seemed to develop some measure of confidence in me when I went through a personal transformation in high school, at the Culver Military Academy in Indiana. In my early adolescence, up to about age fourteen, I was an indifferent student with minimal self-confidence. I ran with a pack of boys and followed them in whatever they did. The result was predictable: I was expelled from Culver during my first year for some serious misbehavior. Fortunately, I was allowed to return the next year. Culver had a brilliant system for developing leadership and stimulating a desire to achieve. This school—and particularly an inspirational track and boxing coach—motivated me to become a serious student and a leader among the cadets. My uncle was visibly proud when I earned some awards and became captain of my company of cadets, and he started talking to me much more seriously about the newspaper business at that time.

At the end of World War II, I was eighteen and at sea in the Merchant Marine. I decided that I would be a fool not to take advantage of the career opportunity my uncle was offering me. I had become intrigued by news and public affairs, and I was an avid reader of newspapers and news magazines. The thought of a career at the hub of the news business had begun to excite me.

I got a firsthand look at the newspaper business during summer vacations—first by working as a copy boy when I was a teenager, and later as a reporter and ad salesman during my years at the University of Virginia. But my love for newspapers probably came from all those years of listening to the Colonel talk about the business—whether in his office, at the dinner table, or at the end of the evening, as he sat in his favorite chair smoking his ever-present Havana cigar and regaling me with stories. He loved his work, and that love turned out to be contagious. It just took me a while to realize that I had caught the bug.

Upon graduating from the Harvard Business School in 1952, I went to work full-time for the Norfolk newspapers, the *Virginian-Pilot* and *Ledger-Dispatch*. After a year in advertising and promotion, I was put in charge of circulation. I soon concluded that the papers' managers had become self-satisfied and resistant to change. True, the papers were making respectable profits, but many of the department heads had been in their jobs for years, and they tended to run their departments as separate fiefdoms. This way of business wasn't a recipe for teamwork, and it seemed clear that teamwork was needed.

Then, in 1954, the role of publisher became vacant. Years earlier, the Colonel had turned over that position to his able general manager, Paul Huber, who successfully guided the papers through the Depression and World War II before dying in 1946. Huber's successor wasn't a strong publisher, and the papers drifted for eight years until he died unexpectedly. Then the Colonel was faced with a very difficult choice: to hire an outsider as publisher or to promote me, his young nephew. Because he was then eighty-one and wanted to see me in charge while he was still alive, he took another big gamble and named me publisher. Overnight, he had made a twenty-seven-year-old responsible for a newspaper company that had about 500 employees and grossed $8.7 million in 1954.

Before I plunged into the job, I asked my uncle for his final advice. "Just keep your bowels loose," he said with a twinkle in his eyes. It wasn't the most genteel figure of speech, but I knew exactly what he meant. This was a lesson you learned quickly as an athlete facing long odds: Stay loose, and just do your best. I've often recalled the Colonel's pithy advice when I've found myself in tight situations or confronted hard decisions.

For the next ten years, while I was still learning the newspaper business, I struggled to reshape management, improve our products, and strengthen the papers' market position. It was a difficult and unsettling task at first. With just two years of full-time experience, I had been placed in charge of people I had formerly worked for, most of whom were thirty to forty years older than I was. Fortunately, the company had an adequate pension plan, and most of these managers were near or past retirement age. In due course, I was able to replace them with my own management team.

I have barely mentioned our broadcasting stations, WTAR-AM and WTAR-TV. The radio station had been managed for many years by Campbell Arnoux, its president and general manager. Arnoux was an able, veteran broadcaster. He had kept the radio station in a strong number one position in the market for years. Soon after World War II, when television was in its infancy,

Arnoux proposed that the company apply for a television license in Norfolk. It's hard to imagine now, but many radio broadcasters in the late 1940s were wary of getting into television because of its high capital costs and unproven programming and advertising appeal. They took a wait-and-see approach. Having faith in Arnoux's broadcasting know-how, my uncle agreed to apply for a television license in 1948.

WTAR-TV went on the air April 2, 1950, the second TV station to broadcast in Virginia. By then, broadcasters and other entrepreneurs were tripping over themselves to apply for licenses in Norfolk and most other cities. Confronted with a flood of competing television applicants, the Federal Communications Commission moved slowly to settle on guidelines for awarding licenses. The Korean War intervened in June 1950, and license awards then were put on hold until November 1953. Thanks to Arnoux's foresight, WTAR-TV had the television market to itself for seven years. When I became the newspapers' publisher in 1954, our broadcasting stations were running smoothly and quite profitably thanks to WTAR-TV's head start. The Colonel's $15,000 bet in 1932 looked pretty good in 1954.

At age eighty-six, five years after having placed his full trust in me, the Colonel died. I feel blessed to have had the benefit of his love and his skillful mentoring for so many years. I believe that his character and values left an indelible imprint, both on me and on Landmark. Throughout my forty-four years at the helm of Landmark, his powerful example remained my benchmark and guidepost.

INTO A NEW INDUSTRY: CABLE

For example: My uncle had given me the opportunity to buy his stock in the company at a generous price after his death, and on a slow payment schedule. This arrangement was very much in the spirit of his sale of stock to his key managers, many years earlier, and it gave me a great personal benefit that I couldn't have enjoyed otherwise. I resolved to do something similar for key managers.

After an examination of the options, I created an executive stock plan, the fundamentals of which haven't changed since its inception. Key managers are offered stock at a formula price with a slow payment plan. Landmark has an option to repurchase the stock, either when a stockholder leaves the company or five years after his or her retirement. The stock price formula uses a multiplier of a five-year moving average of operating earnings; therefore, by design, the formula rewards long-term operating performance. Our plan is in sharp contrast with many stock option plans, which primarily reward short-term stock market performance.

The stock has produced an exceptional investment return for the managers we count on. In addition to the economic benefits to our managers, the stock plan has made them feel and act like owners. And this base of ownership is remarkably broad. Today, even after the repurchase of shares from stockholders no longer active in the company, 227 of our current and retired executives own 32 percent of Landmark's stock.

I mention the stock plan here because it underscores the continuing influence that Sam Slover had on Landmark—especially in those early days when I was still feeling my way. Throughout these learning and rebuilding years, and in fact throughout my tenure at Landmark, I continued to ask myself, What would the Colonel have done in this situation?

Beginning in the late 1950s, I found myself looking for a way to grow the company, much as Colonel Sam had done in his own pioneering days. My first instinct was to look within the newspaper and broadcasting fields, but by this time opportunities in our own fields were limited. Large media companies like Gannett, Knight, and Newhouse were bidding the prices of newspapers well beyond our reach. Circumstances were similar in television broadcasting. Network-affiliated TV stations had become highly profitable. Whenever an attractive station came on the market, it was flooded with rich offers. We didn't have the financial capacity then to build an attractive business paying rich prices in bidding contests to acquire newspapers or stations.

In 1963, therefore, I decided to start looking for a media business that hadn't yet been "discovered." Around this time, Campbell Arnoux suggested that we look into something called "CATV," now known as cable TV, which was then in its infancy.

Cable television was a central antenna service that supplied clear television pictures to small, mostly rural towns that were too distant from television transmitters to receive strong signals. To become a cable operator, you simply acquired a franchise from the local government, built a "head end" (an antenna to receive distant signals and modulate them onto coaxial cables), strung the cables on telephone and power poles, and connected lines to subscribers' homes.

Early cable systems carried three channels. In 1960 twelve channels became the standard—which in many areas represented more capacity than there were signals to be received.

On first blush, I liked the look of this odd business, which seemed pretty simple. The technology was not complicated. Marketing a cable service seemed similar to selling newspapers to subscribers—a business that we knew very well. And in most of these small towns, the service more or less sold itself. Rural people were tired of being out of the cultural mainstream. Just like their city cousins, they wanted good access to those all-powerful monoliths of American culture: CBS, NBC, and ABC.

I asked Dick Roberts, then research director for our newspapers, and Bill Diederich, our controller, to learn as much as they could about cable TV, and, if the field did indeed look attractive, to search for good opportunities. They took up their assignment with alacrity.

Because Diederich and Roberts were key players not only in the development of our cable TV company, but also in the startup of The Weather Channel, I want to introduce them here. I had met Diederich in 1954, when he was a second-year student at the Harvard Business School. He was interested in going into the newspaper business, and he had written to me to ask how I had become publisher of the *Virginian-Pilot* and *Ledger-Star* when I was so young. (The *Ledger-Dispatch* bought the Portsmouth *Star* in 1955 and the merged paper became the *Ledger-Star.*) I wrote back to say that it had helped to have an uncle who owned the place.

Not long thereafter, Diederich had to research and write a "long report" for his Advanced Production Problems course, and he wrote me to see if we had a production problem he could study. I invited him in, and gave him a complex production problem involving all of the papers' departments. He wrote such an incisive evaluation of the problem that we immediately implemented most of his recommended solutions. I was so impressed by Diederich's work, in fact, that I recruited him to join Landmark. He started our first research department, focusing on market and operations research, later helped install our first budget system, and then became corporate controller.

Dick Roberts, my other cable investigator, was a Naval Academy graduate who served for several years on submarines home ported in Norfolk. In 1961, he decided to leave the Navy for a business career and enrolled in graduate business school. He came to see me during his Christmas vacation in 1962, and I soon offered him a job to succeed Diederich as research director.

Roberts invited Bill Daniels—a pioneer in cable TV, an owner of cable systems himself, and the leading broker in the field—to visit us in Norfolk. Daniels gave us a quick seminar on the business, telling us many encouraging things about the business and also warning us of pitfalls. He persuaded us that cable TV could produce very attractive investment returns with only moderate risks. Inspired by Daniels, my colleagues and I let our imaginations roam. We envisaged cable systems that might one day be connected together—probably by microwave—and become the pipelines for transmitting pay television. And might not people one day be willing to pay a fee to see movies, sports events, and theatrical productions in their homes?

We next talked with Fred Lieberman, an entrepreneur who was building cable systems and who also had acquired the rights to other franchises that he found himself unable to finance. He was typical of many of the entrepreneurs then building systems. Not many large companies were in the business in 1964; Cox Enterprises was perhaps the largest. Many of the players looked a lot like Lieberman. He had started in the business as an engineer, working for a contractor building cable systems. Borrowing seed money from relatives, he built his first few small systems himself. Subsequently, by acquiring franchises, selling some, building others, and constantly trading up, he was able to amass a substantial number of cable systems. When the larger companies discovered cable and began bidding the prices up, Lieberman sold out for a handsome sum.

Lieberman offered to sell us an unbuilt franchise in Roanoke Rapids, North Carolina, about ninety miles south of Norfolk. The price was $15,000—but only if we agreed to let Lieberman build the system for us. Dick Roberts conducted a survey of the town and found that 40 percent of those interviewed were eager to get cable. That was better than we expected, so we bought the franchise. I asked Bill Diederich to take charge of building and staffing the system, and his involvement gave me some confidence as we ventured into this new field.

But there was one more hurdle we hadn't foreseen. The city council still had to approve transfer of the franchise to us, and the approval process turned out to be something more than a formality. Dozens of local contractors who were in the business of installing and maintaining TV antennas on house rooftops launched an aggressive campaign to persuade the council *not* to approve the transfer. The stakes were high: It was not uncommon for people in Roanoke Rapids to have twenty-foot or even thirty-foot antenna poles on their houses, and this was a good business for the contractors. In fact, antenna contractors already had started a national trade association, the specific purpose of which was to block the construction of cable systems. The fight in Roanoke Rapids, representative of a larger conflict, soon became bitter.

But the real problem that the antenna industry faced was that the technology simply wasn't good enough. Antennas had to be turned in one direction to get signals from Raleigh, in another direction for Norfolk, and in yet a third direction for Richmond. Reception tended to be unsteady and snowy, even with the large, ungainly antennas on the rooftops. When the winter ice storms came, the antennas grew heavy coats of ice, and sooner or later succumbed. Yes, this ensured a nice stream of repeat business for the antenna contractors, but it also frustrated consumers.

As a result, growing legions of local citizens wanted better TV reception, and they were more than willing to get their unsightly and troublesome antennas off their roofs. We were able to persuade many of these citizens, and voters, to go to bat for us with the council, and as a result, the council finally approved the transfer in 1964.

We found ourselves in relatively uncharted waters. As a newspaper publisher, Landmark had traditionally stayed at arm's length from our local governments, in an effort to protect our editorial independence. In the Roanoke Rapids franchise fight, we found that we had to get deeply embroiled in political maneuvering, dealing with local authorities and entrenched constituencies. We were fortunate that our first such fight was a relatively uncomplicated one. Subsequent battles were not so easy.

Struggles began erupting on other fronts as well. In those days, it was not always easy for cable companies to persuade the telephone and power companies to let them run cables along their existing poles. Some utilities, realizing that they held most of the good cards, were demanding exorbitant rates. Some wanted to get into the business of transmitting television signals themselves. Cable companies retaliated by threatening to install their own poles. In Roanoke Rapids, we engaged in testy negotiations with the telephone and power companies, but eventually we were able to negotiate acceptable agreements. Six years later, in 1970, the FCC finally laid out a set of rules prescribing reasonable pole-rental rates and also prohibiting telephone companies from operating cable systems in their telephone service areas.

Meanwhile, Fred Lieberman referred us to two more franchises that were for sale in the towns of Beckley and Princeton, two county seats in southernmost West Virginia that were nestled in river valleys surrounded by the Allegheny mountains. We bought both franchises for a total of $18,000. Slowly, we began piecing together a media business that could grow alongside our more traditional newspaper and broadcasting businesses.

Bill Diederich, who by then had become vice president and treasurer of Landmark, did a fine job of getting us started with our first few cable systems. It was soon obvious, though, that we needed a full-time management organization dedicated to cable. I hired Rex Bradley, a recently retired Navy Supply Corps Captain whom I had known in graduate school, to be president of the new company, which by now had acquired a new name: TeleCable.

Together, and over time, we learned that building cable systems could be an outstanding investment, particularly for private companies like ours that had the benefit of other profitable businesses. The reason was simple: Cable was a capital-intensive business that could produce high tax losses in early years through accelerated depreciation of construction costs. We could write off these losses immediately against our newspaper profits, and as a private company, we were not concerned about recording high book losses. As a result, our strategy was to concentrate on getting franchises and building our own systems, rather than buying going concerns that might have used up most of their tax write-offs. This allowed us to get a quick return of capital while at the same time we were building valuable cable systems. Meanwhile, subscriber penetration, revenues, and costs were reasonably predictable. In those early cable systems, mostly located in towns where off-the-air television reception was poor, almost everybody in town wanted cable service, and household penetration of more than 90 percent was not unusual.

Bradley mounted an organized effort to acquire new franchises. In 1966, most of the U.S. population lived in cities without cable franchises. In cities, off-the-air reception of local stations was almost always satisfactory. As a result, there was no consumer groundswell in support of cable in large metropolitan areas. Hence our focus continued to be on franchises in smaller cities, where people needed cable to get good TV reception. We won franchises in places like Columbus, Georgia; Spartanburg, South Carolina; and Racine, Wisconsin. We purchased systems that had recently been started in Kokomo, Indiana, and Bloomington–Normal, Illinois.

For the most part, marketing cable across these early systems was a joy. People wanted better TV reception at a reasonable price, and we gave it to them. The pent-up demand for cable service was so great in those early cable communities that operators reported a brand-new phenomenon: "truck chasers." When the cable crew showed up in a neighborhood, people would literally follow them down the street to find out how and when they could get hooked up.

It wasn't that our offerings were all that compelling in those early days. Cable was little more than a master antenna system, retransmitting clear signals from nearby stations, and—in some cases—adding duplicated networks, the occasional independent station, and Public Broadcasting System signals. At the same time, the industry wasn't entirely reactive. Cable operators sometimes tried to make cable more appealing by adding their own programming to fill vacant channels. Most of this was primitive fare—for example, news from The Associated Press wire scrolled in text across the screen, or a local weather channel with the forecasts in text and a stationary camera trained on dials showing temperature and wind speed.

Other offerings ranged from the high-minded to the silly. Many systems televised city council and school board meetings gavel to gavel. Some early systems boasted channels that cablecast live bingo games. One of the earliest systems aimed a camera at a bowl with a goldfish in it. Apparently, subscribers really did sit and watch the goldfish swim around, for when the channel was not on, people called the system to ask what had happened to the goldfish. Collectively, these programs were the first local-origination shows that many systems produced, and they were remarkably popular.

This primitive but lively programming had a major impact in the next stage of industry development, when the bidding for franchises became ferociously competitive, and bidders were compelled to commit to carry local-origination channels.

In many cases, the biggest obstacle to closing the cable sale with the consumer involved convincing people to take down their antennas. We offered rebates to people who would bring in their antennas. These campaigns, combined with the inherent appeal of our products, worked spectacularly well in many cases.

FROM THE MOUNTAINS TO THE CITIES

In 1970, a bold young entrepreneur named Ted Turner conceived a plan to extend the distribution of his struggling independent Atlanta television station, WTCG. (The call letters, capturing Turner's characteristic flair, stood for "Watch This Channel Grow.") Turner's station was losing money because it didn't command a large enough local audience share to compete for advertising with the Atlanta network stations. He reasoned, though, that if he could bulk up WTCG's audience by adding viewers from distant communities, that larger audience would be salable to more advertisers. Federal law did not permit broadcasting stations to extend their reach by building microwave systems, so Turner began

23

encouraging cable systems beyond his signal's reach to build or lease microwave systems to pick up his signal.

On the face of it, Turner's gamble seemed like a long shot. Why would distant cable systems want a signal from an independent station based in Atlanta? It turned out that WTCG's subscriber appeal was surprisingly strong, however, in part because Turner had the programming rights to Atlanta Braves games. At the same time, of course, cable systems were eager for programming to fill those still-empty channels. WTCG plugged a gap nicely.

This was only the first of a number of creative business ideas that Turner developed to capitalize on the promise of cable. His clever scheme not only served him well but also helped effect a structural change in the industry. It encouraged the expansion of cable into larger cities, where people were interested in WTCG's programming. Later, building on their success with offering Turner's station, cable systems began picking up the signal of WGN, the *Chicago Tribune*'s independent station that broadcast Cubs games. Then, in 1972, Home Box Office (HBO) began distributing its signal to cable systems by microwave and thus became the first venture to offer pay television successfully. Subscribers paid their cable system an extra monthly fee for HBO's programming, which consisted mainly of more recent movies than were normally available on television, presented without commercial interruptions.

These new program offerings, delivered to cable systems by microwave, enticed many operators to seek franchises in cities that heretofore had appeared unattractive. But even though products were now available to "push" through this new channel, and consumers were eager to "pull" those products through the channel, serious obstacles to the growth of cable remained. Connecting cities by microwave was costly. Real estate rights to build the microwave towers along the route were expensive, and maintenance was a continuing burden. Heavy rain or electrical interference caused signal problems, including what was known as "rain fade." FCC licenses were required, and the number of frequencies available was limited.

For all these reasons, cable operators were eagerly anticipating the onset of program distribution via satellite. It was obvious that satellites—whose signals could span the country from coast to coast—would eventually provide almost instant nationwide coverage, with much larger channel capacity and at lower costs than the microwave alternative. The most venturesome cable operators intensified their efforts to lock up franchises in the most attractive cities.

We shifted the focus of TeleCable's franchising efforts to medium-sized independent cities, and also to the more affluent suburbs of larger cities. The first of these suburban communities where we invested millions in cable infrastructure were the Kansas suburbs of Kansas City, including Overland Park and ten other contiguous communities. For several nerve-wracking years, we feared that we had a very expensive microwave-based turkey on our hands. We had no strong distant signals, and we were hemorrhaging from the negative cash flow caused by minimal penetration.

This was in the days before HBO went on the satellite. Making the best of a bad situation, we delivered our own version of premium television to Overland Park. We purchased films directly from movie studios, installed a bank of VCRs in our head end, and scheduled back-to-back movies. This tactic generated some added revenues, but it did little to expand our anemic subscriber penetration. When the arrival of the satellites finally enabled us to import more programming, the Kansas suburban systems' penetration accelerated rapidly. Cash flow turned around, and these systems went from turkeys to stars, eventually becoming some of our best performers.

The first satellite transmission of cable programming was on September 30, 1975, when HBO broadcast the heavyweight championship fight between Muhammad Ali and Joe Frazier, billed as "The Thrilla in Manila." After that, HBO became available via satellite to every cable system in the country, including the major urban markets. The next signal to go on the satellite was WTCG's. Turner's brainchild was soon renamed WTBS, Turner Broadcasting System. By 1980, the Christian Broadcasting Network (CBN),

WGN, WOR, ESPN, C-SPAN, USA, Nickelodeon, Showtime, The Movie Channel, Cinemax, and Bravo had begun transmitting by satellite. Cable operators paid monthly fees per subscriber to carry a few of these networks. In addition to giving cable systems more programs to sell, satellite signals were superior in quality to microwave signals.

With the coming of the satellites in 1975, the gold rush for franchises started in earnest. By then, a number of larger companies had replaced the early entrepreneurs as franchise applicants. The competition became feverish—and, unhappily, sometimes unscrupulous. Bidders made extravagant promises of services, on which they were unlikely ever to deliver. The CEO of a large cable company was quoted as saying that he would sign a blank piece of paper, and let the city write the franchise contract around his signature. Why? Because he intended to renegotiate the deal later. There were instances of influence peddling, and—in some cases—bribery of city officials. In a highly publicized case, Irving Kahn, founder of TelePrompTer, the largest cable company, was convicted of paying a $15,000 bribe to city officials in Johnstown, Pennsylvania, and then lying about the bribe, in order to help obtain a franchise for TelePrompTer. Localities did their part to feed the hysteria and raise the stakes, in many cases making unrealistic, even outrageous, demands for services.

At TeleCable we were spared the worst of this. In the suburbs of big cities and in the medium-size cities where we were concentrating our franchising efforts, the politics tended to be cleaner. Construction costs, too, were lower. For the most part, we faced fewer requirements to put our cables underground, and when we did need to put them underground, we found fewer obstacles to construction. And finally, the demographics in these communities were usually more attractive for cable marketing.

But I should be careful not to make our progress in this new business sound like a stroll in the park. We faced many hurdles, including some inside our own organization. As the size of the cities where we won franchises became larger, the capital costs of our cable investments skyrocketed. In addition to capital costs, we faced large operating losses for several years until subscriber revenues caught up with costs. This was true for all new cable systems. The more systems we built, the larger our losses became. At our annual management stockholders' meetings, Rex Bradley would brag, in jest, that the mounting losses were a bullish measure of our growing business.

Many of our newspaper and broadcasting management stockholders—people who had invested their hard-earned savings in their own company, in an important vote of confidence—could not understand why we were investing so heavily in cable. Why didn't we just acquire additional newspapers or television stations, which almost without exception would be more profitable and less risky in the near term? Some of these managers assumed that we were trying to diversify—hedging our bets by spreading our risk across another business.

I have never believed in diversification for these kinds of defensive reasons. Defensive diversification encourages managers to rationalize their investment decisions, and quite often it leads to mediocre returns. I viewed our cable investments as an offensive move. We were entering the business before the cost of doing so became prohibitively high. Once again our status as a privately held company gave us a significant edge. Big start-up losses—which we suffered through—discouraged many large, public companies from entering the field. The CEO of one major, publicly owned newspaper company admitted to me that his company simply couldn't allow these kinds of losses to show up in its quarterly and annual reports. Some years later, when cable became the darling of Wall Street, his company entered at a high cost.

As often as possible, we told our anxious managers that we were convinced that cable's growth potential was extraordinary. Consumers' thirst for more television programming was already well documented, and as of 1965 only 14 percent of American homes had cable. With distribution technology improving, we were convinced that almost all of America's homes could be counted in cable's market potential. The worst that could happen—as we told our management shareholders throughout this long period of investment and losses—seemed to be modest returns. And, we hastened to add, Landmark was staging its investments carefully. We didn't have to "bet the farm" all at once, so we didn't. The risk of a total wipe-out seemed vanishingly small.

In part as a result of our experience in the cable industry, I developed an informal philosophy about new businesses, and I articulated some elementary standards to govern our entry into them. First: Do we expect to get a better long-term return than with other opportunities we have? Second: Are the risks tolerable? Third: Do we understand the business, and have access to the talent to manage it successfully? Fourth: Can we be proud of the business?

Our record has been consistent. Every time we've met all four of these standards, we've succeeded. And every time we've failed to meet even one of these standards, we've failed.

To our in-house skeptics, I pointed out that Landmark could only rarely acquire a media business on the open market. We did buy several newspapers and television stations in the 1960s and 1970s, but none of them by means of the auctions that had become the norm for sales of media businesses. These bidding contests had driven up prices well beyond our point of indifference. We simply couldn't win at an auction. The handful of metropolitan-size papers and stations we acquired in this period were owned by people with whom we had long-term relationships, and with whom we could deal one on one. By and large, these owners were less concerned about profit maximization and more concerned about how a new owner would treat their employees and communities.

In the first of these acquisitions, the *Greensboro (N.C.) Daily News & Record* and WFMY-TV, we reached a verbal understanding with the owners, and both parties signed their names to a one-page agreement. About a week later, another qualified buyer offered to pay several million dollars more than our agreed-upon price. Even though our one-page agreement would never have survived in court, the owners honored it, and we acquired the papers and station at the original price. I like to think that Land-mark would have behaved in exactly the same way had our roles been reversed. I know Sam Slover would have.

We made a few other acquisitions like the Greensboro one, but we continued to focus principally on acquiring cable fran-chises. The pace of franchising was accelerating. Within a few short years, by the beginning of the 1980s, most American cities would award their cable franchises. We needed to move quickly to grab opportunities while they were still there to be grabbed.

THE BATTLE INTENSIFIES

Our hunt for strong franchises was led by Rex Bradley and Alec Purcell, a bright young man who had been hired out of grad-uate business school. He made lists of attractive, unfranchised com-munities. If they learned that a city council or county board of supervisors was preparing to take franchise bids, Bradley would size up the opportunity by visiting local people—the city attorney, the city manager, the mayor, perhaps members of the city council or board of supervisors—to get a feel for local issues and political nuances. He and Purcell would talk with people who appeared to be influential in town and identify the best local lawyer to represent us, which usually meant the lawyer who commanded the most respect and had the best connections. In some cases, they found that town officials had already privately selected the franchise winner, and that they were only going through the motions of an official selection process. In most places, though, the process was legitimate.

TeleCable also sought franchises in some communities where no franchising process was yet underway. Our goal was to persuade local officials that cable would be a true asset for the community and that TeleCable was the best possible operator—and thus that no complicated and time-consuming competition was needed.

Not surprisingly, this pitch didn't work very often. Only in Racine were we able to gain a franchise without competition.

In the early 1970s, when the promise of satellite-delivered programming began to make the big cities appealing as cable markets, media giants like Warner, Westinghouse, and Time Inc. began plunging into the business and quickly heated up the competitiveness and sophistication of franchising. Rex Bradley decided it was time to devote a full-time team to franchising and hired Barney Oldfield to lead the team.

There were usually at least four bidders when an attractive cable franchise came up for bid. Many cities hired consultants who specialized in evaluating applicants and their proposals. Proposals provided detailed technical specifications and demonstrated the applicant's financial capacity to build and operate the system. They supplied evidence of the applicant's ability to operate cable systems, and also of its ability to deliver on its promises. And, of course, the bidders made promises in their proposals, usually how many channels and networks they would carry, and what specific local services they would provide. Although we learned that cable consultants frequently ranked TeleCable number one in terms of technical specifications and "character" (corporate citizenship and willingness and ability to deliver on promises), we increasingly competed with bidders who seemed to be promising more channel capacity and local programming than they could provide.

Our largest challenge came from a new trend: Applicants began to make influential local citizens minority partners in their ventures. By 1971, the trend had become the norm. Some of these equity stakes required only token financial investments by the local shareholders. Others were outright gifts. Most of the equity offers went to people who had direct influence with council members. In the industry, we referred to this practice as "renting a civic leader." Even though this sort of influence buying was lawful, we believed it was unsavory and resisted engaging in the practice.

The net result of our high-minded stance? Even when bid-reviewing consultants ranked TeleCable's proposals number one, applicants with local partners were soundly defeating us, in one franchise battle after another. Clearly, we either had to rethink our position or consciously decide to close down our franchising efforts entirely. We finally found a middle ground: We would take in local partners on condition that they invest pro rata shares of the equity and accept liability for their shares of debt. If the equity investment required was $1 million and a local stockholder owned 1 percent of the venture's stock, that stockholder would have to invest $10,000. And if the debt required was $3 million, the local stockholder would accept liability for $30,000 of the debt. This arrangement was not as attractive as equity "gifts," and we worried that we might have difficulty attracting good local partners to this kind of deal. Our fears proved unfounded, however, and some of the best local citizens, who were also repelled by the sweetheart deals, welcomed the opportunity to make genuine investments in local cable TV. And although we didn't advertise our investment policy, it gave us a leg up in the eyes of some consultants.

We succeeded in winning competitive franchises in Lexington, Kentucky; Springfield, Missouri; and three Dallas suburbs—Arlington, Plano, and Richardson, Texas. Along with our existing Overland Park–Kansas City operation, these systems turned out to be our largest ones. All were attractive cable markets. Springfield was a particularly interesting story. We won the franchise there only after a long struggle. We were a late arrival in the competition, and the city council didn't select us until the fifty-ninth ballot, as the compromise choice in a deadlock between two strong local bidders. But the deal was not yet closed. The city charter required validation of the award by a referendum, which we lost by a handful of votes—probably because the local television stations had opposed the award and had mounted a misleading publicity campaign. The mayor was infuriated. To everyone's astonishment, he persuaded the council to conduct a second referendum—which we won by a wide margin.

In some of our franchise competitions, we benefited from our reputation for being squeaky clean, for keeping our promises, and for being innovative in developing local services. In Overland Park, for example, we had built one of the first two-way cable systems, whereby subscribers could communicate electronically with the cable company or with the host of one of the program channels. Also in Overland Park, we ran some of the first experiments in distance learning, testing the viability of educating the homebound via two-way cable. In a July 2, 1971, story about Tele-Cable's tests, *The New York Times* reported that the experiment "promises in time to turn an ordinary television set into a much more versatile communications device. . . . This opens a range of possible applications so great that scores of small and large companies are vying for cable franchises, convinced that the now-infant industry has a chance of becoming a giant."★

Our two-way system in Overland Park enabled TeleCable's first entry into telephony. We entered a joint venture with Time Inc.'s cable system in Kansas City to operate a competitive local exchange carrier that sold areawide telephone and data service to businesses. Today, Overland Park also uses the two-way capability as part of a computerized traffic-control system.

AN ESTABLISHED PLAYER

I have focused here on the critical struggle to win franchises, but that was only one part of this chapter in our corporate evolution. As far back as 1968, TeleCable's franchising, construction, start-up and operating activities had become so demanding that we realized we needed a manager to oversee the marketing and operation of our systems once they were built. Our investment returns depended heavily on how quickly we could get paying subscribers on line, and then keep them there. We needed a strong

★Boyce Rensberger, "Cable TV: Two-Way Teaching Aid," *New York Times,* 2 July 1971.

sales and marketing effort, good technical performance, and first-rate customer service.

I asked Dick Roberts to move to TeleCable as vice president of operations. Rex had hired three able young managers—Alec Purcell, Gordon Herring, and Jim Key—and an exceptionally strong chief engineer, Nick Worth. This group turned out to be a skillful, aggressive management team. It was equal to or better than any management in the cable business then, and the team did a lot to push TeleCable into the big leagues.

In 1980, TeleCable was the nation's fifteenth largest cable operator with more than 230,000 subscribers, and it was growing rapidly. We had acquired a reputation in the industry for technological development, innovative services, and principled business conduct. In the 1970s, TeleCable had been the first multisystem operator to provide satellite-transmitted programs to all its subscribers. It was also an industry leader in rebuilding its systems to enlarge their channel capacities. We developed a plan—to be implemented between 1980 and 1982—whereby most of our subscribers would have access to more than thirty-six channels. At the same time, we began building the infrastructure for expansion to sixty channels.

Rex Bradley retired in 1977, and Dick Roberts succeeded him as president. Bradley had been successful in creating Tele-Cable's organization from scratch and building or buying twelve cable systems. He had served as chairman of the National Cable and Telecommunications Association (NCTA), the cable industry's national trade association, giving TeleCable a disproportionately large stature in the industry. In his new role, Roberts at first concentrated on building a strong bond of teamwork among Tele-Cable's management, and instilling Landmark's values of emphasizing the development of our staff. Under Roberts's leadership, TeleCable became a leader in adopting advanced technologies that continually expanded our channel capacity and provided a succession of new service offerings to subscribers. Later Roberts also served as chairman of NCTA.

33

The pace of the chase for new franchises was beginning to slow by the early 1980s, as many of the attractive franchises had already been awarded. That left the acquisition of going concerns as the only means to expand TeleCable's geographic reach. But by that time, prices for most systems had escalated dramatically, and our acquisitions became increasingly rare.

Throughout this period, we were bargain hunters, which I realized later was a mistake. Our estimates of subscriber penetration, revenue growth, and final value turned out to be far too conservative. We had opportunities to buy systems for less than $1,000 per subscriber, systems that today are worth $3,500 to $4,000 per subscriber and that have many, many more subscribers than they did twenty years ago.

But I've always resisted the impulse to second-guess these kinds of missed opportunities. In fact, the same price discipline that kept us out of good deals kept us out of many more bad deals. In part thanks to that discipline, TeleCable—which we started with a $15,000 investment in a small-town franchise—had turned into a splendid business. Its revenues and cash flows continued to grow handsomely as we developed new sources of revenues, and as our subscriber numbers grew far beyond expectations.

The advent of satellite distribution of programming prompted pundits to predict that scores, perhaps even hundreds, of new programming channels would be launched to appeal to a wide variety of human interests. Even to the most conservative old-timers in our ranks, cable's potential had become intoxicating. More people would subscribe to more things. Programs that were once considered luxuries would become necessities. An enormous range of information and entertainment would be available in millions of homes. Cable would be at the very heart of these huge changes— and although we were far from the largest player, TeleCable and Landmark were very much in the game.

But once again, the game had changed. So where was our next big opportunity?

CHAPTER TWO

A NEW IDEA

I was enormously encouraged by our success in cable TV. We had entered that business in a relatively early stage of its development, and within a decade we had carved out a respectable niche for ourselves. By 1977, however, cable was beginning to mature, and most of the appealing franchises were taken. I thought we were approaching a time when TeleCable's future growth would come largely from the development of its existing systems. Once again, it was time to start searching for another attractive media business in an early stage of development.

As I noted earlier, I had learned to rely on Bill Diederich, Landmark's chief financial officer, for creative ideas. A tight-fisted and savvy numbers guy, Diederich was also a wellspring of inventiveness. He astonished me with his uncanny ability to sniff out business opportunities long before others saw them. Back when the cable industry was just beginning to grasp the potential of satellites, Diederich was confidently predicting a demand for cable channels dedicated to full-time coverage of news, sports, and weather. Not many people were thinking as clearly as he was back in those days.

So when in the late 1970s I again challenged my Landmark colleagues to join me in looking for new businesses, Diederich came right back at me. He urged us to start a twenty-four-hour-a-day cable news channel, to be delivered via satellite. There was a large potential audience, Diederich argued, of people who didn't want to have to wait until 5 or 6 P.M. for network newscasts. He also believed that the substance of network news was so thin that there was a pent-up demand for in-depth television news programming. And with news as the program, we would always be sure to have fresh content.

I was intrigued. First of all, I loved the news business. Second, I agreed that a twenty-four-hour news channel would likely have a large and potentially loyal audience. Envisioning Landmark as the successful survivor in this business was a big leap for me, however. Viewers would expect network-quality programming, meaning that we would have to compete, at enormous expense, with the three networks' news departments. And almost certainly, at least one of the networks—if not all three—would launch directly competitive cable news channels in an effort to snuff us out. How could they allow an upstart to raid their profitable turf unopposed?

Diederich disagreed. He argued that we could mount a credible news channel for much less than the networks would have to pay for the same kind of service. Because of union work rules, the networks' news departments were notoriously overstaffed. We didn't have to play by those rules. And if we structured our business correctly, we would have no compelling reason to pay the staggering salaries the networks paid their anchors and other "star" performers. Finally, Diederich was convinced that the networks very well might not take us seriously. He predicted that they would take a wait-and-see approach, letting us test the waters before jumping in themselves. Therefore we would have the first-mover advantage, which would give us the time to build strong distribution relationships with the cable operators.

After extended debates, I agreed to explore the news channel concept. I thought it might be possible to enlist a strong news partner—say, the *Washington Post, The New York Times,* Knight-Ridder, or Gannett Co.—and also to contract with The Associated Press to draw upon its extensive worldwide network of news bureaus. The proposed news channel would then have a running start in terms of credibility and resources. I went to New York to try out the idea on Keith Fuller, president of The Associated Press, and to meet with several others involved in network news. Fred Friendly, former president of CBS News and a vocal critic of network news, was one of the thoughtful and informed people who encouraged me to push the idea forward.

FROM NEWS TO WEATHER

The entire inquiry suddenly went into a stall when, in December 1977, I was diagnosed with throat cancer. I began a two-year therapeutic journey that included radiation treatments and two bouts of surgery. Surgeons removed all my vocal cords, so I had to learn a new way of talking through my esophagus. As it turned out, there was good mixed in with the bad: While relearning how to talk, I was reminded that perseverance can overcome seemingly impossible odds. I also developed an enormous respect for the medical professionals who worked so hard and so effectively to help make me well and able to talk again.

This personal setback temporarily halted Landmark's venture into cable programming. And in this fast-moving field, timing was everything. By the time we reentered the fray in 1980, many of the best ideas—including the news channel—had already been spoken for. Ted Turner, ever the pioneer, had launched Cable News Network (CNN). ABC challenged Turner by beginning a news service, and Turner immediately counterchallenged by launching a second channel, Headline News. ABC soon discovered that Turner's head start—and the goodwill he had built up with cable operators—had made him unbeatable. Before long, ABC folded its tent.

Meanwhile, however, all was not smooth sailing in Atlanta. CNN was losing money rapidly, and it was difficult to see how Turner could survive without outside help. I telephoned him at one point to see if he would consider selling part or all of CNN to Landmark. I honestly thought I was making an offer that my old sailing friend would take seriously. Not Ted! He practically bit my ear off over the phone. "What?" he roared. "Would you sell your newspapers?"

So a news channel was off the table. At the suggestion of Bob Haigh, one of Landmark's directors, we organized two new-ventures teams to canvass the media landscape in search of other opportunities enabled by new technologies. One team was led by Bill Diederich, and the other by John O. "Dubby" Wynne. Wynne was a hard-charging young leader who had recently returned east from a stint running one of our West Coast television stations.

Although we were involved in many local media businesses, we didn't see much deal flow involving national businesses. Dubby Wynne, who knew something about venture capital, guessed that venture capitalists would be among the first to hear of innovative programming ventures conceived by people outside the networks' orbits. So both teams began courting venture capitalists in late 1980 in search of new ideas.

Eventually, Wynne's guess panned out. One day in April 1981, a Chicago-based venture capitalist telephoned Bahns Stanley, a member of Bill Diederich's team. He told Stanley about a business plan that he himself was not interested in, but which might match our interests. "I don't know whether it's any good or not," he told Stanley candidly. "A lot of people have said 'no' to it already. But it's based on a business plan that I wrote for an old poker buddy of mine."

The poker buddy turned out to be John Coleman of Chicago. Coleman had been a weathercaster throughout his twenty-three-year television career. His deep voice, communications skills, and Midwestern good looks combined to make him a local celebrity across much of northern Illinois. Although like many TV weathermen of the day he gained early renown for on-camera antics, Coleman's delivery of the weather gradually became more dignified. He took the weather seriously, he seemed to be telling his audience, and they should do the same. In 1977, he had joined ABC's national morning broadcast, *Good Morning America,* where he soon garnered a national reputation for presenting his forecasts with high levels of energy and showmanship.

Coleman's idea was to create a twenty-four-hour national cable network devoted exclusively to weather coverage. He believed that broadcast TV coverage of weather did not fully meet viewers' needs. He had become convinced that the short time devoted to weather on TV—typically about fifteen minutes a day—was hopelessly inadequate, in light of the profound impact that weather had on people's lives. Acting on this conviction, Coleman had begun developing his concept of an all-weather cable network in 1978, figuring out how to program and staff such an enterprise, and searching for a deep-pocketed financial partner.

His most important ally in this effort was a professional meteorologist, Joseph D'Aleo. D'Aleo had relocated temporarily to Chicago in 1980 to help Coleman, who unexpectedly had lost his meteorological producer for his *Good Morning America* segments. (Although the program was based in New York, Coleman's segments—fed through a satellite uplink in Chicago—were seamlessly blended into the nationwide ABC signal. Few viewers realized that host David Hartman and weatherman John Coleman rarely laid eyes on each other.) D'Aleo fully intended to enroll at the University of Wisconsin to finish his doctorate. But his first stint in Chicago was extended, and extended again, and then a second crisis brought him back to Chicago and Coleman.

D'Aleo, by nature a quiet, even shy individual, somehow managed to hit it off with the extroverted Coleman. By force of circumstance, they were spending many long nights at the studio together, squeezing out the time needed to produce segments for *Good Morning America*. Almost inevitably, D'Aleo became involved in the planning for Coleman's national weather network. As he recalls:

> *We would work all night preparing for John's* Good Morning America *performance. Then we'd go down and have breakfast, and then go to his office and have long talks about what it would take to do a weather channel. How many people would we need? How many artists? How many on-air meteorologists? How many off-air people? What kind of programming would we have? That kind of thing. There were a producer and some artists who were involved in the early discussions. He had planned that if this thing took off, they would be part of it.*

Throughout this hectic period, Coleman was also flying around the country, trying to line up a financial partner for his venture. He came extremely close to persuading Dow Jones, publisher of *The Wall Street Journal,* to back him. "We went so far down the road with Dow Jones," D'Aleo recalls, "that we were even looking for housing in the Naperville, Illinois, area." But the publishing giant decided that it had better uses for its money and dropped out of the running.

The picture that emerges of John Coleman, in this period before he found us at Landmark, is of an absolutely driven man. He would work all night on his *GMA* segments, then go to his office to plan for his weather network, then put in some hours for the local Chicago station, and then—if one of his overtures to a prospective backer seemed to be panning out—board a plane for distant parts. "He'd get on that plane to see a potential backer in, say, Colorado," says D'Aleo, "then he'd fly back to Chicago, go home, shower, and come in to work."

We knew none of this at the time, of course. What we knew was that a venture capitalist in Chicago was intrigued enough with Coleman's idea to talk it up to Bahns Stanley, but not excited enough to act on it himself. Stanley's initial reaction, too, was skeptical, but he decided to run the idea by Bill Diederich. Our crafty CFO, liking what he was hearing, immediately encouraged his young colleague to track me down and tell me about it. Stanley reached me in El Cajon, California, where I was visiting a small newspaper we had acquired there. When he sketched out Coleman's idea, I distinctly remembered that Diederich years earlier had predicted not only a round-the-clock news network, but also a "24/7" weather channel. I asked Stanley to set up a meeting with Coleman.

We met the following week in Landmark's boardroom. Along with me on my side of the table were Bill Diederich, Dubby Wynne, Bahns Stanley, Dick Roberts, and Gordon Herring, then head of marketing at TeleCable. Coleman brought his lawyer, Phil Couri, and Mike Ban, an advertising executive who had consulted with him. With passion and enthusiasm, Coleman outlined his concept. His arguments in favor of the plan were strongly reminiscent of those we had used in favor of an all-news channel. Viewers would be able to get national and regional weather information around the clock, whenever they wanted it. They would not have to wait for the six o'clock or eleven o'clock news programs. Cable TV could tell the "weather story" with a depth and quality of coverage that never would be feasible in the broadcast-TV context. Coleman had retained the A. C. Nielsen television ratings and research company to study cable viewers' potential interest in an all-weather channel; the resulting study had indicated that about half of those interviewed would have a significant interest in a twenty-four-hour weather channel.

Gordon Herring, our in-house cable marketing expert, had joined our TeleCable subsidiary in 1970. He brought to the table a unique combination of business smarts, marketing savvy, and a solid technical grounding. He had begun as TeleCable's director of research—which meant that it was his job to hunt up new programming—and subsequently moved into marketing. Thus not only had he sold communities on TeleCable, but he had also sold cable to potential subscribers. Herring was an energetic and resourceful salesman.

At our initial meeting with Coleman, Herring cited some anecdotal experience from TeleCable that seemed to support Coleman's assertions. Many of our cable systems carried the kinds of rudimentary local weather channels described earlier: scrolling text across the screen and dials scanned by cameras showing temperature and wind. In terms of technical complexity, they were only one step up from the goldfish swimming in the bowl. Herring believed that, appearances notwithstanding, these primitive channels had high viewer loyalty. When we periodically surveyed TeleCable's customers, viewers always identified these local weather channels as important sources of satisfaction. Conversely, whenever there were problems with the dials or the character generator that delivered the text, our operators received a remarkable number of complaints about the loss of the "weather channel"—more complaints, in fact, than they got from the loss of any other channel.

As Coleman conceived the weather channel, it would focus mainly on national and regional weather. But Herring believed that for any full-fledged weather network to succeed, it would have to present frequent, detailed local weather information that was relevant to each cable system's customers. Providing that information sounded like a very high hurdle, but Herring thought we could develop the necessary technology. The new technology he envisioned would make it possible for a portion of the same satellite signal that delivered a national weather program to simultaneously deliver discrete local forecasts to each cable system.

Herring had recently served as a member of a Landmark task force that had investigated the feasibility of news and information services using teletext (an electronic means of transmitting printed matter via television signals). Several companies had already run operational experiments with teletext service in Europe. Although the service was not attractive economically, it was feasible technologically. Herring believed we could adapt this technology to build an addressable receiver capable of receiving and storing localized information from a satellite transponder.

Coleman seemed amenable to this expansion of his original concept, although like the rest of us, he had no idea if it ultimately would prove feasible. He pushed on with his proposal. He asked that Landmark put up all the capital that would be needed for the venture. He would provide the necessary management and programming expertise, in return for a minority interest in the venture.

When it came time for me to weigh in, I admitted that I had a very positive reaction to Coleman's concept—especially as modified by Herring—and I said that we would be happy to explore the proposed venture in depth. I had been fascinated by the weather ever since I was a child, after experiencing a damaging hurricane when staying in my uncle's oceanfront cottage in Virginia Beach. The ferocious 1933 storm, eastern Virginia's most damaging hurricane in recorded history, had sneaked up to our doorsteps unannounced. Later in life, I had taken up sailing, and I knew firsthand that getting accurate weather forecasts is critical both for developing racing strategy and for ensuring boating safety. Thus I was predisposed to react enthusiastically to the idea of a twenty-four-hour weather channel. But, of course, we still had to do our homework.

DUE DILIGENCE

I asked Dubby Wynne to lead our due-diligence effort. (For the benefit of my readers who have never bought a business, "due

43

diligence" is simply the painstaking homework that precedes such a deal.) Although we had originally hired Wynne as corporate counsel, we discovered almost immediately that he was a hard worker and tenacious competitor, and that he had potential as a leader and manager. We made him general manager of a TV station in San Jose, in the intensely competitive Bay Area television market, and in the late 1970s called him back to Norfolk to back up Bill Gietz, our broadcasting head, and to help us search for new ventures. When Gietz retired, Wynne became head of broadcasting.

Wynne was assisted by Bahns Stanley and Doug Holladay (a newspaper person who had recently joined Wynne's new-ventures team), and he frequently consulted with Dick Roberts, Gordon Herring, and TeleCable's engineering chief, Nick Worth. Others from Landmark and TeleCable were pulled into the study when they had specific expertise we needed. John Coleman, too, was involved in much of the due diligence, since we were evaluating a potential partnership with him.

Early on, Wynne learned that Coleman had already shopped his weather channel plan extensively. He had been turned down not only by a number of venture capitalists but also by media companies, including NBC and Dow Jones. Given all these rejections of the idea, we wondered, What did they know that we didn't?

While our due diligence was progressing, Wynne and our in-house counsel, Louis Ryan, were also negotiating with Coleman and his lawyer over the shape of an agreement with him. We had already concluded that Landmark had most of the expertise needed to launch and operate a weather channel. Through our newspapers and television stations, we understood the advertising market. Through TeleCable, we understood the cable marketplace, and we had good relationships with the larger cable operators. What we felt least confident about was programming a weather channel and organizing the "back shop" that would be needed to support this kind of specialized programming. We believed that Coleman could supply the programming expertise we needed, and that his stature as a celebrity TV weatherman would open some doors for us in the advertising world.

At a meeting of Landmark's board of directors in July 1981, Wynne and I described the business concept of a weather channel and expressed strong initial interest in the venture.

Here, perhaps, I should underscore the differences in the roles of directors of public companies and private companies—particularly in private companies like Landmark, in which the chief executive officer is the majority stockholder. Public company boards are the final decision-making authorities, absent a stockholder vote to reverse them, which in real life rarely happens. In companies like Landmark, directors and managers recognize that it would be easy for the majority stockholder to be, in effect, the final decision maker on any matter. Indeed, many private companies have pro forma boards that simply conform to legal requirements and "rubber stamp" decisions the majority stockholder has already made.

I purposefully set a different course for Landmark. I sought outside, nonemployee directors who could bring exceptional knowledge and independent judgment to Landmark. Currently we have five such outside directors and four management directors. The outside directors include the retired CEO of a major manufacturing company, a newspaper owner and publisher, a professor at Harvard Business School, and the retired CEO of a cable company. All speak their views frankly, and they have brought extraordinarily valuable knowledge and outside perspective to our management. They have substantial investments in Landmark stock and therefore speak as stockholders and as directors.

We never go to our board simply seeking ratification of a decision we have already made, especially in a realm that might change Landmark's character and direction. Instead, we defer any decisions like starting or entering a new business until we can get the board's frank advice and consent. This practice is unusual, and it is definitely more cumbersome than acting unilaterally. Nevertheless, our independent-minded board has brought us a wealth of priceless ideas and also has saved us from some serious mistakes. They force us to do our homework and bring our best ideas to the table. For their part, several of our outside directors have told me that they get more satisfaction from being on our board than from the public-company boards they have served on. They believe they have more impact on Landmark because we sincerely seek and value their advice.

So in that supportive but critical spirit, our directors sat us down in July 1981 and interrogated us about our new idea for a weather channel. Several directors expressed more skepticism than enthusiasm. At the end of the discussion, however, they encouraged us to continue with due diligence—cautiously, was the message I heard, authorized us to negotiate an agreement with Coleman, and OK'd our proposal to lease a satellite transponder, which we needed to deliver our signal to cable systems. We knew at the time that these decisions were weighty; we had no idea how weighty they would prove to be.

Moving forward with our due diligence, we made a long list of issues that remained to be explored. Eight of these we identified as critical: Would cable operators give us a channel? Would they pay us to distribute the channel? How many viewers would watch a weather channel—how often and for how long? Would this kind of programming appeal to national advertisers? How large an audience and what viewership ratings would we need to appeal to advertisers? Could we develop the technology needed to deliver local forecasts to each cable system? Could we get access to a scarce satellite transponder? What would our costs be? (Later I'll discuss the cost side of the due-diligence effort.) How much revenue could we expect?

Many of these questions focused us on the need to understand, as fully as we could, the fast-moving world of cable television.

UNDERSTANDING THE CABLE UNIVERSE

At the beginning of 1981, there were approximately 18 million cable subscribers in the United States, constituting about 23 percent of households with television sets. Most of these subscribers were in smaller communities with twelve-channel cable systems.

But the pace of cable construction was then accelerating rapidly, and industry analysts expected the wiring of larger markets to generate about 26 million new cable subscribers by 1990. Almost all these new systems would carry between thirty and fifty-four channels. Meanwhile, many of the twelve-channel systems were planning "rebuilds" to allow for more channels. We believed these channel upgrades, along with new cable construction, would create the opportunity for a weather channel to gain wide distribution in a rapidly growing cable marketplace.

HBO, six years old in 1981, was the primary driver of cable penetration in many of the major markets, giving viewers television access to reasonably new movies without commercial interruption. The independent stations—WTBS (Atlanta), WGN (Chicago), and WOR (New York)—had strong appeal in markets with transient populations who had lived in other parts of the country. ESPN had just started in 1979, but its sports-only programming already was proving very popular with males. USA Network, which started in 1980, had a particularly strong appeal to women. In 1979, Nickelodeon became a major hit with children, and in 1981, MTV established itself as a strong draw for teenagers.

We knew full well that competition for channel space in the twelve-channel systems, which included most operating systems in 1980 and 1981, was ferocious. If we went ahead, we would be competing for channel space with all existing programming, as well as with all the new and proposed program services, including Disney, Lifetime, the Financial News Network, The Nashville Network, and Arts& Entertainment. Meanwhile, of course, the first wave of niche cable programmers, such as ESPN, CNN, Nickelodeon, and MTV, were also trying to extend their penetrations.

But we had an ace up our sleeves, as we contemplated launching ourselves into this fierce competition. Most of the twelve-channel systems already had a channel reserved for weather.

47

Replacing an existing weather channel with our own weather channel seemed like a reasonable prospect, assuming that our product was superior to the existing fare. None of our other competitors could present themselves as replacing an inferior service, and we intended to take full advantage of this differentiating factor.

Meanwhile, many new cable systems, almost all of which would have much larger channel capacity, would be awarding franchises soon. We were convinced that a weather channel could be, and would be, sold as a public service. And at the same time, we thought our weather channel would occupy such a narrow niche that competitors would not be drawn into our space—at least not immediately. We knew we needed *time* to establish ourselves, and we thought we might just get it.

We thought through our value proposition very carefully in this due-diligence phase. The most attractive advertiser-supported networks—ESPN, CNN, and USA—were able to charge cable operators a fee to carry their services. And in 1981, these three networks were the only ones that could command such fees. At the other end of the spectrum, some of the proposed networks were offering to pay to be carried. We were somewhere in the middle: We couldn't afford to pay for carriage, nor could we expect to charge operators for carrying a weather channel. Like broadcast networks and stations, we would have to depend on advertising for all of our revenue.

But the picture was not necessarily bleak. Our programming costs, we were convinced, would be low. We wouldn't be required to pay for the rights to sports events or movies. If we could hit on the right approach to programming—compelling and inexpensive—we ought to be able to do all right.

Gordon Herring discussed the weather-channel concept with many of his counterparts in other cable companies. At first blush, their response was less than enthusiastic. But when Herring reminded them that they could replace an antiquated utility service with a combination of live programming and frequent local weather information, most of them began to warm to the idea.

Based on these reactions, Herring concluded that most cable operators who already carried local text-based weather channels would replace them with our weather channel. It seemed likely, moreover, that new cable systems, as well as systems that were adding channel capacity, would rapidly adopt a free weather channel. And these two latter kinds of systems would account for almost all the future growth in cable subscribers. We continued to like what we were seeing.

UNDERSTANDING OUR AUDIENCE

We knew that advertising revenue would determine the success or failure of our proposed weather channel. Thus we focused on what we knew, or could learn, about our prospective audience, and what kind of ratings we might generate.

The key measure advertisers use to judge a television program's appeal and value is audience ratings—the estimated percentage of available television homes watching a program at a given time. Traditionally, advertisers have relied on A. C. Nielsen as the source of national network television ratings. Even people far removed from the media world know the power that the phrase "Nielsen ratings" holds for TV moguls.

Estimating the size of our potential audience, and by extension our potential ad revenues, was a precarious task at best. It involved stacking up a series of uncertain estimates—how many subscribers would have access to our channel, how many of them would watch the channel at any time, how long would they stay tuned, and how frequently would they watch? We came up with a wide range of estimates for each of these factors. Of necessity, we were piling estimates on top of each other, hoping that our calculations had something to do with reality.

We had few hard facts to work with. We realized that we had to depend largely on our gut instincts about consumers' weather information needs and about how much weather-based programming would appeal to them. As an interim measure, we came up with a range of ratings estimates—best case, best guess, and worst case.

We also were not sure whether viewers would sit through national weather forecasts to wait for their local forecasts. One Landmark director asked, pointedly, "Won't a viewer in Keokuk, Iowa, be bored to death if he's really only interested in local weather?" Bahns Stanley responded that national surveys showed that 13 million people travel more than a hundred miles every day, and weather information is of particular interest to travelers. At least some of those Iowans would want to know what the weather looked like elsewhere.

In keeping with a typical due-diligence process, we dutifully made lots of calculations. And then, without a great deal of confidence, we settled on best-guess estimates of audience ratings that, if they panned out, would put us somewhat below the rating then claimed by Ted Turner's CNN.

UNDERSTANDING ADVERTISING

Advertising on the fledgling cable networks—approximately $45 million in total billings in 1980—was dwarfed by advertising revenues in established media like newspapers, with $15.6 billion, and broadcast television, with $11.3 billion. But cable industry observers predicted that cable advertising would double in 1981 and reach $2.2 billion by 1990. Toward the end of our due diligence, we were convinced that these estimates were conservative. We believed that in ten years, cable channels would be taking many millions of viewers away from the broadcast networks, and we expected advertisers to follow the viewers.

What led us to this conclusion? Already, advertisers were eagerly seeking leverage in their periodic negotiations with the Big Three broadcast networks, whose advertising rates per thousand viewers had more than doubled in ten years. Some cable networks were offering rates that were less than a third of Big Three ad costs. Many advertisers who could not afford network spots of up to $150,000 each could afford the price of national cable spots, which ranged from several hundred to several thousand dollars. And some cable networks, especially those aimed at narrower demographic audiences, enabled advertisers to target specific groups more efficiently.

Of course, these arguments were sales pitches, but they were supported by our interviews with advertising agency executives in New York. Dubby Wynne and Bahns Stanley visited a number of agencies, sometimes accompanied by John Coleman. At that time, only a few people were selling cable advertising. There was next to no research, and people in the ad community were just beginning to experiment with cable. Most agencies in those days had an in-house "expert" on cable, and we talked to all of them. As it turned out, we probably should have paid less attention to some of them. As Stanley explains, "These guys were feeling their way through the dark, so it was the sightless leading the blind to some degree. We didn't realize the lack of clout they had within their own agencies. They couldn't drive behavior of the people controlling budgets."

Almost everywhere we went, we heard strong endorsements of the general idea of cable advertising. We heard confirmation of our expectations of growth in the cable industry. We even heard some favorable opinions about the weather concept. Unfortunately, we didn't realize then how little faith we should place in those opinions.

While due diligence was proceeding, Gordon Herring came up with another brilliant insight. Like so many great ideas, this one seems obvious in hindsight. It dawned on Herring that the same transponder capacity that could be used to deliver local weather forecasts—a key underpinning of our plan—could also be used by national advertisers to localize their commercials. Advertisers could list their local dealers, for example, or promote special offers aimed at local markets.

No other network had this capability, and we thought that the ability to localize commercials would make at least some advertisers clap their hands with delight. It certainly excited us. It gave our little network a unique selling proposition—a "USP," in advertising lingo—that we thought would grab advertisers' attention. Many national advertisers, moreover, offered cooperative advertising funds to local or regional dealer groups. We envisioned tapping into these funds for additional revenue. Our optimism about the value of localized commercials was heightened by a new round of interviews at the advertising agencies.

When I asked Herring where he got the idea for localized commercials, he thought for a moment, and then answered:

> *It came to me out of the blue one day, when I was brainstorming with Nick Worth about other things we could do with the new technology we were creating.*
>
> *But you'd also have to say that it came out of our experience. About a year before we were even thinking about The Weather Channel, I was in Racine trying to help our folks there get an advertising sales effort going on our local origination channels. The regional advertising manager for A&P agreed to buy the crawl [the scrolling text] on our existing automated weather channel. He decided to run a special on hams, but forgot to tell the local store about it. When the store experienced a run on hams, and ultimately ran out of hams, they realized that the crawl was a tremendous advertising tool.*

Again, hindsight is both easy and infallible. The localized commercials became a huge leg up for what would become The Weather Channel. It may have been the single most important unique advantage that helped our new venture survive and prosper.

Meanwhile, we faced a near-term barrier that would hurt our ability to sell ads: the lack of audience ratings for the foreseeable future. Nielsen wouldn't even provide ratings for a cable network until it had penetrated at least 15 percent of TV households nationwide. At that time, WTBS was the only cable network with ratings. Advertisers resisted buying spots without ratings, and we estimated that our weather channel would not be rated for three years.

In the beginning, we would have to rely on what we called "concept selling." We would concentrate our sales efforts on advertisers whose products seemed to overlap with weather in some way—cough medicines, travel-related products like tires and batteries, motel chains, and so on. We realized that this kind of selling would require our salespeople to be smarter or more sophisticated than the typical salesperson. They would need to go beyond the agency media buyers and sell our weather concept directly to the potential clients' advertising departments. We knew that going directly to these prospective clients would offend many people in the agencies, who sought to control all media relationships for these ad buyers, but we saw no other options. Later, we learned that there were anywhere from five to ten people involved in these kinds of decisions, and we had to sell at every one of these levels. Needless to say, this huge challenge required persistent and creative selling.

After all the footwork and analysis, we made raw guesses about how much advertising revenue we could expect. We believed the optimistic projections about the growth of advertising revenues on cable—including our own optimistic projections— and concluded that we ought to be able to capture at least a 2 to 3 percent share of cable advertising.

It was a shot in the dark. And that's how unsophisticated we really were, making the most important assumption we would have to make about our venture's economic viability. In the end, I was encouraged more by my instincts than by all our analysis. The U.S. television advertising market was enormous, $11.3 billion and growing. A national weather channel would have to get only about 0.1 percent of that market to break even. If the demand for our kind of weather service was as large as I expected, how could we miss?

Later, of course, we learned it would not be quite that easy.

CHAPTER THREE

BUILDING THE DATA PATH

E arly in our due diligence, even though we were
venturing into uncharted territory, we found
ourselves becoming more and more optimistic
about our infant Weather Channel's chances.
Some of the critical questions we were exploring seemed to be
yielding encouraging answers. For example, we were increasingly
confident that we could gain widespread cable distribution, make
weather programming that was appealing both to viewers and
advertisers, and attract enough of the kinds of viewers advertisers
would want to reach.

Of course, I'd like to be able to claim that our growing sense of optimism was based on solid facts and hard-nosed analysis. Unfortunately, that's not entirely true. By and large, we had to go with our gut.

We did know, though, that we desperately needed several things if we were to have any chance of succeeding. One was a perch on a suitable satellite, which would allow us to distribute our programming to hundreds of cable systems nationwide. Another was access to a usable form of weather information. A third was a technology that would enable us to deliver unique local weather forecasts to each of these cable systems.

The competition for space on satellites was ferocious and intensifying. Procuring the necessary weather information would require a new kind of public/private partnership. And to our knowledge, the locally addressable technology we needed didn't exist anywhere in the world. Getting any of these things would be tough, and we knew that we had to get them all. We had to elbow our way onto a satellite, strike a deal with the federal government, and become world-class inventors.

GETTING TO KNOW SATELLITES

The cable industry today relies largely on satellite technology to provide clear pictures to its subscribers. But in the 1960s and well into the 1970s, before satellites became available for commercial use, many operators used land-based microwave technologies to pick up and relay signals originating in distant places. Microwave transmission posed many problems, however, so when HBO successfully used a satellite to transmit the Ali–Frazier heavyweight title match to subscribers in 1975, the industry rejoiced. HBO used an uplink to send its signal to a satellite "parked" 23,000 miles above the earth, and the satellite rebroadcast that signal nationwide. (Such satellites are said to be in "geostationary," or "geosynchronous," orbit, which simply means that they stay in a constant position relative to the earth, permitting continuous coverage of a particular piece of geography.) Operators who had installed an appropriate satellite "dish" on the ground picked up and rebroadcast the signal.

Of course, no single program provider could pay the astronomical costs of launching and maintaining a communications satellite. So each satellite supported a number of "transponders," each of which retransmitted a different signal back to earth. Early generations of satellites had twelve transponders; later ones had twenty-four. Different commercial entities leased the rights to use individual transponders.

In the pioneering satellite days of the late 1970s, cable operators needed a separate dish for each satellite they were tapping into. These dishes weren't cheap, originally costing between $75,000 and $100,000. Program providers therefore transmitted their signals from a satellite for which the cable operators already had a dish. A new entrant into cable programming like our proposed Weather Channel could conceivably set up shop on another satellite—but if it did so, it was likely to find itself under pressure to provide free dishes to cable operators, at up to $100,000 a pop.

In the trade, satellites are called "birds." When new program entrants made the rounds of the cable operators, looking for systems willing to sign up for the new service, they sooner or later would hear the all-important questions: "Which bird are you on? Do you have your slot yet?"

The bird we chose was RCA's Satcom I, launched in 1975 and quickly thereafter occupied by the strongest cable programmers like HBO and the Turner networks. We knew that we wanted to be on Satcom I, which reached 95 percent of cable households in the United States. If we could get space on that satellite, we would be sending a strong message to the cable industry that we were serious about our new venture. Unfortunately, Satcom I's twenty-four transponders were sold out. Our preferred bird had no room for us.

AN OPPORTUNITY ARISES

In June 1981, while we were deep in negotiations with John Coleman and trying to figure out whether his business plan was viable, we learned that the lease for transponder 21 on Satcom I was being put up for auction.

The reasons, which were complex, reflected the rapid evolution of the cable industry in that period. A consortium of four leading movie studios, along with Getty Oil, had set up a company called Premiere Television. As its founders saw it, Premiere would provide subscription television services to the entire cable industry, serving as the intermediary between Hollywood and cable operators. Premiere would enjoy a clear competitive advantage: It would award itself a six-month TV exclusive on the movies its owners already controlled. This setup would amount to a death sentence for established competitors like HBO, Showtime, and The Movie Channel. Premiere set about building a $2.7 million studio in Bristol, Connecticut, to house the venture.

Not surprisingly, the existing players protested loudly, and the Justice Department agreed to review the scheme. Early in 1981, the Feds ruled that the Premiere scheme violated antitrust laws. And so in June, Premiere announced that the lease on transponder 21 was for sale.

There was one wrinkle. The previous owner of the transponder had subleased two hours of evening prime time—8:00 P.M. to 10:00 P.M., Eastern Standard Time—to Home Theatre Network (HTN), a mini-pay service owned by Group W. The organization that took over Premiere's lease would have to honor this sublease. From our vantage point in Norfolk, we thought we could live with this restriction. Although we dearly wanted to be a twenty-four-hour-a-day service, our market research had shown that evening prime time was unlikely to be a peak viewing period for The Weather Channel. We also thought there might be a way to use technology to continue to transmit weather data throughout the evening.

In any case, if we wanted to be on Satcom I, we didn't have any other options. Even with the HTN complication, the competition for transponder 21 promised to get hot quickly. Through back-channel sources, we learned that at least seven other groups were interested in bidding on the transponder. Most of these companies were bigger and better known than Landmark. Many had deeper pockets.

But Landmark had several advantages of its own. For one thing, although our pockets weren't necessarily the deepest, we were free to dig as deeply into them as we wanted—one of the advantages of being a privately held corporation. Wall Street wouldn't react to our strategic moves, so we could make moves. If we had to take a short-term hit to position ourselves for long-term gain, well, so be it.

A second ace up our sleeve was Gordon Herring. Herring was closely attuned to both cable operators' needs and subscribers' preferences. After a decade at TeleCable, moreover, he also knew many of the key players in the cable industry, including Burt Harris, president of Premiere Television. Although we certainly couldn't expect to trade on this relationship—Harris would get the best deal he could for the transponder lease, in any case—we felt confident that we wouldn't get lost in the shuffle.

Harris soon announced the ground rules of his informal auction. The asking price at the start of the auction was $15 million, which would include both the all-important transponder and the newly constructed studio in Connecticut, out of which the all-sports network ESPN was already operating. Initial bids were due on Friday, July 10, 1981, at noon, Pacific Daylight Time, at Premiere's Los Angeles headquarters. Premiere would then negotiate with the top bidders in order to get the best deal.

One of the most important factors in winning an auction is knowing whom you're likely to be bidding against. We guessed that our strongest potential competitor might be Group W, which dearly wanted to expand its Home Theatre Network—with its two-hour-per-day toehold on transponder 21—to a round-the-clock service.

Two facts supported this guess. First, HTN was making money, and it seemed logical for Group W to build on this profitable base. Second, cable operators were putting pressure on "part-time" programmers to move toward full-time schedules.

A second critical success factor in winning an auction is timing. Gordon Herring, who acted as our agent throughout this process, decided that he would wait until the last minute to submit the Landmark bid. Doing so would help us determine the right entry point and perhaps prevent another bidder from using us as a "stalking horse."

CLOSING THE DEAL

At 11:30 A.M. on July 10, a half-hour before the bidding deadline, we sent our bid to Burt Harris via telegram. We bid $8 million for transponder 21 on Satcom I but left the Bristol studio out of the bid, because we weren't interested in it. We expressed our willingness to assume the HTN sublease for two hours a day of prime time.

Harris called Gordon Herring a few hours later to say that our bid was good enough to get us in the running. He also told us that we were one of seven bidders, and that our bid was at least $2 million lower than the high bid. On the other hand, Harris said, certain aspects of our bid were attractive, and he wanted to keep talking to us. He also said that he wanted to extend the auction by one week to see if he could get a better price for his company's very valuable transponder lease. Finally, he mentioned in passing that he would be out of contact on Monday, and that he planned to meet with the highest bidder in New York on Tuesday.

Here's where some careful sleuthing by Herring paid off in a significant way. He had learned through industry contacts that Group W's chairman, Dan Ritchie, would probably have to give his personal OK to any increase in his company's bid. Herring also found out that Ritchie was planning to be at a family wedding over the weekend, and therefore that he would be very hard to reach. By midnight Friday, Herring had decided that if we were going to win this auction for Landmark, we would have to do so over the weekend.

"And by Saturday morning," Herring recalls, "after a sleepless night, I decided that we should raise our bid to $12 million and agree to purchase the studio equipment in Connecticut at the same time." He called Dubby Wynne at home and learned that he and I were playing tennis together at a nearby club. Herring then phoned the club, and a tennis pro called us off the court to the phone. Wynne listened to Herring's recommendation, and then repeated it to me with Herring still on the line. "Do it," I said.

Herring plunged ahead. He called Burt Harris the first thing Saturday morning with an unexpected offer. "I told him that we weren't interested in participating in a long, drawn-out auction," he says. "Instead, we wanted to make a preemptive bid that he could take to his board immediately." The terms: $12 million, including the studio, but with a twelve-hour deadline on the offer.

Harris said that he needed to get his board's permission, which he would try to do as quickly as possible. He also asked for time to contact Getty, one of Premiere's owners, which had expressed a strong interest in buying the Bristol studio. Herring made it clear, once again, that we didn't want or need the studio. Within hours, Premiere's president succeeded on both fronts. Through Harris, Getty offered to buy back the studio from Landmark for $1.5 million—which would drop our final price down to $10.5 million. Before the end of the day, Harris and Herring had worked out a way for Landmark to buy and sell the studio. This turned out to be the final piece needed to make Premiere happy and to persuade them to accept our bid.

I will always savor the recollection of the phone call I got that night at a dinner party, when a very excited Gordon Herring was able to catch up with me and inform me of his amazing coup. Of course, I shared his excitement. Against long odds, The Weather

Channel now had a home on Satcom I! Mostly through Herring's skill, tenacity, and pure nerve, we had met one of our two prerequisites for success. Now we could focus on the other prerequisite: delivering reliable local weather information to cable systems all over the country. More broadly, I was proud that we had created the kind of environment within which someone like Gordon Herring knew that he could take intelligent risks and make commitments—even big ones—in Landmark's name.

THE NEXT CHALLENGE: LOCAL WEATHER

In our initial meeting with John Coleman, Gordon Herring had said, in no uncertain terms, that TeleCable would have no interest in the weather-channel concept *unless* it included frequent local weather information. Soon after that meeting, Herring asked TeleCable's Nick Worth to join him in exploring how we could come up with the necessary technology to deliver local weather forecasts to each cable system.

Worth, an engineer who had been with TeleCable since 1973, was a logical choice to be involved in the technical side of our due diligence. He understood intimately how cable systems worked, and he also had a good feel for what TeleCable's subscribers did and didn't want to see. Fundamentally, the technical challenge involved collecting data from a profusion of National Weather Service reports of local conditions and forecasts, using that information to create hundreds or thousands of pages of text display, transmitting that huge body of information through a data channel to a satellite, and then retransmitting that information earthward. The retransmitted information would have to be "tagged" in such a way that each local system could grab its own small piece of the overall data stream, thus obtaining several pages of text that provided the local conditions and forecast. On the receiving end—the "head end" of each cable system—we would need a device that could do this selective grabbing.

And of course, all this localized information somehow would have to be interspersed with the main video signal that our weather channel would be providing nationwide. In effect, we needed to find a way to send computer-generated text messages in and around our video programming while making sure that both were reliable.

The more Herring and Worth thought about this challenge, the more they became convinced that a critical piece of the necessary system already existed. For several years, a Salt Lake City–based company, Compuvid, had been manufacturing a device that several TeleCable systems were using. This device served as the brains behind each system's dedicated teletext weather channel. It used local weather sensors to create character-generated text displays, and it could switch from a video signal to a text display and back again. At that point, the Compuvid unit represented the technological state of the art for locally operated weather channels. "What was missing," explains Worth, "was the satellite front end. If we could marry a satellite front end to the Compuvid unit, we'd be home free."

In the course of these discussions, two important things developed almost simultaneously. First, John Coleman and Landmark entered into a formal agreement to launch a nationwide weather channel. (More on that in the next chapter.) Second, Gordon Herring scored his transponder coup. Now that we had satellite space and a formal agreement to launch a weather channel, Herring's and Worth's investigations had to go on a fast track, using the best resources that Landmark had at its disposal. So the two men "worked the system" to recruit additional people to join their team. Ultimately, because they had to return to their duties at TeleCable, the newcomers would take primary responsibility for the overall development project.

The first of the new recruits was a brilliant technologist, Alan Galumbeck. I enjoy telling how Landmark recruited him, because the story underscores the importance of throwing a tight net over talent wherever you find it. Our chief financial officer, Bill

Diederich—as you'll recall, one of the original champions of our entry into the programming field—was the father of thirteen children and was therefore a very careful shopper. And as I've said before, he was by nature a thrifty and systematic person. So when he set out to make a major purchase, he always researched it thoroughly. As a colleague once said, "Bill buys a set of storm windows the same way you or I would buy NBC." By the time Diederich got to a particular sales counter, he could tell the difference between a good salesperson and a bad one. If someone didn't know his or her stuff—or worse, tried to blow smoke over Diederich—no sale.

So one day in the early months of 1966, Diederich went into the Sears store, on 21st Street in Norfolk, in search of a slide projector. A colleague had told him that the kid behind the camera counter really knew his stuff, and our CFO decided to put this kid through his paces. Diederich was so impressed by the young Alan Galumbeck—who was then working his way through Old Dominion University's electrical engineering program by moonlighting at Sears—that he not only bought a projector but recommended that we get Galumbeck in for an interview.

Ultimately, we stole Galumbeck away from both Old Dominion and Sears. The move had enormous long-term implications for both Landmark and The Weather Channel. Still in his twenties, Galumbeck set up our first effective business data-processing system. He later became production manager for our Norfolk newspaper business and helped design and build a new printing plant, which included what was then the longest newspaper press line in the world. At the end of 1978, he became our first "Director of New Technologies," focusing on computer technologies as they pertained to the newspaper business. As a result, Galumbeck was close at hand in 1981 when Herring and Worth went looking for skilled allies.

A second newcomer to the development team was Doyle Thompson. Thompson was a pioneer and near-legendary figure in the broadcasting world, who capped his career by serving as

National President of the Society of Broadcast Engineers. He started in his television career in 1949, when he built WFMY-TV in Greensboro, North Carolina, for the Greensboro News Company. With Thompson's help, WFMY became the first television station in the Carolinas to carry live broadcasts—a notable badge of distinction in the early days of TV. When we acquired the Greensboro News Company in 1965, Thompson was one of the skilled professionals who came along.

Herring and Worth were focusing mainly on the technical challenge of creating local forecasts across hundreds of local cable systems nationwide. They had not forgotten, of course, that our proposed weather channel would need a studio, production facility, and satellite earth station for the live signal that would be cablecast to all the subscribing systems. Someone would have to design and build a kind of facility that was brand new to most of us. We thought first of Doyle Thompson. Unfortunately, we recently had lost Thompson's services when, in March 1981, we sold our Norfolk TV station, WTAR-TV, to Knight-Ridder. Dubby Wynne and I huddled on this problem and decided to take an indirect approach. Thompson was then only about two weeks into his new job with Knight-Ridder and wasn't likely to jump ship back to us so quickly. So we called him and casually asked him if he'd be willing to help us out with our weather channel. He said that he'd be happy to tell us what people and equipment we would need.

What we didn't know was that Thompson was already interested in rejoining our company. He didn't see a clear path for advancement within Knight-Ridder, and he missed his former colleagues. Our conversation turned out to be part consultation, part reunion, and part a gentle wooing process. As he recently recalled in an interview:

> So I did my homework, and met with Dubby and Frank. I went
> into Frank's office, and I was telling them, "OK, you'll need
> this number of cameras, and this is what they'll cost. And you'll
> need these lenses, and here's what they'll cost." I was going down

the list. And every time I looked up, the two of them were look-
ing at me, grinning.

Anyway, to make the story short, I was back with Land-
mark from that day forward.

Our successful reenlistment of Thompson meant that the rest
of the technical team could concentrate on the satellite end of the
larger challenge, while Thompson almost single-handedly stitched
together the studio facilities and uplink-related technologies.

We knew, in the summer and fall of 1981, that we had the
core of a good technical team. We knew that if our scheme was to
succeed, all these technologies would have to converge sometime
soon. But we didn't know exactly *how* they would converge. Nor
did we know whether they could converge fast enough. Someone
else might come up with the same idea, and we knew for sure that
the world didn't need two weather channels.

Meanwhile, new cable systems were being launched, and
existing systems were expanding. We had to get channel space on
these new and expanding systems as soon as possible, or we might
never get it. We had months—not years—in which to overcome
our technological challenges.

DEFINING THE TASK

The existing Compuvid unit was part computer and part television device. An operator keyed in the text on a keyboard, and
the Compuvid device stored this textual information in digital
form. The unit then locked onto the video input and superim-
posed the text over that input.

In the scheme that Herring and Worth were now putting
together, people wouldn't be sitting at keyboards all around the
country. Instead, the studio that Doyle Thompson was building
would "capture" weather information provided by the National
Weather Service. Exactly how this would happen was still a large

unknown. Somehow, we would use this information to create and send hundreds of localized messages up to our satellite—along with the shared national feed, of course—and the satellite would broadcast both the national signal and several hundred localized messages to subscribing cable systems. Each cable system would download the national signal and also "pick off" its own specific local signal, and a substantially enhanced version of the Compuvid device would figure out how and when to merge that signal.

The challenge was to combine an analog TV signal with a digital text signal. After exploring several alternatives, Herring and Worth proposed to squeeze the digital information into something called the "vertical blanking interval." Simply put, the VBI is a regularly recurring "hole" in the beam of electrons that makes up a television signal. Much work had already been done using the VBI to embed a data channel in a video satellite feed, some using the teletext system with which Landmark was already familiar. But we still had a lot to learn.

At this point, Alan Galumbeck took over primary responsibility for the development project. Fortunately for us all, he had a knack for breaking down complex processes into manageable parts. As he recalls:

> I approached this task the same way I approach any other such challenge. I look at the project from the point of view of the data: What is the information that has to be conveyed? And based on that, how do we manage the data, and manipulate the data, and get it into the form we need on both ends?

Using this framework—building the data path—Galumbeck decided that he had to do three things. First, he had to figure out how to get the necessary weather data from the National Weather Service into our studio. Second, he had to determine how to make that information "addressable" for each subscribing cable system. Doyle Thompson would find a way to get the complete package—video and teletext—up to the satellite, and RCA, owner of Satcom I, would get it back down to earth. Then would come Galumbeck's third challenge: enabling the individual cable systems' head ends to grab and decode their respective signals.

Galumbeck decided that Compuvid could take the lead in developing the head-end system, which by this point had a catchy name: the "Satellite Transponder Addressable Receiver," or WeatherSTAR. "It seemed that given the specifications for what needed to be done," he recalls, "they would be able to build the WeatherSTAR."

Galumbeck still would have to ride herd on Compuvid—and then some, as it turned out. But for the time being, he would focus on the front end: where the data would come from, and what form it would take.

GETTING THE DATA

In a sense, we always knew where the data would come from: the National Weather Service.

By 1981, the National Weather Service (NWS) and its predecessor agencies had been in business for more than a century. They were not the first in the weather field, of course. Observers had been gathering and interpreting weather data for centuries. Most of that work, however, focused on climatology. People needed to know, for example, when the first killing frost of the fall was likely to be, and when it was safe to plant in the spring. The systematic study of climate gave tentative answers to these questions.

Predicting the weather on a day-to-day basis was much less of a focus. In fact, giving advance notice about the weather was effectively impossible until the telegraph was invented in 1844. Only then could information about the weather finally travel faster than the weather itself. And so the science of forecasting was born.

A decade before the Civil War, the Smithsonian Institution established a network of weather-reporting stations in the eastern half of the country. Rudimentary reports were processed in Washington and displayed on a large map for the benefit of visitors to the institution. Part of an 1858 report by Smithsonian director Joseph Henry foreshadowed something like The Weather Channel: "This map is not only of interest to visitors in exhibiting the kind of weather which their friends at a distance are experiencing, but is also of importance in determining at a glance the probable changes which may soon be expected."★

This first weather network foundered during the Civil War. It wasn't until the late 1860s that a serious effort was made to put the federal government back into the weather business. The always turbulent Great Lakes experienced a particularly bad weather year in 1869, when almost two thousand ships were lost. This led to the establishment a year later of a "Division of Telegrams and Reports for the Benefit of Commerce," whose focus quickly spread beyond the Great Lakes to embrace the country's rivers and coasts.

Within a decade, as a direct result of the completion of four transcontinental railroads—all lined by telegraph poles—the Signal Office was able to produce serviceable weather maps that covered the entire continent. In 1891, the "Weather Bureau" was recreated within the Department of Agriculture, and began a process of decentralization that greatly improved the quality of local and regional weather information. Almost two hundred local stations of the Weather Bureau produced either local forecasts or weather maps, or both. Over ensuing decades, that number more than doubled. The rise of commercial radio also helped disseminate the bureau's increasingly accurate forecasts.

The first seven decades of the twentieth century saw steady improvements in the science of meteorology and forecasting. Weather balloons explored the upper atmosphere beginning in the late 1930s. Radar, developed in great secrecy during World War II, soon was applied to the study of precipitation and storm detection. Starting in the 1950s, computers were called upon to run

★Mark Monmonier, *Air Apparent* (Chicago: University of Chicago Press, 1999), 41.

newly developed weather-prediction models. On April 1, 1960, Tiros I—the first weather satellite—was launched into orbit 725 kilometers above the earth, giving ground-based observers new insights into the weather.

Beginning in the 1960s, private weather companies began selling specialized services to businesses and industries with a special interest in the weather: airlines, utilities, agriculture, and so on. One of these pioneering companies, Weather Services Corporation, eventually spawned a company that plays an important role later in this chapter.

Meanwhile, the Weather Bureau—renamed the National Weather Service (NWS) in 1970, and housed within the newly organized National Oceanic and Atmospheric Administration— searched for an appropriate role in a changing context. For many years, the NWS had focused on gathering and interpreting weather-related data from its "listening posts" around the country, which by the 1970s numbered about five hundred. The dissemination of data, by contrast, was deemed to be the job of the private sector. This strategy made sense, in that it kept the government mostly out of the media business. But it did little to put the NWS's name in front of the voting public.

So the NWS was failing, even as it was succeeding. Many of the weather experts on radio and TV used NWS data as the basis for their forecasts, but few gave the NWS credit for its vital contribution. The meteorologists at NWS felt an understandable resentment toward the on-air personalities who earned fame and fortune recycling valuable NWS information, for the most part without attribution.

Post-Watergate disenchantment with government in general, and with the federal government in particular, led to recurrent calls for elimination or privatization of government functions. Both the Carter and Reagan administrations targeted the 5,000-person NWS, arguing that weather forecasting was a function that the private sector could and should take over.

But both administrations failed to take into account a wily bureaucrat named Dr. Richard E. Hallgren. Dick Hallgren was a former IBM-er who had come to the government in 1964 and became head of the NWS in 1979. In each of his first three years on the job, budgets submitted to Congress by the Executive Branch called for cuts to the NWS. Hallgren worked a carefully cultivated network of congressional allies to fight off each round of proposed cuts. The way to cut the NWS was to shut down local stations. The way to stop the cuts was to announce in which congressional districts the cuts would come. But by the summer of 1981, Hallgren knew he needed additional allies.

And this was when John Coleman asked Hallgren for a meeting. According to Hallgren, Coleman began by making the case, strongly, that the National Weather Service needed The Weather Channel. Coleman described a nationwide cable network presenting weather information twenty-four hours a day, seven days a week, with the NWS prominently acknowledged as the source of the forecasts.

Coleman told Hallgren that a key part of his plan involved displaying NWS severe-weather warnings and watches instantaneously—a public service that, again, would serve the purposes of both the NWS and our fledgling network. Hallgren readily agreed to this concept; the prospect of a television screen suddenly turning bright red and broadcasting an NWS tornado warning, almost in the instant that warning was generated, was enormously appealing to the head of the Weather Service. But Hallgren asked for assurances that The Weather Channel wouldn't tinker with (or worse, fail to pass along) these high-stakes messages. And to Coleman's dismay, Hallgren said that for the plan to work, The Weather Channel would have to take steps to tap into the NOAA Weather Wire Service—a national teletype-based pipeline of NWS-generated data—at *every node* on that network. Doing so would ensure that The Weather Channel would not overlook any watches or warnings, but it would be expensive.

Coleman, meanwhile, had a major stipulation of his own. For the whole system to work, he explained, the NWS had to agree to a substantial change in the way it did business. At that time, each of the five hundred or so local NWS stations around the country prepared its forecasts differently. Many used the same "rip-and-read" format as did live radio. But if The Weather Channel was going to succeed in its ambitious scheme to gather and retransmit these hundreds of local forecasts, all forecasts would have to be in the same format. No more local idiosyncrasies, said Coleman; from now on, the National Weather Service's outputs would have to be standardized from coast to coast. And they would have to adopt specific protocols that would make them understandable to, and usable by, our computer network.

Hallgren recalls:

> *What John didn't know was that for quite a while, I had been looking at the wide variety of formats in which the Weather Service issued its forecasts. Now, variety is good, to the extent that it reflects different kinds of weather or different ways of communicating in different parts of the country. In fact, if you get too standardized, you may stop communicating with some people. But there were something like fifty different formats being used nationwide, and I really wasn't happy with that variety.*
>
> *The best example concerned probability of precipitation. When they bundled "today, tonight, and tomorrow," which was a common format, they'd say, "Probability of precipitation today, 50 percent; tonight, 60 percent; and tomorrow, 70 percent." Well, people have a limited capacity for absorbing information, and that's a very confusing way of presenting it. So I was interested in making changes.*

Changing these formats, and especially adopting specific formatting conventions dictated by The Weather Channel's computer system, most likely would raise hackles all across the vast NWS organization. But instinctively, Hallgren felt it was a good trade, and he was confident that he could bring his troops along.

At the end of the meeting, both parties expressed a willingness to continue the discussion. As it turned out, this meeting was the first of many rounds of negotiations between NWS and The Weather Channel, which were to extend over many months and expand to include a large number of players. Increasingly, as these negotiations progressed, we at The Weather Channel gained confidence that we could strike a deal that would give us access to NWS data. What we weren't so sure of—until late enough in the game to make us very nervous—was that this information would come in a format we could use.

MOVING AND ADDRESSING THE DATA

An informal task force soon began meeting to tackle the problems of how to move and address the NWS data. Our representatives included Alan Galumbeck and Director of Meteorology Joe D'Aleo. The NWS's chief negotiators were Deputy Director Joe Friday and meteorologist Ed Gross, Hallgren's two most trusted lieutenants. "After one of these meetings with Coleman," Gross recalls, "Dick turned to us and said, 'Do something. Get something done.'" A critical third "seat" at the table was occupied by Todd Glickman, who represented a Bedford, Massachusetts–based company, WSI Corporation.

Glickman was sitting at the table because WSI, a spinoff of the Weather Services Corporation, specialized in capturing and providing weather data through computer links. The company had become a leader in its field by developing methods of taking in vast quantities of information, storing it in databases, and providing it to customers in an easily accessible form.

By the time we hooked up with them, WSI already had access to much of the weather-related data that The Weather Channel would need, including the "zone" (or regional) forecasts that were accessible through the NOAA Weather Wire. Hallgren had insisted that we tie directly into this network. But for us at

The Weather Channel to tap directly into the Weather Wire, and the upgraded "Family of Services" system that would soon replace it, would be like taking a drink from a fire hose: too much, too fast. It quickly became clear that hiring WSI to serve as a data intermediary made a lot of sense.

Then came the tougher part. How could the zone forecasts be "addressed" so that they would come into our computer system in a format suitable for transmitting up to Satcom I, retransmitting nationwide, and then being decoded by the Weather-STAR on each cable head end? In other words, how could we ensure that when you're sitting in your living room in Wichita, you get Wichita's current conditions and not El Paso's?

Defining these protocols fell to Alan Galumbeck and WSI's chief computer whiz, Paul Bayer. Together they devised a scheme whereby messages could be addressed to a single cable system; a single county; a single forecast zone; a series of two or more systems, counties, or zones; or all of the above. Zone forecasts, as well as special messages such as watches and warnings, would be preceded by special codes that would allow WeatherSTARs around the country to pick off their specific information. Galumbeck recalls the process:

> *I did most of the work on developing the data format. I hit upon the notion of hierarchical processing, which from my perspective came purely out of the data. This was one of the things that made the process patentable, and which as far as I know had not been done before.*

Because for us the basic building block of the hierarchy would be counties, Galumbeck became an expert on them. "I became more familiar with counties," he says ruefully, "than I ever wanted to become." But this knowledge had to be captured in a database, so that we could accurately address county-based information coming in from the NWS to subscribing cable systems. As the database got more complicated, Galumbeck had to start worrying about finding an affordable computer with plenty of real-time processing capacity. After scrutinizing the available machines, Galumbeck acquired a pair of Digital Equipment Corporation PDP 1144 computers, installed them in our main newspaper computer room in Norfolk, and hired a team of four software engineers to implement his overall design for the STAR host computer system.

Meanwhile, Ed Gross took on the task of getting NWS stations across the country to adopt a uniform approach to their forecasting. Simply put, he had to persuade them to stop forecasting various aspects of the weather day-by-day (temperature today, tonight, tomorrow; chance of precipitation today, tonight, tomorrow; and so on) and instead give the complete picture for *today* (temperature, chance of precipitation, etc.), then the complete picture for *tonight,* and then the complete picture for *tomorrow.* John Coleman had called this a "flow forecast," meaning that the forecast would follow the flow of time. As Gross recalls, effecting this conversion was tougher than it might sound:

> *When we started proposing to change our forecasts to conform to The Weather Channel's needs, there was a revolution. I mean, even in headquarters, there were a couple of people who were trying to circumvent what we were doing. Joe Friday actually had to kick one guy out. So although Joe and Dick really felt it was time to change this, there was lots of resistance. It was amazing. I got all these nasty letters, including some pictures of me with little knives stuck in.*

Gross hit upon an experiment designed to move the plan forward. He recruited Jim Volkemer—then the meteorologist in charge in Portland, Maine—to run a local trial of the new approach. "And although Jim started out as a skeptic," Gross says, "he came back and said, 'Hey, Ed, this is great! It's exactly what we needed!'"

The NWS's representatives felt that they were moving at lightning speed, overcoming decades of tradition in just a few months. Meanwhile, The Weather Channel team was getting nervous. The fall of 1981 went by, and then much of the winter of 1981–82, and we didn't see the NWS making much progress. Getting the data in a correct format was absolutely critical to us, and we had no control over that critical variable. An excerpt from a February 1982 letter from John Coleman to Dick Hallgren makes the point succinctly:

> *We continue to be concerned that we have budgeted, planned staff and facility, and put our operation in place based on an expectation that the National Weather Service forecasts will be formatted in a way that our computer can properly directly convert them to the television display, and that the National Weather Service may not be able to deliver the forecast in a manner that meets those requirements.* ★

By that time, we had publicly announced our launch date: May 2, 1982. But as Coleman's letter goes on to explain, until we were sure that NWS would deliver, we couldn't be very specific about exactly what The Weather Channel would be putting on the air in ten weeks' time.

As it turned out, our concerns were misplaced. Although we didn't realize it at the time, Dick Hallgren had ample incentives to make the deal work. Once again, he was under budgetary pressure. A *New York Times* article from March recounted in some detail the ongoing battles over the future of the Weather Service. "The Weather Service takes its responsibility to protect the safety of life and property very seriously," Hallgren told the *Times,* "and I know our people are not very happy."★★ Over the short term, his people weren't happy about The Weather Channel, either. But

---

★John Coleman, letter to Richard Hallgren, 22 February 1982.

★★"45 Weather Posts Given a Reprieve; Outcry Brings Shift by U.S.," *New York Times,* 8 March 1982.

Hallgren knew that the near-term discomfort caused by our demands eventually would be outweighed by the benefits that we would provide to each other, and to the nation. So one way or another, our allies at NWS were going to deliver the goods.

BUILDING THE WEATHER CHANNEL'S NERVE CENTER

Following Alan Galumbeck's problem-solving road map—where will the data come from, what has to happen to it, where does it have to go next, and how will it get there?—the next big hurdle was the creation of a suitable studio facility. And although we had a seasoned veteran, Doyle Thompson, on that job, creating our new home from scratch gave us plenty of exciting moments.

Early on, we picked Atlanta as our home city. The choice was largely driven by John Coleman's needs: He had to be in a city with a reliable ABC satellite uplink, so that he could keep delivering the *Good Morning America* segments to which he was contractually obligated for several more years. This same ABC contract strictly limited his appearances on other all networks, including our own. In addition, Coleman argued, and we agreed, that The Weather Channel should locate itself in a temperate climate—to minimize the risk of being shut down by bad weather, when our services might be needed most urgently—and at the hub of a good transportation network. Atlanta also presented quality-of-life advantages, and was less aggressively a "union town" than most northern cities.

Doyle Thompson made his first visit to Atlanta in September 1981. Our recently leased space was at 2840 Mt. Wilkinson Parkway, in a modern commercial development north of Atlanta. A month or so earlier, John Coleman had sketched out his vision for the studio. Perhaps reflecting his strong sense of the need for the business to economize—at least in some areas—the sketch showed the entire studio area fitting into one relatively small room, with a small number of offices around the periphery. The cameras would be located in an equipment area adjacent to the studios, poking and shooting through holes in the wall. Thompson showed the sketch to several of us, making the case that Coleman's vision was inadequate. We readily agreed. Through these discussions, the studio and its related facilities began to grow to a more realistic size.

Body counts are never more than a rough measure. But the minutes from several meetings of Landmark's board of directors give some sense of how quickly our vision was changing. Coleman's original estimate of the size of the staff, made in the summer of 1981, was 65. By October, that number was climbing toward 100. Two months later, the total was more than 120. Doyle Thompson had already built several studios from scratch, so he more or less knew what he was getting into. On the other hand, The Weather Channel was a moving target, and all the movement was from smaller to larger. For example, our equipment list grew along with our studio, our power requirements grew along with our equipment list, and our UPS (uninterruptible power supply) systems grew along with our power requirements.

And so on, and so on. Of necessity, Thompson operated more or less without a budget. Looking back, I find it hard to imagine how we could have finished the job without someone like Thompson, whom we knew and trusted, on the ground in Atlanta. He protected the "critical path" of the design and construction process, and he also minded the treasury.

Remember, too, that this was all taking place in the context of explosive growth in the TV and cable industries. Thompson couldn't do all the work himself, and he had a hard time finding qualified people to help him. He remembers: "The biggest problem I had was finding qualified technical people. Every TV station in the U.S. was looking for engineers and technicians to help build up their electronic news-gathering capabilities. So I was advertising, and going to talk with people wherever I could. It was extremely difficult."

Another problem that Thompson had to solve was getting a good satellite uplink, and then getting a clear path from that site—most likely on the top of a nearby hill—to Mt. Wilkinson Parkway. Thompson was talking one day with an engineer from GE Americom, which owned a satellite uplink facility on the top of Mt. Wilkinson itself, a few miles from our studio site. It turned out that GE was willing to lease that facility, which had formerly handled a huge volume of coast-to-coast phone traffic. Thompson quickly called Dubby Wynne, who negotiated a good lease price for us, and we had our uplink facility: a 30-foot parabolic dish aimed at Satcom I and transmitting around 5,000 watts of microwave power.

Thompson had already resigned himself to using a series of microwave relays to connect our studio with the uplink facility. "We will have to go by air," an entry in his notebook puts it, although he knew that the microwave links would not be as robust as a good old-fashioned underground cable. Then we discovered that our mountaintop purchase included a very special bonus: Southern Bell offered us the opportunity to pull a fiber-optic cable through their huge conduit, which ran down the mountainside and beneath the neighborhoods that sat between the mountain and our studio. Most important, the conduit went under a number of major thoroughfares—streets that we couldn't possibly have dug up to lay our own cable.

But even with this big advantage, the run was extraordinarily long—about a mile and a half—and it seemed impossible to fish a cable that long through the phone company conduit. Thompson solved this problem by tapping into the conduit roughly halfway along our run, pulling the cable in from both ends to the middle, and using a microscopic welding technique to join the two bundles of fiber. We later learned that this was probably the longest continuous run of fiber-optic cable in the world at the time. Sometimes it helps not to know that you're attempting the impossible.

STRUGGLES WITH THE STAR

For much of the fall and early winter of 1981, Compuvid did most of the development work on the WeatherSTAR more or less on its own, with lots of phone calls and occasional supervisory visits from Alan Galumbeck and other technical people from The Weather Channel. Then, in the week between Christmas and New Year's Day, Compuvid invited representatives from The Weather Channel to come take a look at its all-important technology.

To put it kindly, the demonstration was less than a brilliant success. Doyle Thompson, our TV veteran, said flatly that the quality of the video signal coming out of the WeatherSTAR was nowhere near FCC broadcast standards and was therefore unacceptable.

Of course, it wasn't clear whether programming that was intended to be cablecast actually had to conform to any particular standard, broadcast or otherwise. Nevertheless, everyone in The Weather Channel's delegation agreed that if Thompson saw a problem, then upgrading the quality of the WeatherSTAR's signal was a priority. "The only way I knew to be safe," Galumbeck recalls, "was to have a signal in response to which Doyle would say, 'Yep, that's a valid broadcast signal.'"

Through continual processes of trial and error, Thompson, Galumbeck, and Compuvid engineers gradually got the Weather-STAR into a condition that was good enough to go with. Our technical people deserve enormous credit for doing two paradoxical things at once: setting high standards, and also bending those standards when the clock demanded immediate action.

RUSHING DOWN THE ROAD

By the spring of 1982—in other words, just in time—we had most of the technical components of The Weather Channel in place, at least in a rudimentary form.

In retrospect, I'm sure that we tried to do too much, too fast. We often put the cart before the horse, and then asked the horse to run down the road at breakneck speeds. For example: We grabbed transponder 21 on Satcom I well before it was clear that we had the information we needed to put up there, or a good way to get the information back down to the ground. We committed millions of dollars to an idea that we couldn't even represent very well. I distinctly remember the Landmark board meeting in October 1981 when we showed a video simulation of what we thought The Weather Channel's product might look like—assuming that all of our complicated, interrelated plans managed to come together in the right way, at the right time. After a few minutes of silence, one of our board members said that, first of all, he hated the music. And second, if our meteorologists actually talked that fast on the air, he for one would continue to get his weather information from the newspapers.

Without a doubt, we put a rickety technology into play well before it was robust enough to do the job for which it was intended. We spent the next few years fixing the WeatherSTAR's many problems. I'm pretty sure we beat up our partners at Compuvid, who did much of the heavy lifting, a little too forcefully.

On the other hand, I'm convinced that if we hadn't acted as aggressively as we did—if we hadn't spent the money, rushed down the road, and pushed ourselves and our partners to make our self-imposed May 1982 launch deadline—The Weather Channel might never have been born.

CHAPTER FOUR

BIRTHING PAINS

B y the end of June 1981, we had a large investment in a satellite transponder on Satcom I,
cable's most exclusive neighborhood, and we
were scrambling to figure out how we could
develop the "black box" we needed to enable cable operators to
receive local weather forecasts.

On July 6, 1981, we reached closure on another major unre-
solved issue: a set of agreements with John Coleman. Wynne and
our corporate counsel, Louis Ryan, had been engaged for several
weeks in off-and-on negotiations with Coleman and his lawyer,

Phil Couri, over the shape of two agreements. One was a management and consulting agreement between the new venture and Coleman's own management company. The other was a stockholders' agreement between Landmark and Coleman, defining how each would acquire stock in the venture.

Much more work remained to be done before our weather channel could go on the air, of course. We had to find operators who would actually commit to show our product. We had to find advertisers who would support it. We had to figure out exactly what our programming was going to look like, and then hire and train people who could produce and deliver that programming. We had to build our studio and solve our technical problems— which we had only begun to define—and get ourselves on the air with as much flair as possible.

These were the birthing pains of The Weather Channel, and they were considerable.

STRIKING A DEAL

At Landmark, we have always tried to make sure that the outcomes of negotiations come as close as possible to fulfilling the needs of all the parties, and that business agreements produce win-win results over the long term. On paper, those words look a little sanctimonious. But they're true, nonetheless, and we believe in them. We've learned from painful experience that shotgun weddings produce unhappy offspring. Unfortunately, the Landmark-Coleman negotiations, and the agreements that grew out of them, made this point many times over. Those agreements explain a great deal of what eventually came to pass.

Our problems, which in retrospect could have killed the experiment in its cradle, cropped up very early, probably because both parties came to the table with unrealistic expectations. John Coleman believed that because he came up with the concept of a weather channel, he should be able to control its development and operation. We countered that Landmark should have ultimate authority for strategic decisions because we would be financing all the venture's operating and capital needs—and thus were assuming all the financial risks—and at the same time we would be supplying the essential technologies, the cable industry contacts, and several of the people who would be most critical to the enterprise.

From the beginning of our talks, it was abundantly clear that Coleman was obsessed with starting a weather channel. And the truth is that even before our due diligence was finished, I had become similarly obsessed. Now, both Coleman and I believed we had to be the first mover, doing everything possible to preempt a competitor. And yet we had some fundamental differences staring up at us from the table, and a proper settlement of those differences threatened to take a lot of time. As it turned out, the only resolution that we could get to in a hurry was a bad one: We agreed that if an impasse arose over operational control or strategy, the two parties would divorce. We further agreed that Coleman would have operational control of the venture as long as he met a series of specified financial targets. If he failed to meet these profit targets after one year and subsequent years, Landmark would have the right to terminate his management agreement and fire him.

In hindsight, I should have recognized the high risks inherent in this kind of agreement. All the parties at the table had contributed to creating an adversarial, legalistic climate. The tenor of the negotiations should have been a flashing yellow caution light, but none of us thought we could afford to slow down. We soon discovered that we had chosen a bad way to structure our risky start-up venture, particularly because a great deal of money and pride were at stake.

The financial agreement we reached was rather complex. We established two classes of stock. Landmark purchased 80 shares of Class A voting stock for $80 and Coleman purchased 20 shares for $20. That $20 would later provide a strange punctuation mark in our relationship with Coleman. Landmark purchased 1.2 million shares of Class B nonvoting stock at $1 per share, and Coleman was issued 75,000 shares of Class B stock in exchange for his business plan. Coleman also received six subscription agreements that gave him the opportunity to purchase up to 225,000 additional shares of Class B stock for $1 per share if the venture achieved specified targets for revenue and operating income (net revenues less all expenses) over a five-year period. In other words, Coleman could end up owning 20 percent of The Weather Channel if he hit financial targets that were more conservative than his own projections.

We also took steps to help Coleman purchase his Class B stock. Coming up with the cash for such a purchase is often an insurmountable challenge for the "idea man" in these kinds of relationships. We agreed that if the venture hit its targets, Coleman would receive a cash bonus totaling twice the amount he would need to purchase that year's allotment of stock. He thus would have enough money to pay taxes on the bonus and buy the stock. He could also receive an additional cash bonus in any year in which the venture exceeded 125 percent of its operating income projections.

Complicated as these conversations were, it wasn't until we focused on the management agreement that relations really became strained. The agreement that resulted from some testy sessions reflected Coleman's strong need for control, and also his concern that Landmark might wind up bullying him at some point. Our agreement provided that Coleman would be chairman of the board, president, and "chief executive and operational officer with total operational responsibility." As long as the agreement remained in effect, the contract read, "neither Landmark nor the Board of Directors will unreasonably restrict the responsibilities or authority of Coleman."

Of course, we didn't give away complete control of the store. Landmark could cancel the agreement—thus terminating Coleman's role—after any year in which the venture failed to achieve at least 85 percent of the operating income projection the agreement specified. The projection for the first year of operation was a loss of $924,000, and the projection for the second year was a profit of just over $2.7 million. If the agreement were cancelled, Landmark would pay Coleman a $250,000 cancellation fee and purchase his stock. In other words, even though Landmark would own 80 percent of the voting stock, Coleman's operational control would be assured as long as the venture met our financial projections—which set a lower hurdle than Coleman's own projections. Coleman also had the authority to appoint two of the venture's four directors, and thus he could block us from removing him or restricting his powers arbitrarily.

Over the past twenty years, I have often looked back in amazement that we handed over so much control of a precarious venture to a man we hardly knew. We had not checked Coleman's references carefully, and now we were pinning all our expensive hopes on him. The only way I can explain our precipitous actions is to say that I was overcome by "deal psyche"—the urge to get the deal done. Even though I had always cautioned my colleagues against falling prey to deal psyche, the thought of an around-the-clock weather channel riveted my attention, and John Coleman was a hell of a salesman.

A few weeks later, when journalists expressed strong skepticism about our scheme, my passion for the deal began to ebb. Belatedly, I found myself worrying about Coleman's ability to manage this venture. We had rationalized away the management question, in large part because we placed such a high value on both Coleman's weather expertise and his "star" quality. We believed that both ingredients were critical to the success of our weather channel. We wanted Coleman to pass muster, and so he did.

WHY SO CONFIDENT?

Because our financial projections in the agreements were both based on, and lower than, Coleman's own projections, Coleman was extremely confident that a weather channel could achieve those numbers. Bahns Stanley had been working for weeks

87

on making independent projections for us. The critical questions related to estimating revenues. How much distribution from cable systems could we expect? How much acceptance by viewers and advertisers did we believe we could get? Depending upon assumptions, these revenue estimates produced a wide range of results.

Meanwhile, on the cost side of the ledger, we were confident of our ability to estimate the costs relating to technology, sales, and marketing. This was Mistake No. 1. We also had more or less accepted Coleman's estimates of programming costs—Mistake No. 2, and a big one! As it turned out, we had woefully underestimated all these costs, particularly the programming and production costs. As Stanley explains:

> *We were trying to calculate what it would take to run a 24/7 business. When we finally went on the air, we had more than twice as many people on the payroll as Coleman had initially estimated. The basic problem was that nobody in America had ever done a weather segment for more than two or three minutes at a time, and we were going to get people to do live television twenty-four hours a day.*
>
> *Also, we had to organize a production factory where we would create graphics twenty-four hours a day. Again there were no models for that. It's no surprise that we were sloppy at the beginning. From the data in, to the creation of products, to the on-air presentation, to the act of pumping it out the building— all these things were sloppy. There were so many points of contact, and so many stresses on the system, that simply didn't exist anywhere else.*

Even our most pessimistic projections showed attractive investment returns. No, we didn't think of this venture as a "slam dunk," because we knew we had to do a lot of things right for it to succeed. But I honestly can't remember being more excited or optimistic about any other business deal we have ever considered. Years later, of course, our optimism finally proved to be justified—

but not before our venture had passed through months and months of chaos and despair. And as will become clear, our success ultimately depended on circumstances we did not even consider.

Why did I think we had a realistic chance of success when most others in the media business thought we were nuts? I had an instinctive belief in the value of the product. I believed it was important. And industry surveys repeatedly showed that the weather segments of local newscasts were the principal magnets for news program viewers. I believed that we could think like cable operators, and that we could take advantage of our strong ties within the cable community. In John Coleman and Dubby Wynne, we had two hard drivers who moved quickly to get things done. In Gordon Herring and Nick Worth, we had two experienced hands who thought creatively about the use of technology. In Alan Galumbeck and Doyle Thompson, we had strong resources in both digital and analog technologies.

But as "deal psyche" started to wear off, I began to worry. Given our status as a private company, I wasn't overly concerned about the public consequences of failure. No one likes to look foolish, but you can't steer the ship with your vanity. The internal consequences of failure were quite another matter, and here my principal concerns were not financial.

For many years before 1981, I had been trying to create an entrepreneurial culture within Landmark. We had started up a number of innovative product extensions in our local and regional markets, and we had been a pioneer in developing cable TV systems. But this weather channel would be our first national business. It would be larger and more visible than anything we had tried before. Success would breed newer, broader opportunities and reinforce the budding entrepreneurial spirit within our organization. A conspicuous failure, conversely, might well make us run scared and also narrow the scope of opportunities that we could pursue with comfort.

Yes, we put more of our money on the table every day. But what I really had in the front of my mind was the potential impact

on our company of hitting a home run, or striking out ignomin-
iously, on the national stage.

GOING PUBLIC

In any case, we weren't planning to hide our light under a
bushel. Coleman and Wynne thought it was important to announce our planned venture quickly and visibly, while the interest
generated by our acquisition of transponder 21 was still reasonably
high. We scheduled a press conference in Manhattan's Park Lane
Hotel for July 30, 1981, and retained a nationally known New
York–based public relations firm (at a fancy price) to get the most
mileage from the event. To our surprise, what we received from
this high-priced talent was a superficial, even amateurish, collection of press releases and press-kit materials. Their mock-ups didn't
come close to depicting how a round-the-clock weather channel
could appeal to viewers. In fact, they tended to reinforce the first-
blush reaction that twenty-four hours of weather, seven days a
week, would be drier than attic dust.

On a tight deadline, therefore, we had to produce our own
materials from scratch. I turned this task over to Jim Mays, Landmark's director of communications. Mays had been a newspaper
photographer and a sports columnist, and—until Landmark sold its
Norfolk television station, WTAR-TV—a television news director. Approaching this public relations task with a newshound's
insight and perspective, Mays produced some very effective press
information. He didn't have time to make it slick, but he told our
story clearly and with a healthy dose of excitement.

On the day before our New York press conference, John
Coleman and I checked out the ballroom facilities of the Park
Lane Hotel and went through a dry run of the conference, at
which he and I were both scheduled to speak. In retrospect, that
day was probably the high-water mark of our excitement and
optimism about the venture. All of us who had been intimately

involved in what had transpired up to that date—the negotiations, the transponder wars, the early technology investigations—now solidly believed that we were about to unveil a winning cable concept. I hosted a festive dinner with Coleman, Wynne, Herring, Stanley, and Mays to celebrate the next day's public christening of The Weather Channel. This was the "wild enthusiasm" phase of a new venture, in full bloom.

Coleman had done his homework for the press conference. On a recent recruitment trip to the West Coast, he had stopped in the studio of our Las Vegas station, KLAS-TV. He wanted to put together a short videotaped sample of The Weather Channel's proposed programming. He persuaded two young meteorologists whom he was trying to recruit—and who hadn't actually signed up with us yet—to serve as his on-camera talent. (Coleman's contract with *Good Morning America* largely restricted him from appearing on the air for The Weather Channel). But because we really hadn't thought through our programming yet, the taping session was unproductive and dragged on for hours and hours. Frustration levels got higher and higher, and tempers wore thin. Hugh Eaton, one of our Landmark colleagues who would later help manage The Weather Channel, recalls what happened next:

> *John was really tired, because by this point, it was 7:00 or 8:00 P.M., and he was used to getting up really early to do his* Good Morning America *segments. So he was really dragging, and his eyes were drooping. But he was driven to get this thing done, and these two guys just couldn't make him happy. So he said, "Let me show you what I'm talking about."*
>
> *And he got up there in front of that camera, and it was incredible. I mean, he came alive. He had energy. He made the thing sing, and live. It was a transformation like you couldn't believe.*

But the resulting tape didn't come close to overcoming the skepticism we encountered at the conference the next day. Nor did Coleman's lively explanation of the high interest in TV weather, and our opportunity to fill an obvious void, and so on. Nor, for that matter, did my own brief comments. The assembled reporters simply couldn't grasp why we would want to waste a scarce transponder on such a dull subject. Most couldn't get beyond the misperception that we were expecting people to watch weather over and over again. In retrospect, I can see that they were stuck in a broadcasting mentality while we were talking about narrowcasting. It was not the best time I've ever had at the Park Lane.

To be fair, I should say that the trade press reported the event more or less as straight news, which was probably the best outcome we could have hoped for. But our public announcement also unleashed the first trickle in what would become a flood of jokes about, even ridicule of, The Weather Channel. Television critics in the print media were especially tough on us. Meanwhile, the dominant reaction of my friends in other media companies was one of wonderment. A few more or less implied that I was out of my mind. Dan Burke, the president of Capital Cities/ABC, found a kind way to put it. "Well, Frank," he said, "You've got a lot of guts."

Despite these reactions, we pressed forward vigorously. As noted, Coleman and Wynne set a target date for going on the air on May 2, 1982, then just over nine months away. The May date coincided with the opening of the annual convention of the National Cable Television Association, where we definitely needed to make a splash and stake out our turf. "If you're going to make your debut," as one of my colleagues put it, "make it at Carnegie Hall." Considering the work that we still had ahead of us, the date was highly optimistic.

BUILDING A STAFF

One of the first challenges we faced was building a staff. This happened in a couple of ways simultaneously, reflecting the fact that we were under time pressure, and also that the two "camps" (Landmark and Coleman) had their own ideas about what was needed.

An important early hire was Landmark's own Hugh Eaton. When John Coleman made the prototype Weather Channel video in Las Vegas, Eaton was there, too, waiting for Coleman to interview him. Under the terms of our agreement with Coleman, Landmark was to select, and Coleman approve, The Weather Channel's vice president for business affairs, who would have responsibility for the financial control of the company. Dubby Wynne and I asked Eaton, a long-time Landmark executive in finance and human resources, to fill this position at The Weather Channel, where he would also head up human resources. Eaton had high ethical standards and strong people skills, and we hoped he would be able to instill some of Landmark's values in the brand-new Weather Channel organization. But Coleman had to approve the choice, so Eaton accompanied him to Las Vegas, and passed the "audition." This is the way it was done, in those frantic early days: everything at once.

I've already described the role Doyle Thompson played in setting up our Atlanta studio and uplink facility. Coleman had previously proposed a Midwestern candidate for this key post, but our technical people were highly skeptical of this candidate, and pushed for Thompson instead. He was another known quantity, with strong skills in the technical side of broadcasting, whom we were happy to be able to inject into The Weather Channel.

Coleman had only limited experience in the world of business, and he knew he needed Dubby Wynne's help identifying and recruiting people for some of the other senior management slots. Both Coleman and Wynne wanted to fill the cable affiliate sales management position with someone who had cable TV experience; but people with that experience were rare in those days, and The Weather Channel was not viewed as the strongest proposition in the industry. As an alternative, Wynne proposed Dean Waite, the publisher of one of Landmark's small daily newspapers, who was regarded as particularly strong in generating sales. Coleman agreed to this choice, as well.

Coleman also put forward his own candidates. For example, he proposed to hire Mike Ban, a Chicago-based advertising executive who had helped him develop his original business plan, as vice president for advertising sales. Ban was vice president of advertising for paint manufacturer Sherwin-Williams, and he had a strong grasp of advertising, particularly from the client's point of view. Wynne was concerned about Ban's lack of sales management experience, but he found him personable and knowledgeable, and ultimately he concurred with Coleman's selection.

Coleman also recruited Joe D'Aleo, who kept deferring his dreams of finishing his Ph.D. as he continued to help Coleman with *Good Morning America* in Chicago. D'Aleo signed on as director of meteorology, which meant that he was in charge of both the on-camera and off-camera meteorology staff. These meteorologists, of whom Coleman originally expected to hire about fifty, would be at the heart of the new venture. D'Aleo would help Coleman recruit and train the staff—although Coleman insisted on personally interviewing all candidates for positions as on-camera meteorologists—and he also would work closely with Coleman on the design of our programming.

The formal recruitment of the meteorology staff started with ads in the December 1981 issues of the *Bulletin of the American Meteorological Society* and *Broadcasting* magazine. These ads generated a flood of resumés, tapes, and phone calls from weather people all over the country. Not surprisingly, the levels of experience and professionalism varied widely. As D'Aleo recalls, "Some of the tapes we'd watch and say, 'Ah! We've got to have that one! He's perfect!' And others were laughable. They were probably the first tapes that some of these young people had ever produced, and some of them were really rough. I wish we had saved them."

Coleman and D'Aleo made a conscious effort to recruit people from different geographical backgrounds. Similarly, they tried to recruit people with experience with meteorological extremes:

tornadoes, tropical storms, heavy snows, and so on. They also tried to hire graduates of several different meteorology schools, on the theory that each school taught things a little differently, and that The Weather Channel would benefit from the widest possible range of skilled approaches.

One of their recruits was Dennis Smith, a tall, outgoing young man with craggy features and a shock of brown hair. I'll cast Smith as a typical recruit, although the fact that he's still with us more than two decades later suggests that he was an above-average talent. Smith had had a half-dozen years of on-camera experience working as a weather person at local stations in Oklahoma City and Wichita, Kansas. He loved his work, but he didn't like some of the unpleasant surprises that came with working the weather beat in a broadcast context. For example, it wasn't unusual for Smith to work hard on a three-minute weather segment, only to have it cut to a minute if a late-breaking news story—or maybe some exciting sports footage of local interest—needed more time. So when he spotted one of our ads in *Broadcasting,* he thought it might be worth making a phone call. As he recalls:

> *So I came down in late 1981 and had an interview with John [Coleman]. I knew of him from seeing him on* Good Morning America, *so that was kind of exciting. And it was even more exciting when I got to talk to him about the prospects of where this thing was going. He was very passionate, very excited. He was very much like he was on the air: exuberant, bubbly. That same kind of excitement came out while we were talking. So I said, "Hey, this is different. I'm willing to take a chance. I want to see what happens."*

Slowly, the team came together. Coleman and D'Aleo recruited both on-air and off-camera meteorologists in roughly equal numbers—about two dozen in each group, initially. The off-camera people would help supply the revised forecasts, interpretive material, and short and long features that the on-camera meteorologists would depend on to fill our soon-to-be-gaping

24/7 pipeline. Although Coleman himself didn't have a degree in meteorology, he insisted on hiring only trained meteorologists, rather than the "talking heads," often picked for their good looks or on-camera antics, who were then delivering the weather on many TV stations.

Coleman's personal charisma played an important role in this recruitment. "He was tremendously attractive, in terms of signing up the on-camera meteorologists," recalls Hugh Eaton. "It was easy for him to sign up those guys and women from all over the country." Meanwhile, another Coleman recruit—art director Pam Peniston, a colleague from Chicago—began hiring the artists who would prepare the visual materials the meteorologists needed.

Our schedule was unforgiving. The senior managers began operating out of Atlanta in late 1981. The official date-of-hire for most of The Weather Channel's employees was March 1, 1982. We were committed to going on the air just over two months after that. Our studio wasn't yet complete, our technology was not yet perfected, and our programming still existed mainly in Coleman's and D'Aleo's minds. Meanwhile, we had to hit the streets in search of cable operators who would commit to putting our product on their networks.

GOING AFTER DISTRIBUTION

Again, time was the enemy. We all felt intense pressure to launch our channel quickly: before someone else got the notion to start a weather channel, and before vacant channels were committed to other programming services. Coleman was especially anxious about the threat of competition. He kept reporting rumors about other groups who were allegedly considering a weather channel. Fortunately, none of these rumors ever panned out. On the other hand, new program services were being announced almost weekly, and there was a fierce, intensifying competition for channels.

As early as September 1981, therefore, Coleman and Tele-Cable's Gordon Herring began calling on the nation's dozen largest cable operators, seeking support and channel commitments. Herring and Coleman soon proved to be an effective team. Herring had friendly contacts with many of his counterparts at other cable companies—that is, the people mainly responsible for programming and marketing their systems. Coleman, I'll say again, was a marvelous spokesman for his cause. He pushed The Weather Channel with a missionary's zeal. He never failed to emphasize the public service that the channel would provide, often closing his sales pitch by exclaiming dramatically, *"The Weather Channel will save lives!"*

But the cable operators were a savvy bunch, and not particularly susceptible to passionate oratory from Coleman or anybody else. They liked our "cable-friendly" contract, on which we had spent a lot of time. Again, our experience as cable operators helped us a lot in this realm. We knew how to write a contract they'd like. They were happy to give our sales team a fair hearing. Then, after The Weather Channel left the room, they weighed their options carefully. As Herring recalls:

> *I'd say the initial reaction from most operators was positive, but not exactly extreme excitement, since The Weather Channel was pretty much of a utility product. The operators liked the fact that it would be free, and that on most systems it would replace an automated service that was less than sophisticated.*

But we were competing with every new programming service for channel space. These included Disney, Lifetime, Playboy, Financial News Network, Arts & Entertainment, The Nashville Network, and several regional sports channels. At the same time, we were competing with the first wave of programmers—such as ESPN, CNN, Nickelodeon, MTV, and others—that were aggressively trying to extend their distribution.

Dubby Wynne knew what Coleman and Herring were up against. He was therefore a little surprised by their early successes, which grew in part out of better market conditions than we had expected. "We are finding that there are far more dedicated weather channels in 12-channel systems than we had estimated," he wrote in an October report to the Landmark board. "It seems clear that we will start with a much higher cable household total than we earlier thought—perhaps 4 million. This is critically important in establishing credibility with advertisers."

After much hard work by Coleman, Herring, and others, seven of the top twelve companies committed 2.5 million cable households to us. When we exhibited at two cable conventions, we received encouraging responses during meetings with the two largest operators, TelePrompTer and American Television and Communication Corp. They liked our pitch, they told us, and they were looking forward to seeing our product prove itself on the air.

It was becoming increasingly clear, in other words, that a great deal would be riding on our launch. By scheduling it to coincide with the first day of the annual convention of the National Cable Television Association, in Las Vegas, we would get another important chance to woo and win more distribution customers, including some of the nation's biggest.

SEARCHING FOR ADVERTISERS

During this same period, Mike Ban began organizing a staff of six or seven ad sales representatives. He hoped to have at least four people in New York and two in Chicago. One outstanding hire was Mike Eckert, a successful radio ad salesman in Chicago, whom Ban picked to head the Chicago office. Chicago quickly emerged as our most successful sales office, and Eckert emerged as a man to watch.

Ultimately, our advertising sales would depend on how many viewers we had, how often they tuned in, and how long they watched. We did not expect the average viewer to stay with us long—perhaps five minutes at a time. We hoped that viewers would tune us in several times a day, and we also hoped that with creative programming, we could gradually stretch the time they stayed with us. But in our start-up phase, all of this was guesswork. For several years—at least until we reached Nielsen's minimum 15 million households—we wouldn't be able to prove to advertisers that anyone was actually watching their commercials. We shared with this problem all but the biggest cable programmers at that time. Cable advertising had to be bought experimentally, and on faith.

I was optimistic about our audience appeal. I believed instinctively that there was a large untapped interest in weather, and that we could build upon, and maybe even build, that interest. My main worry was that viewers might not watch us long enough to be attractive to advertisers. And once again, we wouldn't know that until we went on the air.

Through a lot of hard work, the sales staff managed to sign up four advertisers to be on the air with us when we launched: American Express, Quaker Oats, Eastman Kodak, and Hyatt Hotels. Because it was extremely important to have advertisers on the air from Day One, we offered these four companies very low introductory rates.

PROGRAMMING AND TRAINING: TWO MORE BIG BITES

In the months before they started bringing people to Atlanta—that is, at the end of 1981 and the beginning of 1982—Coleman and D'Aleo sat down with some producers and artists and laid out what they thought our program elements should be. They created storyboards for the various features, to be used in the initial training of both on-air and off-air meteorologists.

These storyboards, which D'Aleo was able to retrieve from his files more than twenty years later, provide an interesting window into how our tiny programming group was thinking about their initial challenge. The boards indicate how long each segment was supposed to last, how many on-camera images might appear during that segment, and—in a rough cartoon format—how the on-camera meteorologists might interact with those images. Some of these segments are readily recognizable today. The "national forecast," for example, was expected to take a minute and a half, and to require up to nine frames of artwork. According to the storyboard, "The series starts with maps in motion followed by our choice of one or more additional forecast maps," such as highs and lows, relative humidity, hours of sunshine, and so on

Other segments are more exotic. The "Talk to the Weatherman" segment, also anticipated to last a minute and a half, would feature "one or more weather channel meteorologists who will be available to chat with and answer questions on the phone live with our viewers." That concept didn't make the final cut, although for several years we did maintain an answering machine on a toll-free phone line, on which viewers could record a question that we might later answer on the air. This gave us plenty of time to get good answers to the questions we chose to answer.

A thirty-second segment, envisioned as a contest, was called "Trivia Corner." According to the caption on this storyboard, "Talent poses questions about weather past, present, or future. Mostly serious, a few whimsical, to be answered by viewers on our 800 toll-free number." One accompanying cartoon shows a Clark Kent–like meteorologist with a huge book—"Weather Records"— open on the desk in front of him as he poses a knotty question to the viewers. The other cartoon depicts a text slide of the question he is posing: "Q: In what state did the single greatest storm snowfall occur? Call 800-WEATHER." Again, this particular segment didn't make the final cut.

Looking at these storyboards today, I'm struck by how relatively homespun and unpretentious our initial vision was. This unassuming image was in part deliberate: We wanted viewers to feel that our staff members were friendly, accessible, solid citizens. But I'm sure this quality also reflected the personalities of the people and institutions involved in the venture. For all his ambition and energy, John Coleman was a Midwesterner at heart: hard-working, literal and linear, and maybe even a little corny. Joe D'Aleo was deliberate and thoughtful and never wore his ego on his sleeve. And Landmark's influence was anything but flamboyant. Collectively, we weren't the most colorful cable programmers.

Coleman and D'Aleo also spent a considerable amount of time thinking through the content and pace of programming, over the course of the day and the week. One early memo divided the available time slots as follows:

- Morning Drive (Monday through Friday, 5 A.M. to 11 A.M.)
- Morning (Saturday and Sunday, 5 A.M. to 11 A.M.)
- Daytime (11 A.M. to 5 P.M.)
- Evening (5 P.M. to 11 P.M.)
- Late Night (11 P.M. to 5 A.M.)

Drive-time programming was supposed to consist, among other things, of "fast-paced, short segments," with a heavy emphasis on today's weather, and with no lifestyle features. Saturday and Sunday mornings, as well as the daytime slot, would include longer features, lifestyle stories ("skier's forecast"), and less frequent local weather. By evening, according to the memo, we would "pick up the pace again," because we were "competing with local and national news and prime time programming." And in the late night, we'd focus on the West Coast, "assuming east coast is asleep," showing lots of satellite views of the western U.S. and Pacific, and international weather with an "Asia emphasis."

We eventually put most of these plans into practice, although not in as formulaic a way as this memo might suggest. To some extent, we blocked out the programming along the lines suggested by this grid. But we also followed the lead of our advertisers—scarce as they were, in the early days!—who sometimes wanted to sponsor a particular segment at a particular time of day. And finally, we gradually began matching particular on-screen staffers' talents and personalities with particular time slots. The high-energy people tended to wind up in the high-energy time slots, like drive time and early evening, and the more soothing types wound up on the afternoon and weekend shifts. Things evolved as we got smarter.

Our storyboards and programming schedules were first put to use on March 1, 1982, our formal "Orientation Day." It was the first day of work for most of our troops. Coleman gave a brief pep talk to the newly assembled team, and then he turned the meeting over to Director of Meteorology D'Aleo. D'Aleo, who had been a meteorology professor and had a strong academic bent, presented what he called a "history lesson," with a special emphasis on weather forecasting. "Once a teacher, always a teacher," he explained.

He also distributed a five-paragraph document he called a mission statement, which I'll reproduce here in its entirety:

> The mission and principal goal of THE WEATHER CHANNEL is to become the nation's primary and best source for weather information—to provide a valuable and needed service to our customer—the viewer, the cable operator, and the advertiser.
>
> To become the nation's primary and best choice for weather information, THE WEATHER CHANNEL will employ both the best available technology and good people. We will use these resources to gather, transform, and deliver useful, accurate information and present that information on a timely basis and in an understandable, interesting, and personable (entertaining) way. Ultimately, to succeed, we must also be dependable. Our credibility as an information service demands that we deliver vital information whenever and wherever we are needed. Through our programming, we should both inform and educate. We should strive to elevate the understanding of the viewer and in this way increase the usefulness and demand for our product.
>
> Fulfilling these goals and achieving our mission will require the commitment, dedication, hard work, and teamwork of all THE WEATHER CHANNEL employees. In return,

*THE WEATHER CHANNEL must provide the resources necessary
to do the job, a pleasant and secure environment, the opportunity
for achievement and growth, and recognition and reward for
accomplishment.*

*By working together to achieve these goals, we will make
this a great company and a successful cable service.*

This mission statement genuinely reflected our intentions
and aspirations. Unfortunately, it made promises that we weren't
able to keep in the early days. Remember that Doyle Thompson
was then building our new studio and production facility from
scratch. On Orientation Day, our new troops walked into a cav-
ernous room that was mostly empty. We were still scrambling to
provide the "resources necessary to do the job," as well as a "pleasant and secure environment." Most of the necessary equipment
didn't start arriving until mid-March, which meant that for most of
our first month of operations, training was difficult. There are only
so many times you can read through storyboards with enthusiasm.

By April, though, we were beginning to live up to our promises. The studio, production facility, and uplink to the satellite
were mostly in place and working. Now our on-camera meteorologists were actually "on camera," working with D'Aleo to polish
up both their own delivery and the program content.

For the entire month of April, we were practicing on the air,
and Doyle Thompson occasionally threw our signal up to the
satellite as part of a systems test. Someone with the right dish and
a little technical know-how could have watched our programming evolve in real time, minus the local forecasts, the delivery of
which our technical group was still hammering out. I don't think
many people found us—which is just as well, because this practice
programming was pretty rough.

We encouraged, and expected, the on-camera meteorologists to be their own producers. Thus they had to make the transition from Weather Channel novices to experts in a very short
time. Most succeeded admirably. A related goal involved getting

these meteorologists—all formerly "local talents"—to think of the entire nation as their "beat." As D'Aleo puts it, "We stressed with our on-camera people that we had to be everybody's local weatherman. We said, 'Don't talk about the weather there, and the weather here. You're there. You're the weatherman in Sioux Falls. You're also the weatherman in Portland and Atlanta.'"

Gradually, and none too fast for our collective comfort, the people and the programming came together. But many questions remained. One of them involved these maps and slides that were supposed to be appearing on screen with our on-camera meteorologists. Who was going to be generating them, and how—and what would they look like?

GETTING THE LOOK RIGHT

So while all these other activities were going on, we also were recruiting and training a cadre of artists to create computer-generated materials for the on-camera staff. From a vantage point at the dawn of the twenty-first century, it's hard to imagine what this involved in the early months of 1982. Today, we are bombarded with computer-generated artwork more or less constantly: on TV, at our computer workstations, in bars, restaurants, and convenience stores, and—most recently—in elevators. It wasn't always so! In 1982, the Apple Macintosh computer was still several years away from being born. Few graphic artists had ever touched a computer.

So John Coleman's art director, Pam Peniston, had her work cut out for her. She put the word out in the Atlanta area that a new TV company wanted to hire artists who were willing to produce program-related slides on computers. One of the artists who heard about this strange opportunity was a young printmaker, Victoria Webb. Hooking up with The Weather Channel, she recalls, was a complete accident:

It was a fluke. This was April of '82. I was working in a graph-
ics studio doing prints, and there was a guy there who was a
newspaper cartoonist. He happened to know somebody at
TWC, and knew they were hiring artists. So he just mentioned
it one day, and I thought, "Hey, it would be kind of cool to work
on a computer." I had no idea what that meant, but it sounded
more interesting than what I was doing.

Webb's entree was more or less typical of the dozen or so
people whom Peniston rounded up. Several, like Webb, had fine-
arts backgrounds. Others were graphic artists specializing in commercial design and graphics. One spray-painted vans for a living.
But this seemingly motley crew was destined for great things.

Doyle Thompson, the designer and builder of our studio,
was anything but a computer jock. Back in those days, TV was
analog, computers were digital, and the twain rarely met. Nevertheless, he sized up the limited choices then on the market and
took his best shot. He purchased several Aurora computers—
which featured a rudimentary form of animation, useful for making active-looking title slides—and also several Colorgraphic
machines, the best computer then available for making maps. Early
on, Thompson also purchased a Quantel Paintbox, a proprietary
hardware and software system with a color monitor and keyboard-
based inputs. Although Paintbox, developed in the United Kingdom, emerged as one of the best tools ever created for graphic
designers and computer artists, we had Serial No. 1 in the United
States, which put us well out on the bleeding edge of technology.

All our computer systems crashed more or less constantly.
Most often, it was Thompson who had to get them working
again. As he recalls:

One problem was the unit that we used for all our backgrounds.
It was supposed to be on the air twenty-four hours a day, seven
days a week. Well, it would crash, and we couldn't get it to

work. So I'd be at the studio in the middle of the night, with a phone line open to Great Britain, waiting for them to come in. This is the type of thing we had to put up with, and it's one reason why I went prematurely gray.

The effort paid off. In short order, our artists became computer artists. They figured out how to run their still-primitive software. They learned how to work with the meteorologists—both on camera and off—and how to generate slides on tight timetables. Perhaps most important, they came together as a cohesive team, and they generated a "look" for The Weather Channel that was visually sophisticated without being slick. Within a year of going on the air, we would be winning a disproportionate number of prestigious awards from the Broadcast Design Association.

ON THE AIR: JUST BARELY

The late spring of 1982 was a challenging and exciting time for me. After the many months of therapy and practice that followed my throat surgery, I hoped I was ready to resume my public speaking. My new voice was necessarily guttural, and I was concerned that people might have trouble understanding me. And I feared that my voice might give out in the middle of a talk. But I knew that I needed to begin addressing groups of people again.

I soon got the call. In April, I was elected chairman of the board of The Associated Press, the world's largest newsgathering organization, and toward the end of that month I found myself addressing the AP's annual meeting in San Francisco. My reentry into the public dialog was successful, and reassuring, but the AP chairmanship came with a basketful of management challenges. The AP is a cooperative owned by its member newspapers and broadcasters. Its market position was so strong that the organization had become a bit self-satisfied and resistant to change. Now, facing the onslaught of a revolution in communications technologies and competition from a variety of new sources, the AP needed a swift wake-up call. I enjoyed the challenge and the talented people I was associated with, but it occupied much of my time over the next five years.

Just a few days after the AP meeting, I flew to Las Vegas, where—on May 2, 1982—I would speak again, this time officially launching The Weather Channel. The venue, as noted earlier, was the National Cable Television Association's annual convention, attended each year by several thousand cable operators and suppliers. We aimed to capture the imagination of operators and the press by displaying our unique programming live. Richard Hallgren, director of the National Weather Service, had agreed to attend the event, informally conferring his blessing on our efforts. Dubby Wynne would serve as the master of ceremonies. John Coleman, speaking on a live hookup from Atlanta, would once again try to "sell" our baby. I would speak briefly and throw the switch, we would take to the air, and our Weather Channel would be a reality.

That was the plan. And as far as the audience ever knew, we pulled it off without a hitch. Behind the scenes, though, the reality was a whole lot more complicated: funny, hair-raising, and occasionally a little bit bizarre.

The idea was simple enough. We would rent the huge ballroom at the Las Vegas Convention Center. In that hall, we'd have a large-screen video as well as a dozen video monitors located around the periphery of the room. The Las Vegas team, including Dubby Wynne and me, would perform the in-person duties. John Coleman, in Atlanta, would talk to the crowd in Las Vegas by means of the large screen. When I threw the switch, the monitors around the room would show actual Weather Channel product from a dozen locations around the country. The main signal, of course, would be identical on all twelve monitors: the live feed from Atlanta. But the local information on each set would be different, reflecting the fact that each of these sets—equipped with its own WeatherSTAR, and standing in for different local systems around the country—was pulling down a different signal from the satellite.

Of course, it wasn't quite that easy. Bahns Stanley had contracted with a supplier of satellite-receiving services to set up a small dish outside the building to supply the Atlanta feed to the ballroom. As soon as our team pulled down the satellite signal, though, they knew it was completely unsatisfactory, evidently because of an enormous amount of telephone microwave interference in and around the convention center. TeleCable engineer Nick Worth spent half a day before the convention opened trying to find an interference filter that would clean up the signal. Nothing worked.

At the end of that discouraging day, Nick Worth, Bahns Stanley, and Gordon Herring were sitting in the empty ballroom, trying to come up with a plan. Sitting there with them was a small, somewhat portly man, whom Worth thinks may have been an employee of Centel, the local phone company, but whom Herring remembers as a staffer with a video production company in the convention center. No one seems to have caught his name. Worth later came to refer to him as "the leprechaun," and so he has entered company lore. One of our dispirited team members pointed out that KLAS-TV, Landmark's Las Vegas TV station, had brand-new satellite links only a few miles away.

"That might as well be on the far side of the moon," Worth said glumly.

"Not necessarily," piped up the leprechaun. "Centel has a video line between KLAS and the convention center. I know a couple of guys who could fire it up for you. But it's going to cost some money to get those guys out at night."

"How much?"

"Oh, at least a couple of hundred dollars," said the leprechaun, solemnly.

At this point, we had committed something northward of $20 million to the venture. Herring said, "Not a problem. Go find your friends now."

Away went the leprechaun. Herring and Worth piled into their rental car and sped down the road to KLAS. They walked in off the street and asked to speak to the engineer on duty. As Worth recalls:

Now, even though we were all employed by divisions of the same parent company, Landmark, we didn't know anybody at that station, and they didn't know us. In fact, we were reluctant to tell them we were with TeleCable, figuring they might say, "Oh, the hell with you cable guys! Get out of here!" We decided ahead of time that we'd say we were from Landmark.

So it's early evening, and we come in off the street after management has gone home. We roust out the engineer on duty, and say, "Hey, we need you guys to reorient your seven-meter dish to pick up The Weather Channel."

After making one or two phone calls, they did just that. They were tremendously cooperative. They reoriented the dish, got a beautiful signal locked in, and hooked it up to the Centel video feed. So we hopped in our car and went back to the convention center.

With encouragement from the leprechaun, the Centel crew already had a truck parked outside the center, perhaps a thousand feet from the ballroom. By the time Worth and Herring got there, they had a respectable signal from KLAS, which they were still tuning up and balancing. But how would the signal get from the street to the ballroom? The leprechaun cautioned Herring and Worth that the unionized convention center staff might not be as cooperative as Centel had been. So Herring and Worth set out to string the cable themselves, stealthily. "I recall climbing up on top of a roof," Worth remembers. "I recall going through a kitchen and sweet-talking the cooks, running cable underneath the stoves and sinks to keep the cable out of the way as much as possible. And at some point, I just laid it right across the floor, and pointed it out to the kitchen staff so they wouldn't trip over it."

Our low-profile wiring crew finally got the cable—and therefore the satellite signal—into the ballroom. Eagerly, they hooked up the TV set, pushed the right buttons, and got . . . another horrible image, almost obliterated by electronic snow. The signal loss over the run of the cables was too great. Once again, it looked like all our efforts had been in vain. And once again, the leprechaun showed up.

"You know," he said matter-of-factly, "what you need is a Dynair minimop."

Worth knew immediately what he was talking about. A mini-mop is a video amplifier that restores lost video signal, as well as an equalizer that restores the balance of that signal. But simply knowing about it, as Worth explains, wasn't enough:

> Now, we're not talking broadcast standard equipment, here. We're talking something off the second shelf, at best, and of course, we don't have anything of the kind sitting around. But sure enough, the Leprechaun reaches into his bag, and pulls out a Dynair minimop.
>
> Imagine that you're stranded on a desert island, and an airplane passes overhead. You say to yourself, "Gosh, if I only had a two-way radio to communicate with that pilot." And one of your fellow castaways pulls one out of his hip pocket and says, "Oh, you mean like one of these?"
>
> To this day, I believe our leprechaun was sent there to help us out. I grabbed the mini-mop, hooked it up, we balanced the line, and all of a sudden, voila, we had a beautiful signal in the ballroom.

With a strong signal finally in place, everything appeared to be on track. We had set up a dummy "switch" for me to throw, with an official-looking switch box, complete with dummy wires tucked into the apron of the dais. On a prearranged signal, someone in Atlanta would throw the real switch. The following morning, we did a dry run, which went off more or less seamlessly. The clock ticked down to launch time. With less than an hour to go, we combed our hair, straightened our ties, and prepared to make television history.

Then came a distressing phone call from Atlanta. A member of the Atlanta-based crew had just noticed that all of the Weather-STARs in the country—including the dozen in our Las Vegas ballroom—had their clocks set to Eastern Time. A nationwide audience was about to get a weather report from a company that couldn't tell time west of Indiana. Our software engineers in Atlanta dove into the WeatherSTAR code, looking for the bug that was setting the STARs' internal clocks incorrectly. Working frantically, they pulled off a small miracle. One by one, the monitors around the ballroom reset their internal clocks with time to spare.

Then came the next surprise. As Gordon Herring remembers it:

> About fifteen minutes before the launch, a reporter was wandering around the room and got back behind the stage. There, he managed to trip over the main power cord, taking down all the lights, all the WeatherSTARs, and everything else that was powered with alternating current. Dubby Wynne was furious. We had to race from one STAR to the next resetting all the addresses and refreshing all the information, just minutes before the doors were supposed to open to let the public in.

Once again, the last-minute bandage stuck. When compared to these last-minute plot twists, the launch itself was almost anticlimactic. The crowds filed in. Dubby Wynne, who had calmed down by now, welcomed our guests, who numbered almost a thousand, and announced that we had signed affiliation agreements for 4.2 million subscribers. This was a record for cable networks at launch. Dick Hallgren spoke of the National Weather Service's support for the venture. John Coleman—on video from Atlanta—described the programming and introduced meteorologists and other key staffers. We took questions from the press.

Finally, the moment came. I made a few remarks, and then reached for the switch that would "turn on" the service. "Now I will throw a switch," I intoned as dramatically as possible, "to launch a weather forecast *that will never end*." It seemed fitting at the time, but that boast was a bit of showmanship that nearly came back to haunt me, a year later.

When I threw the switch, the real switch in Atlanta was thrown at the same time. The blue-and-white Weather Channel logo fish-hooked out of a black background to the center of the screen, as upbeat pop music began to play. A voiceover stressed that this new service was "brought to you by your local cable system." Two earnest and mustachioed young meteorologists— Bruce Edwards and Andre Bernier, who had won their coveted "premiere show" slots by lottery—came on the air, introduced themselves, and got right down to business.

"Headlining the weather news," Edwards announced, "it was a high-plains heat wave today!" Up came a stylized rendition of Mount Rushmore, colored in hot yellows and oranges. The world's most comprehensive television weather report was underway.

CHAPTER FIVE

FLIRTING WITH EXTINCTION

Launching a new venture is one thing; helping that venture succeed is another thing entirely.

When we went on the air on May 2, 1982, we knew that we had barely beaten our self-imposed deadline. And we had beaten that deadline only selectively. Owing to delivery delays and failures of the WeatherSTARs in the field, only a few of the 4.2 million subscribers whom we had under contract actually began receiving local forecasts when I flipped that switch in Las Vegas. For many months thereafter, we were still scrambling to fix the design flaws in the WeatherSTAR and its related technologies, and to get more STARs into the field.

We also had to look for opportunities to make the STAR do more for our customers.

Meanwhile, we had to come to terms with an increasingly bleak financial picture. In our prelaunch planning, we had carefully reduced John Coleman's revenue estimates and increased his cost projections. As our voluminous red ink was now telling us, we hadn't done enough of either. It didn't matter that we were adding many new subscribers every week. In fact, each new subscribing system required another small but measurable outlay of capital. Until we had ratings, we couldn't generate significant ad revenues.

Most troubling of all was our rapidly deteriorating relationship with our chief executive officer, John Coleman. In our Weather Channel drama, Coleman had written a part for himself that, sadly, he proved unable to play. In Atlanta, morale sagged dangerously. As Wynne and I began contemplating a leadership change at The Weather Channel, we knew we had to abide by the agreements we had reached with Coleman in the summer of 1981. But the rigidity of those agreements, and their implicit tilt toward adversarialism, now came back to haunt us.

TECHNOLOGICAL WOES AND FIXES

The technical scares that we experienced before our May 1982 launch turned out to be minor compared to the problems we encountered after we went on the air. The first STAR units Compuvid produced were undependable and plagued with problems. Collectively, these problems represented our first major operational crisis. It was critical to our credibility and reputation that we diagnose and solve the STAR's problems quickly, and that we provide high-quality service in the process.

One of our biggest snafus involved unreliability in the data stream that fed the localized information. Our whole plan to broadcast local conditions and forecasts depended on sending a steady stream of digitized, "teletext-based" information up to the satellite in the vertical blanking interval (VBI) of the main Weather Channel video signal. Each WeatherSTAR around the country would then pick off its own preaddressed signal, which it would pull down into that particular cable system's head end and transform into on-screen text.

Almost from the start, local cable systems complained about receiving scrambled-up teletext messages. Mysteriously, individual characters would fill the entire screen. Words would be strangely distorted. The variety of complaints seemed to indicate that more than one thing was going wrong.

Alan Galumbeck, our engineering genius, hit on a scheme that solved part of the problem. He figured out a way to transmit all the teletext data twice, more or less concurrently. The receiving WeatherSTAR could compare the duplicated messages, and— if only one error was detected—could correct the error. If it detected more than one error, the receiving equipment would simply ignore that round of messages entirely and wait for the next updated transmission. It took only about twenty minutes to go through the cycle of forecasts nationwide, so missing one cycle was rarely a calamity, or even particularly noticeable.

The frequency of errors abated somewhat as a result of this intervention, but Galumbeck still thought we were getting more errors than we should have. Working with his counterparts at Compuvid, he homed in on a problem with something called the "tank circuit." In layman's terms, this was the electronic holding tank in which the WeatherSTAR captured the incoming teletext message. Within the tank circuit was a wire coil, which at first had a "Q" (quality) rating of about 60. Suspecting that this was not good enough, Galumbeck and the Compuvid engineers sub-stituted a coil with a Q rating of 90, and the change seemed to help somewhat. The revised design was incorporated into the WeatherSTARs then being manufactured.

Then Compuvid got a visit from an engineer from Signet-ics, a British company that had designed the chip set for the underlying teletext circuitry. As Galumbeck recalls, the British engineer had strong opinions on the subject of coils and Q ratings:

> He came in, looked at what we were doing, and said, "You guys are crazy. You need a Q of at least 250!" Maybe that's not the exactly right number, but it was somewhere way up there. In other words, we needed a far higher-quality coil than we had been using. He pointed us toward a vendor, we got in a few samples, stuck them in, and it made all the difference in the world.
>
> Within the first twelve months, we cycled all the STARs back through the factory to have the coil in their tank circuit upgraded.

Down the hallway in Atlanta, meanwhile, our veteran broadcast engineer Doyle Thompson was working on another aspect of the corrupted teletext messages. Thompson noticed that a disproportionate number of complaints were coming from northern climates in the winter. What did this pattern mean? The dishes that pull satellite messages out of the sky are parabolas. The signal from the satellite arrives as a flat wave, which hits the parabolic surface of the dish, which in turn focuses the signal on the antenna's focal point. At that exact spot is located the antenna's low-noise amplifier, which boosts and relays the signal. *Precision* is critical.

When a freezing rain or a heavy snow starts to fall, the bottom of a satellite dish fills up more than the top of that dish. The parabola's shape begins to change, and the signal begins to miss the focal point. In other words, precision goes out the window, noise gets into the overall signal, and teletext information is likely to be the first part of the signal that is affected adversely. After fielding enough of these calls, Thompson recalls, he and his colleagues learned what to tell the anxious cable operator: "I'd say, 'Go out and hit your dish with a hammer.' Or, 'Try sweeping your dish out with a broom.' And they'd go outside in the snow and hit their dish with a hammer, come back inside, and say, 'Wow! You fixed it!'"

A similar problem came to be known as the Case of the Dirt Daubers. Each WeatherSTAR installation came equipped with a series of local sensors for wind speed, direction, temperature, and rainfall. Their inputs were tied into the local WeatherSTAR, and they were intended to give precise, real-time local readings. Then a strange and strikingly consistent complaint started coming in: Something's wrong! Our WeatherSTAR is reporting twice as much rainfall as it should!

It took Thompson a while to figure this one out. The gauge that measured rainfall was little more than a miniature teeter-totter. A funnel caught the rain and directed it toward a little bucket on either end of the teeter-totter. When the bucket got full, it would drop, and the mechanism would hit a micro-switch that recorded one-hundredth of an inch of rainfall. Then the water would drain out of a little hole in the bottom of the bucket, and the process would start over, filling up the other bucket. Unless, as Thompson explains, Mother Nature interfered:

> There's a type of wasp called a dirt dauber. The dirt daubers
> didn't understand that this little hole was not designed for them.
> They would go in and build their nests on the teeter-totter.
> The incoming water would tip the thing one way, and the weight
> of the mud would tip it back the other way again. Two clicks for
> the price of one.

One of the biggest challenges Galumbeck and Doyle faced was that these kinds of problems were intermittent. Some showed up in some places but not others. Some only showed up rarely. Thus imposing a blanket "fix" was difficult, or even risky. For example, some cable systems experienced difficulty when they put their WeatherSTAR equipment on the same tower from which they picked off their on-air signals. The "Channel 2" frequency, in particular, seemed to be adversely affected by having a STAR in the vicinity. After much investigation, Galumbeck and his colleagues discovered that although the WeatherSTAR conformed to

FCC radiation standards in terms of what was escaping from the unit, the STAR was nevertheless energetically radiating outward through its sensors and wreaking havoc on Channel 2's VHF frequency. The Weather Channel engineers scrambled to seal up the STARs more effectively. They also added a "doughnut" of ferrite beads—which helped absorb very high frequencies—to all the leads going into and out of the STARs.

These are examples of just some of the kinds of problems we tackled in the early months of operation. We were able to correct the most serious STAR failures in a few weeks, but it's fair to say that we were patching the STAR more or less continuously for a year. We also began planning for new generations of STARs, a process of upgrading that continues to this day. Doyle Thompson set up a service desk to receive and follow through on complaints from cable operators and viewers. When we could identify a simple wiring problem, we would send the operator a new circuit board by overnight delivery. If that didn't solve the problem, we sent a new STAR, and the cable company would send its suspect unit back to the manufacturer to be rebuilt.

Some problems remained internal but were no less troubling. For example, our host computer experienced its share of glitches. This computer was a complex, real-time system with nearly a hundred separate programs working simultaneously. Like most of the rest of our systems, we had developed it in a great hurry, and as a result it was buggy. The problems caused by the bugs tended to cascade, which very often led to a crash. The computer would stop processing, and our rivers of data—incoming and outgoing— would stop flowing. A loud, persistent alarm would ring, and an operator would flip a switch that engaged our backup system. But this backup was so crude and erratic that the staff almost immediately dubbed it "RATS"—"STAR" backwards. No one at The Weather Channel breathed easily until RATS was put back into the electronic closet.

Some of our technical people now think that we went on the air before we had perfected our technology, and that as a result we looked amateurish. No doubt that's true. But if our choice was to be the "first mover" in weather or to be perfect at launch, I believe we made the right choice.

When all else failed, we had the benefit of a pretty forgiving customer base. By the early 1980s, cable operators had developed a realistic attitude about new equipment: They expected trouble. The real question that they wanted answered was, "When trouble crops up that's of your making, what are you going to do about it, and how quickly?" We felt that our dedication to quick, no-fault problem solving would buy forgiveness from the operators who were affected. We also committed ourselves to reducing the STAR's failure rate—which averaged 15 percent in our first year of operations—to 1 percent in Year Two.

BEATING THE BUSHES

In our first six months, we were adding 125,000 new subscribers per week, and most reacted favorably to our service. Still, we were too small to qualify for Nielsen ratings, so we had no way to prove to advertisers that anyone was actually watching The Weather Channel. It now appeared that our rate of subscriber growth, although very respectable, would leave us without ratings for much longer than we had projected. Since we were providing our programming free of charge to the cable operators, we needed to generate as many ad dollars as possible.

In the economic climate of 1982, this was a tough assignment. The country was only beginning to recover from a sharp economic decline. The Weather Channel was viewed as an experiment, and in hard economic times, ad dollars for experiments are difficult to find.

More broadly, cable television advertising was still mostly an experiment. In the fall of 1982, the entire cable advertising budget nationwide was about $150 million, or less than 1 percent of all advertising dollars. And we figured that to break even, we needed at least $13 million in annual revenue—in other words, almost 10 percent of all the available cable ad dollars. We wouldn't get that, or even half of that. But there were other ways of looking at our situation. If the economy took off, and if ad dollars started shifting away from other media and into cable, the overall pot might grow considerably. One industry estimate that we saw toward the end of 1982 suggested that cable advertising might reach $1.5 billion by 1990. We hoped we could get 1 percent of that.

Meanwhile, we had to stay alive. Within three months of our launch, we were falling so far behind our revenue and cost targets that Dubby Wynne decided that he had to devote his full time to The Weather Channel. Dick Barry, Landmark's president, agreed to assume Wynne's broadcasting responsibilities temporarily. Wynne and John Coleman agreed that Wynne would take over direct supervision of cable and advertising sales.

Wynne found some cause for hope. Surveys of subscribers in our TeleCable systems were giving us some rough estimates of viewing habits. True, many of those surveyed were not yet aware of The Weather Channel. On the other hand, those who had developed the "Weather Channel habit" appeared to be watching us more frequently than we had expected.

In an internal study of three TeleCable markets, for example, we found that our daily cumulative audience was 34 percent. In other words, just over a third of the cable subscribers surveyed watched The Weather Channel at least once every day. Our weekly "cume" was 58 percent. The average length of view was between nine and ten minutes. More than 80 percent of viewers liked our service, 8 percent disliked it, and 9 percent had no opinion.

Unfortunately, none of this information helped us sell ads. Most advertisers told us to come back when we had our first Nielsen ratings. So our salespeople were forced to compete with one hand tied behind their backs. Established competitors like ESPN, CNN, USA, and WTBS already had their Nielsens and thus could sell advertising more easily. But since sales by the numbers weren't possible for us, the only sales strategy open to us was "concept" sales. In other words, companies bought time on The Weather Channel because they believed in the idea of the service and either liked having their company affiliated with that service or wanted to sponsor a specific segment that tied into their products or services. American Express, for example, sponsored "travel weather." American Motors Corporation sponsored our ski reports associated with the Winter Olympics.

We did have one unique advantage. Using our teletext system, we were able to give advertisers a way to combine targeted local messages with their commercials. A tire company, for example, could promote its new all-weather radial in a general way, and that ad could be supplemented by specific text-based information about where to get the tire locally. Mike Eckert and his Chicago sales office sold this service very effectively. A big break came when United Airlines signed a one-year contract, under the terms of which United would use our local tags to plug specific flight schedules in different markets. The United sale was an important morale booster and credibility builder for the sales staff, who began citing that account as a bellwether.

Good news came in dribs and drabs. In the fall of 1982, General Foods knocked on our door and asked how to buy a schedule of ads. "They came to us," Wynne told our board in December, "and that is just about unprecedented." But this was the rare exception. Mike Ban, our vice president of advertising sales, was estimating ad sales of $7.4 million for 1983. Early in that year, Dubby Wynne told our board, flatly, "We won't make it."

Bad news, indeed. Operating expenses were now $14 to $15 million a year, more than double the expense targets in our agreement with Coleman. Operating losses were almost $1 million a month.

We were not alone in running heavy losses. *The Wall Street Journal* reported that ESPN was losing $20 million a year, and Ted Turner had told me that WTBS was subsidizing CNN. But that was cold comfort, at best. If these established cable "old timers," with their Nielsen ratings and their respectable ad sales, couldn't turn the corner, how could we hope to succeed?

THE MAKINGS OF A TRAIN WRECK

A more immediate problem now presented itself. As early as the summer of 1982, only a few short months after our launch, Dubby Wynne and I began to feel uneasy about John Coleman's command-and-control management style, which in our opinion grew out of his overall lack of management experience. Further, chasms seemed to be opening up between the people Coleman had recruited and the people who had come from Landmark. Charges of favoritism and scapegoating were in the air. Key people were becoming demoralized, and staff morale was deteriorating.

A consultant whom Landmark had used for years to conduct employee attitude and opinion surveys paid a visit to The Weather Channel in this time period. The findings were worse than we had anticipated. "I've been doing these surveys for thirty years," he told Hugh Eaton, "and these are the worst results I've ever seen." At Landmark, we prided ourselves on providing a satisfying and rewarding workplace; now one of our divisions was telling us we had failed miserably. The quantitative measures were equally discouraging, and the trends were all going in the wrong direction. Expenses were running far in excess of Coleman's estimates. Just two months after we went on the air, Coleman wrote, in a memo to Wynne, "It has been difficult in light of our overall operating costs to come to grips with the reality that in several areas I underestimated staff required to conduct our programming, production and network operations." Accordingly, he wanted to add at least eighteen more people to the payroll, which was already much bigger than he had originally projected.

At least two things were going wrong here. First, we were beginning to realize the costs of our inexperience in judging the kind of organization required to operate a complex, twenty-four-hour-a-day, seven-day-a-week national programming enterprise. Second, we were paying a steep price for not hiring an experienced general manager to operate the venture.

As things went from bad to worse, in-house Landmark staff began to express more and more skepticism about The Weather Channel's chances for success. The same thing had happened early in the days of TeleCable, when we made huge investments in cable franchises without seeing much return, so we weren't overly surprised when the complaints started. But with the bad news mounting, we had to wonder whether our critics had it right. Some managers doubted whether people even wanted to have weather information available all the time. Others wondered how The Weather Channel fit in with the rest of Landmark's businesses. The Weather Channel was a national business, while everything else we did was local. Did we really know how to do national?

Most of the questioning was in good humor, but sometimes it had a little edge. At our annual meeting of management shareholders in the spring of 1983, some of our broadcasting managers spoofed us with a video they produced, purported to introduce Landmark's next new venture: *The Time Channel*—"the exact time whenever you want it!" Another wag asked, pointedly, "Why are we coining money in Las Vegas"—home of our profitable TV station, KLAS—"and gambling it away in Atlanta?"

By early April, it was clear that 1983 advertising revenues would come in far below Mike Ban's $7.4 million projection. In fact, they might not even reach $4 million. It was increasingly hard to foresee an economic return from The Weather Channel. Meanwhile, we faced a serious threat of a union-organizing drive—prompted, we believed, by a tense and unhappy internal atmosphere.

The on-camera meteorologists were a case in point. As a result of water-cooler conversations, they soon discovered that even though they all had more or less the same job, their pay scales varied widely. Those who had come from major media markets were still being paid on their former scale, while those who had been recruited from smaller markets might be earning only half as much. This was one of the disadvantages of assembling a staff from a wide variety of TV markets across the country and having no relevant experience in making these pieces fit together.

The meteorologists also complained about scheduling and alleged preferential treatment in the assignment of work schedules. Some believed that favorites were rewarded with good time slots, and that others were "punished" with less desirable slots. As Hugh Eaton recalls, "I had [on-camera meteorologists,] grown men and women, sitting in my office in tears because they were so frustrated either with the schedule, or the stress that was being put upon them."

Eaton's reference to "stress" raises a whole other set of issues. The Weather Channel's meteorologists included individuals who had relocated to Atlanta from all over the country, in many cases with young families. They had left situations in which they were local or regional celebrities, only to become relatively anonymous Weather Channel staffers. At the same time, they had gone from being on camera only a few minutes a day—at 6:00 P.M., and again at 11—to being on the air up to four hours in an eight-hour shift. They also were their own producers, so they had to spec and stack on the computer all the slides that they wanted to use during the next hour. In short, they were working much harder than they had ever worked in their lives, getting little recognition for it, and being compensated arbitrarily.

These morale problems illustrated the lack of experienced, skilled management. By the early months of 1983, Wynne and I became convinced, reluctantly, that we had to assume full control of the management of The Weather Channel—which meant that we had to relieve Coleman of his management authority.

Our agreement with Coleman gave us the right to remove him after the first year of operation if The Weather Channel did not reach 87.5 percent of the contractual target for operating income. Since the network was going to fall far short of this target, we assumed that we could ask him to leave any time after May 2, 1983.

Despite the clear provisions in our agreement with Coleman, we fully expected him to become hostile when faced with the prospect of being ousted. At the same time, we very much wanted to avoid such ill will. Wynne and I thought Coleman's knowledge of weather programming, and his proven talent for promoting The Weather Channel, could continue to be valuable assets if we could persuade him to accept another role at the network. In a one-on-one meeting in April, therefore, I asked Coleman to step aside from an operating role but remain as chairman. I proposed to give him a substantial pay increase to become our principal spokesman to advertisers, the cable industry, and the public, and to consult on programming. In that capacity, he would still be seen as the "father" of The Weather Channel, and he would be able to retain his stock.

I thought this arrangement might be the best of all possible worlds for Coleman. He would be doing what he did best—performing—while drawing attention to The Weather Channel, which very much needed an energetic and credible spokesperson. On April 18, Wynne reiterated this proposal in writing to Coleman.

Coleman, however, rejected the proposal out of hand. At our next meeting, he said that he intended to remain the chief executive of The Weather Channel, with full operating control. That much, he said, was not negotiable. He was willing to hire a president who would report to him. We stuck to our guns, though, reminding him that under the terms of our agreement, we had the right to remove him and call in his stock in the following month.

The meeting ended on a tense, sour note. Wynne and I feared that this impasse might have an unhappy ending for both parties. We also tried to figure out exactly what Coleman might be thinking. In light of his contractual position, he was on shaky ground at best. We couldn't understand his refusal to discuss any change in his operating authority.

After this meeting, negotiations went from testy to tense. Communications degenerated into formal memos and letters. Coleman began asserting that Landmark had caused The Weather Channel's extraordinary cost overruns—a claim that didn't jibe with the facts. Wynne's last letter to Coleman, dated May 5, 1983, made it clear that we intended to call in his voting stock and eliminate any restriction on our ability to control The Weather Channel. We then called a meeting of shareholders for June 30, and we notified Coleman that the purpose of the meeting was to elect new directors. Clearly, we were headed for a train wreck.

THE COURTS INTERVENE

On June 27, John Coleman filed a suit in Georgia, seeking an injunction to prevent us from removing him and changing his status. A hearing before a judge was set for 2:30 the next afternoon in Atlanta. Although we had fully expected Coleman to go to court, we were stunned by this preemptive strike to enjoin us. Neither of us could comprehend what serious argument he could make to annul the clear terms of our agreement. We guessed that he was mainly seeking a delay.

We rushed to the airport to catch a flight to Atlanta, where we met our Virginia attorneys—Conrad Shumadine and Rebecca Smith—at the offices of King and Spalding, the law firm representing us in Atlanta. The Atlanta attorney who had been preparing to handle any legal action Coleman might take was away on vacation, so he had turned the case over to a partner, Ralph Levy, who now had to be brought up to speed late that night.

Coleman had submitted an affidavit to the court in which he made many allegations that we vigorously disputed. He claimed, for example, that we had violated our agreement with him, and that we had made it impossible for him to achieve the performance targets he needed to meet to ensure that we could not diminish his authority. He alleged that Wynne and I had required him to

126

make large expenditures in excess of the contractual targets. He alleged that we had stripped him of authority for the cable and advertising sales departments, thus eliminating his control over these departments' expenditures and the revenues they could generate. Finally, Coleman asserted that Wynne had verbally assured him that these changes would not affect his interests or position with The Weather Channel, or his ability to acquire additional stock. In fact, he claimed, we had promised to amend his agreement to reflect these changes.

Wynne and I worked with our attorneys long into the night and early morning before the next day's hearing. With tension, frustration, and a strong sense of urgency, we prepared written responses to Coleman's claims and readied ourselves for the next day's courtroom testimony.

Under oath, I told a story very different from Coleman's. I testified that on several occasions since our agreements had been signed, I had talked about their provisions with Coleman, and that at no time did either he or I propose any change in those provisions. I said that our investment in The Weather Channel had already exceeded $32 million, and that continuation of the venture was requiring an additional investment of $850,000 per month. We were no longer willing to give Coleman unfettered control over these substantial investments that Landmark was making. If the court denied our ability to exercise our right to terminate Coleman's management control, I testified, it would force Landmark to leave its investment in the hands of a manager in whom it had no confidence. Thus Landmark would be in the untenable position of having to decide whether to abandon its investment or to continue to place $850,000 per month at the disposal of someone whom we could not control in any meaningful way.

Wynne introduced a series of letters and memorandums between Coleman and himself, which in our opinion proved that Coleman, not Landmark personnel, had proposed the cost increases in question. To show that Landmark had not interfered with Coleman's management prerogatives, Wynne presented a memorandum Coleman had sent to the staff, just two months after launch, stating that he had requested direct hands-on assistance from Wynne and other Landmark staff, and that Wynne would devote his full time to "helping us at The Weather Channel as long as there is a need."

The hearing before Judge Dorothy Robinson was held in the Superior Court of Cobb County, Georgia, where The Weather Channel is headquartered. To our surprise, the courtroom was packed with observers, many of them Weather Channel employees. Coleman had spread the word of the hearing, and employees had come to see what the dispute was all about. Not surprisingly, the atmosphere was tense, and the mounting hostility between Coleman and Wynne was all too obvious.

As we expected, Coleman's skills as a showman made him an appealing witness—particularly so, it seemed, to Judge Robinson. Just twenty-four hours later, she entered a temporary restraining order preventing Landmark from taking any action to change the membership of The Weather Channel's board, remove Coleman as chief executive, or reduce his stock ownership. "There are substantial issues," the judge opined, "concerning the interpretation of the provisions of the agreements among the parties."

After a quick huddle, our lawyers told us what the judge's ruling meant. Most likely, we would have to prove in an evidentiary trial that our agreements gave us the right to remove Coleman. We were confident that we could ultimately prove that we had that right. But a full-fledged trial, with the likelihood of several rounds of appeals, was likely to paralyze us for months.

The sheer fact of the legal proceeding changed our calculations about our cable network's chances of survival. The Atlanta newspapers reported our testimony about The Weather Channel's precarious financial condition, and the Associated Press picked it up and immediately distributed our tale of woe on their national wire. In subsequent days and weeks, cable and broadcasting trade publications elaborated on the story, so that an increasingly gloomy picture of The Weather Channel's likely fate spread throughout the cable industry. At the same time, other new cable networks, including CBS's cultural channel and ABC's news channel, were shutting down. The smell of death was in the air. By publicly revealing our financial distress, we seemed to be almost guaranteeing that no new cable systems would pick us up—and that our existing systems would take the first opportunity to bail out on us.

Many at Landmark shared this dismal outlook, as did a number of anxious onlookers at The Weather Channel. We seemed to be in a hopeless position—bogged down in a lawsuit waiting for a trial, with no change in management and, most important, with no realistic scenarios for turning around The Weather Channel. Every day we were bleeding additional red ink.

And even assuming that we could straighten out the situation with John Coleman, what could we do to save The Weather Channel? The only way we could imagine earning additional revenue would be to charge cable operators for carrying our programming. But we didn't consider this seemingly hopeless prospect seriously. With new cable networks being launched almost every month, it was a buyer's market for cable operators. In this climate, we thought there was no chance that cable operators would pay us for our product.

So even as we were engaged in litigation with Coleman, Wynne and I were spending many hours searching for a way to save The Weather Channel. We explored options with Bill Diederich, Landmark president Dick Barry, Gordon Herring, Dick Roberts, and others. None of us could conceive a plan for reviving the venture. Finally, I told the Landmark board that we should close The Weather Channel. This decision hurt, a lot. It would be the first time Landmark had failed, totally, at a venture in which we had invested so much hope and pride as well as money.

But how, exactly, could we shut down the network? As a result of the judge's restraining order, we weren't steering our own ship. In our affiliation agreements, for example, we had promised to give cable operators ninety days' notice if we intended to close the network. We fully intended to honor this promise, just as we intended to give our employees a generous amount of notice so they could make plans. But by court order, Coleman was still in charge. We were paralyzed.

Wynne and I felt trapped in a situation we had not foreseen, and we couldn't figure out how to break the impasse. In an attempt to get some fresh ideas, we convened a meeting of senior partners of our Virginia attorneys, who had not yet been involved in the matter. An idea finally emerged that, in hindsight, seemed obvious. If we truly believed we had to shut down The Weather Channel, why not cut off the money flow that was keeping it alive? The court had ordered us to preserve the status quo until after a trial on the merits of Coleman's complaint. But we saw no way that the court or Coleman could compel us to continue sending money to Atlanta. Without an infusion of almost $1 million a month from Landmark, The Weather Channel would quickly slide into involuntary bankruptcy.

Nevertheless, we decided that we didn't want to go that route for the moment. Accordingly, I gave Coleman notice of a board meeting to be held July 11, at which we would propose an orderly plan of liquidation so we could fulfill our contractual and moral responsibilities. This wasn't a ploy, or a gambit, or a smokescreen. We were dead serious. Psychologically and emotionally, my colleagues and I had already written off The Weather Channel—as well as the $32 million that we had invested in it so far. As we saw it, all that remained was to give our once-promising offspring a proper burial.

After a four-day delay that Coleman had requested, the board meeting commenced Friday, July 15, in our attorneys' offices. All four members of the board were present: Coleman, Phil Couri (also Coleman's lawyer), Dubby Wynne, and I. In addition, we had invited Louis Ryan, Landmark's secretary and general counsel, and Dick Barry. Coleman, as chief executive officer, chaired the meeting.

Coleman began by stating that Landmark would be better served by the sale of its interest rather than by the liquidation of

The Weather Channel. He then asked me to state the reasons for the meeting.

I presented a written resolution outlining the steps we proposed to take to liquidate The Weather Channel in a responsible way. The board voted on the resolution and tied: Wynne and I voted for it, and Coleman and Couri voted against it. We were clearly in a standoff. Because Coleman's reason for delaying the meeting was to develop alternatives, I then asked him what those alternatives were, and that we were prepared to consider any suggestions he might have.

There was a long pause. I realized that Coleman must have thought I had been bluffing about closing The Weather Channel, and now—faced with the finality and stark terms of my resolution—he was stunned. Clearly, he hadn't planned on this turn of events, and he had no alternatives to present. Couri then proposed a recess of the meeting, and we agreed.

When we resumed the meeting after two hours, Couri presented a plan that would keep The Weather Channel operating for up to six months, during which time Coleman would have an option to buy the network. I immediately responded that we were unwilling to provide deficit financing for another six months. We would, however, consider a thirty-day option.

After another recess, we offered Coleman a plan for the thirty-day option: The price would be $4 million for the assets, $15 million for the transponder, and up to $1 million to cover additional operating deficits we would incur for the thirty-day period. Coleman would have to dismiss his lawsuit with prejudice immediately, sell 100 percent of his stock to Landmark immediately, and he and Couri would have to resign from the board immediately. Landmark and Coleman would agree to release all claims they might have against each other. Coleman could remain as president and in charge of operations throughout the option period, during which he presumably would be arranging for another money partner to replace Landmark. We agreed that we would keep the existing transponder if Coleman could find a cheaper one.

The meeting recessed again. This time the recess lasted almost forty hours, until the morning of Sunday, July 17. Throughout the recess there was an incessant stream of telephone calls and informal meetings, with lawyers present, to negotiate the details and to draft the thirty-day option and settlement agreements, resignations, mutual releases, dismissal of the lawsuit, and other necessary agreements. By late Saturday morning it was clear that we might be headed toward an agreement, although a great many important details remained to be worked out.

Deciding that our negotiating hand would be stronger if I—as Landmark's final authority—was not present, I resigned from the board. Dick Barry was elected to fill my seat. I flew to Norfolk, leaving Barry, who is also an attorney, with authority to lead our negotiations and make final decisions. Not only was Barry known for his cool head, but he didn't have the kind of emotional attachment to The Weather Channel that Dubby Wynne and I shared. In view of the mutual hostility between himself and Coleman, Wynne also decided not to participate in the negotiations. Barry called for legal reinforcements, and Tom Johnson, a senior partner with our Norfolk attorneys, flew in to join the team Saturday morning. Johnson is blessed with a keen sense of humor and a fine legal mind and is a meticulous draftsman of agreements. Landmark's interests were in good hands.

During those two exhausting days and nights of almost continuous negotiating and drafting and redrafting of documents, members of both teams would slip out to grab a nap in nearby offices. The negotiators discovered on Saturday morning that the building managers of the downtown office building in which the summit was being held turned off the air conditioning on Friday afternoons at 5:00 P.M. and didn't turn it on again until Monday morning. (For an unpleasant experience, try camping out in a sealed office building in downtown Atlanta in mid-July.) People got snappish and testy. I later learned that as dawn was breaking on Sunday morning, Barry and Ryan—in an effort to speed up the process—began literally snatching out of Johnson's hands the documents that he was still perfecting.

Finally, after almost two days of tense negotiations, tedious document drafting, stale air, and sleep deprivation, an agreement was reached with Coleman, and all the documents were executed. The deal was struck on a note of comic relief. Coleman had paid $1 per share for his twenty shares of Class A voting stock, so Louis Ryan took a $20 bill out of his wallet and handed it to Coleman as payment for his stock. The Weather Channel was essentially insolvent, so Coleman received nothing for his 75,000 shares of Class B nonvoting stock, for which he had paid nothing. But there was the matter of consideration for the mutual releases we had exchanged. The amount agreed upon was $10. Ryan handed Coleman a $10 bill, and then Coleman handed the same $10 bill back to Ryan. That small gesture evoked a chuckle from both sides, and it helped offset some of the ill will that had built up over the preceding weeks.

The marathon board meeting—for that's what it was, technically—finally adjourned at 7:45 Sunday morning. All my Landmark colleagues who had participated were heartsick about the outcome of our venture, which was now completely out of our hands—at least for the thirty-day option period. Wynne and I, who had put so much of ourselves into The Weather Channel, were particularly depressed. The worst part of it all was that we shared an awful, sinking feeling that we could have done something differently, if only we had been clever enough to think of it.

In a letter to Landmark's board of directors—one of the toughest letters I've had to write in my business career—I explained the terms of the settlement. I summarized the bottom line as follows:

> Coleman has 30 days to find another backer for TWC. If he does, we are out, at a substantial loss. If he does not, we believe Coleman will be out of our lives and we will be in control of TWC's

destiny. Either way involves a painful loss for Landmark, but
both ways are better than the continued deadlock and destructive
litigation. Our best hope is that Coleman can find a buyer.

That last sentence accurately expressed how I felt on July 18, 1983. The $1 million Coleman was obligated to put up when he exercised the option would repay us for the costs of operating The Weather Channel for the second thirty days until he had to close. The other payment would reimburse us partially for the capital costs of equipping the business. Most of the more than $32 million we had already invested, however, would be forever lost. If Coleman did not exercise his option and we continued to operate The Weather Channel, we would continue to lose almost $1 million a month. It seemed that we then would be faced with the unhappy task of shutting down The Weather Channel, with all the additional costs and human miseries associated with that onerous duty.

With that in mind, we told Coleman that we wanted to help him find another partner, and we resolved to do nothing that might interfere, or even look like it was interfering, with his search for financial backing. Wynne wrote to The Weather Channel's managers individually, asking them to cooperate fully with Coleman and instructing them not to say anything to any outside contacts about The Weather Channel's operations, Coleman's plans, Landmark's plans, or anything about the litigation beyond what already had been released publicly. He also asked them to write memos to the file describing any outside contacts.

So now we had done it: We had written off The Weather Channel. We honestly hoped Coleman could find a backer to continue the venture—but at the same time, we doubted he could do it. The Weather Channel had never been an easy sell, and he now would be attempting to sell damaged goods.

We began planning for a proper funeral. To treat The Weather Channel staff as humanely as possible, we decided to offer jobs at Landmark to former Landmark employees who had taken a chance on The Weather Channel, and that we would give other Weather Channel employees ninety days' notice. We also made plans to give our subscribing systems ninety days' notice. We knew it would be tough, though, to hold together enough of a demoralized staff to provide even a minimum level of service for those final ninety days.

Among the staff in Atlanta, rumors were flying. Some heard that Coleman had already lined up a backer. Others had it on good authority that The Weather Channel was already dead. Both of these guesses, and the others that were afoot in this tense period, were just that: guesses. As it turned out, they were both wrong. But despite the overwhelming disappointment and uncertainty that prevailed, most staff members continued to perform their work professionally. I'm proud to recall that our programming—the public face of The Weather Channel—never reflected our internal turmoil.

Dick Barry was the only one of us in Norfolk to have any contact with John Coleman during the option period, and he thought Coleman was optimistic about his prospects for finding a financial partner. A few cable operators called Wynne and me to ask what Landmark intended to do with The Weather Channel if Coleman could not exercise his option. Our answer was always the same: We could not discuss Landmark's plans. Several callers told us they were not interested in investing in The Weather Channel, but they definitely wanted the programming to continue. We did not interpret these comments as a serious invitation for us to charge fees. Beyond these few calls, we had no indication of how Coleman was faring in his search for a backer.

As the end of the option period approached, we saw no signs that Coleman had found a partner. We prepared to put our liquidation plans into motion.

Then, on August 15, without advance notice to us, John Coleman released the following memorandum to The Weather Channel's staff:

Goodbye.
My option expires at 5 P.M. today. I am unable to obtain funding, so it will not be exercised.

Thank you.
You have given me incredible support. You are all excellent at what you do.

Good luck.
Landmark now totally owns and controls The Weather Channel. Good luck to each of you.

So long.
Actually this is just a so long. In this small world, we will meet again.

It was a surprisingly restrained benediction. We were enormously relieved, but we had nothing to celebrate. It was time to prepare the ground for a burial.

CHAPTER SIX

THE FAST LANE

In hindsight, success almost always looks inevitable. The right people do the right things at the right time. Then the winner steps up to the podium, shares credit with all the right people, graciously acknowledges the applause, and takes home the trophy.

That wasn't the way it went at The Weather Channel.

By the summer of 1983, the venture that had begun with such high hopes a little more than a year earlier was nearly dead. Our best hope, that John Coleman would find somebody to buy The Weather Channel and take it off our hands, had evaporated. We would have to shut the network down as honorably and humanely as possible.

Not surprisingly, other programmers took the opportunity to try to hire away some of our very talented people. Some employees did jump ship, but most didn't. Most—including one of our young affiliate managers, Tamara Zinn, who had previously worked at ESPN—believed that we would somehow find a way to keep going. As she recently told an interviewer:

> *I got a call from somebody at ESPN during the whole Coleman and Landmark struggle. They said, "Tamara, get out of there while you can! Come back to work for us, because you're not going to have a job much longer."*
>
> *I didn't know Frank Batten that well, but I just said, "From what I know of him, I just cannot imagine that he'd sell this network. I just don't believe it." I just had the confidence that if there was any way for him to continue, he would, because it was that important to him.*

But the cold fact was that even I had already given up on our expensive baby. Now would come the fire sale—or worse, the public execution and burial.

What followed instead was a miraculous turnaround, initially made possible by the unexpected willingness of cable operators to pay a fee for our service. That bought us time. And for the next decade or so, we worked extremely hard to improve our management practices, build an able, motivated organization, sell ads, and improve our programming. And in this same ten-year period—from roughly the mid-1980s to the mid-1990s—we rode an unbelievable wave of growth in the cable industry, which far surpassed even our own optimistic projections.

But our success was anything but inevitable.

SAVED BY SUB FEES

While John Coleman was scrambling to find a financial backer within his option period, Dubby Wynne and I continued to make our contingency plans for shutting down The Weather Channel. Then something remarkable happened. Out of the blue, several of our largest cable customers sought out one or the other of us and provided a startling and unexpected perspective. The gist of their message was, "We don't want to invest in The Weather Channel, but we don't want to lose it, either. If subscriber fees are what's required to keep it going, we would consider paying them."

"Subscriber fees" (also known as carriage fees) are a per-capita fee the cable operator pays to some, but not all, cable programmers. ESPN, for example, has always commanded a fee from operators, reasoning (1) that ESPN is hugely popular with cable viewers, and (2) that the sports network has high costs because it pays a great deal for the rights to its programming. Similarly, operators already were paying carriage fees to CNN and USA. The precedent for carriage fees, at least in some areas of programming, was already well established.

But as spare cable channels started filling up, and as a wide variety of new cable program services were announced, operators began flatly rejecting the idea of paying new fees. (In our original due-diligence investigations, operators had told us there was no way we could expect to get fees. We would have to make our way by earning advertising revenues.) In fact, the demand for channel space was becoming so intense that some new programming services were offering to pay cable systems to carry them.

The idea that operators were offering subscriber fees absolutely stunned me. Dubby Wynne, too, was taken aback. When he and I were comparing notes on the overtures several operators had made to us, I said, "We'd better take one last look so see whether there's still hope for The Weather Channel."

So even as we continued our contingency planning for shutting down the channel, we also began talking privately about how we could quickly test our prospects for collecting fee revenues. How could we follow up on the informal overtures we had been receiving from the field? How much fee revenue would we need, within what time frame, to give The Weather Channel a chance to succeed? How could we get it?

These discussions had to remain strictly among ourselves, of course, until Coleman's option expired. We did not want to be accused of interfering in our former colleague's hunt for funding. After that unhappy milestone was behind us, I reconvened the group that had initially advised us on entering the venture—Dubby Wynne, Dick Barry, and Bill Diederich from Landmark, and TeleCable executives Gordon Herring and Dick Roberts—for a formal brainstorming session.

Roberts and Herring, our in-house cable experts, said they believed that the prospects for collecting fees from operators were much brighter than in the recent past. Cable operators had become well aware that their futures depended on offering more attractive programming. Most of the multiple system operators were building new systems in larger markets. Their new systems had more channels—thirty-five was typical; as many as fifty or sixty was not uncommon. In most of these markets, Roberts and Herring said, television viewers already had access to reasonably good reception of the three commercial networks, a public broad-casting station, and an independent station or two. Operators of these systems knew that to sell their cable service, they had to offer customers a diverse menu of programs that they could not find elsewhere.

Operators needed periodic fee increases to cover their esca-lating costs. By extension, they needed a continuing supply of new programs to justify their continuing value to customers. Meanwhile, construction programs in larger markets were very expensive, and most cable companies already had heavily lever-aged balance sheets. In fact, they were carrying much more debt than was typical in consumer-service businesses, and their lenders also had begun to be aware of the critical need for appealing new programming.

Against this backdrop, a troubling new development was putting operators on edge. Several of the most ballyhooed new cable networks were shutting down, in some cases even before their first products could go out over the wires and airwaves. For example, CBS had invested heavily to acquire programming and promote a new arts and cultural network for cable. The venerable broadcaster's belated foray into cable commanded a lot of media attention, but the new venture died before getting off the ground. Similarly, another network that had received widespread industry attention—RCTV (Rockefeller Center TV)—announced that it was closing before it opened.

Roberts and Herring had heard that multiple system operators were finding these highly publicized closures unsettling. Lenders, meanwhile, were growing apprehensive about putting up the huge sums required to wire the larger cable markets. In this climate, the prospect of losing yet another network—and one that had already cultivated viewers—was likely to be unwelcome, and even scary, to cable operators.

After we talked through our case for fees, Roberts and Herring advised us to go to the multiple system operators and lay all our cards on the table—including showing our financial results, if necessary. In that spirit, we sketched the broad outlines of a fee plan. We decided we would present it to cable operators as a referendum on the future of The Weather Channel: *You, the operators, will decide whether or not our service will survive.* We would continue to operate the network for three months, which would give us enough time to determine whether operators with at least 80 percent of our subscriber base would agree to our fee plan. If they did, we would guarantee to keep The Weather Channel in operation for at least another year. And finally, we would share with the multiple system operators our honest belief that some kind of reasonable fee structure would ensure the channel's long-term survival. If they would help us, we could make it.

After that meeting, we started devising the specifics of a fee plan. We wanted it to be simple and cheap enough to avoid complicated negotiations, and to encourage quick agreement. We settled on a rate of 5 cents per subscriber; we knew it was competitively low, but it probably would allow us to break even in about three years. (CNN was charging around 15 cents per month per subscriber, which was on the high side; USA Network was in the middle of the range, at about 10 cents per month per subscriber.) Later, after we made a number of presentations to operators and negotiated several agreements, we decided to offer discounted rates for systems in the larger markets. Diederich argued forcefully that we must get large numbers in major markets, since this was the audience that was most attractive to advertisers.

Dubby Wynne, Doug Holladay, and Bahns Stanley, the members of the new-ventures team who had originally "landed" The Weather Channel concept, nearly lived on airlines during that three-month period, as they contacted almost all the largest multiple system operators.

Holladay recalls that they decided to approach Bill Daniels first. Daniels, who was head of Colorado-based United Cable, had been our first advisor on entering the cable business, and had called me during Coleman's option period and expressed strong support for The Weather Channel. He was seen as the "dean of cable operators" by his cable-operator peers, and he commanded enormous respect within the industry. Wynne and Holladay believed that if Daniels became an advocate for our cause, he could quickly get us in to see many CEOs of the top cable companies. This was important, because unlike, say, the programming directors, CEOs could make quick commitments and could commit on behalf of all their systems.

Holladay called it right: While Wynne and Holladay were in their meeting with Daniels, he picked up the phone and called four of his counterparts, who headed some of the largest multiple system operators in the country. Within a week, Wynne and Holladay were able to visit all four operators whom Daniels had called.

In these and other early meetings, sometimes attended by Bahns Stanley, we got strong confirmation that Roberts's and Herring's advice was on target. Stanley recalls an interesting conversation that he and Wynne had with one operator, whom we had identified, incorrectly, as a potentially difficult sell:

"You know," he said to me, "we're going to say yes to your pro-
posal to pay fees. And the reason why we're going to say yes is
that we've noticed that every time a network goes dark, our
interest rates go up. And that's because Wall Street and the
investment community figure that the thing that will drive cable
is differentiated programming. We're expecting to have to borrow
hundreds of millions from lenders, and it's cheaper to pay you
than to take yet another interest-rate increase."

While Wynne and Holladay were on the road scrounging for
fees, we got another dollop of good luck. A market research firm,
East Lansing Research Associates, released an independent study
in July 1983, just before our three-month, live-or-die phase began.
Unexpectedly, the study ranked The Weather Channel as "the
most satisfying" to viewers of eighteen cable networks. More than
60 percent of the viewers surveyed said they were "very satisfied"
with The Weather Channel, a remarkable rating for a network
that had been on the air just a year. All the more remarkable was
the fact that we were beating cable powerhouses WTBS and
ESPN, which ranked as the two next most satisfying channels.
Since we had asked cable operators to help decide our fate, we
made sure they learned of this news, citing it as impartial corrob-
oration of The Weather Channel's perceived value. We also hoped
that news of the survey would fall into the hands of institutions
that were lending huge sums of money to cable operators.

All the time that we were going through the long trauma of
litigation with Coleman, we were sure that the public airing of
our precarious financial condition was driving a stake through our
little venture's heart. As it turned out, we had it exactly backward.
Savvy cable operators had followed our legal travails with some
interest, and by the time we arrived on their doorsteps, they readily accepted our assertion that subscriber fees were the only means
of keeping The Weather Channel alive. Of course, some of them
tried to negotiate our proposed fees downward. But Wynne and

Holladay showed them that our proposed fee structure, modest as it was, wouldn't allow us to break even for several years.

Another dynamic was at play here. Our traveling emissaries were closely associated with TeleCable, Landmark's cable subsidiary, which had an excellent reputation in the industry. To our delight, we found that our sister cable company's credibility carried over to The Weather Channel. Cable operators might not have liked hearing that subscriber fees were necessary, but they were likely to believe it if they heard it from someone like Dubby Wynne. A sales call has the strongest foundation possible when the person you're calling on is predisposed to believe you when you speak.

We were asking for the fees to begin at the start of the following year, 1984. Fortunately, the timing of our calls was just right. We were calling on the operators in the middle of their budgeting cycle. If we had arrived just a month or two later, many operators would have insisted on delaying fee payments until the following year, and that probably would have killed us.

Well before our self-imposed deadline of three months, Wynne became convinced that our fee proposal would succeed. He had sequenced our operator presentations carefully, making sure that we called first on operators who had expressed satisfaction with the channel—and particularly those who were seeking new franchises in key markets and already had included The Weather Channel in their bid proposals. By calling on operators who were likely to give our plan quick approval, we tried to generate a groundswell of support in the industry, which would give us some momentum before we approached operators we thought might be the most difficult to "sell."

In fact, such a groundswell did materialize. Not a single operator rejected our fee proposal. A few of the largest approved the plan at headquarters but then required us also to get the approval of the managers of each system in their group. Holladay then traveled from city to city, calling on each of these system managers—a task that put him back on airplanes for another three weeks. But even before this phase was over, Dubby Wynne felt confident enough to announce—on September 21, 1983—that the industry had accepted our fee plan. "We are appreciative of the cable operators' vote of confidence in The Weather Channel," Wynne said in a public statement. "We were fortunate to conclude so many agreements in such a short time." By the end of 1983, fifteen of the largest cable companies had signed new three-year, fee-based contracts with The Weather Channel.

Success was by no means assured, but we stood to receive $4 million in subscriber fees in 1984. Extrapolating from that base, we thought that we could break even in 1986. Needless to say, all of us who had been intimately involved with The Weather Channel got a tremendous boost. The black cloud that had been hovering over our heads lifted. We were back in business.

Retelling this story, I'm struck by how lucky we were. Our timing was perfect, both in terms of larger industry trends and the annual budget cycle. Our legal woes—so humiliating in real time—served as a great credibility builder. Out of the blue came a consumer study showing we were as well liked as we claimed to be. Luck, luck, and more luck.

But luck favors the prepared mind, and it takes root in the plowed ground. Over many years of hard work and fair dealing, we had built our reputation in the cable industry. We knew that industry intimately, and its major players knew us. We knew where to go, what to say, and how to say it.

We also had the benefit of incredibly dedicated and tenacious people, only some of whom I've named here. Faced with a grim outlook for The Weather Channel and fading prospects for their individual careers, they never abandoned their faith in the channel, and they never quit. In fact, they fought like cornered tigers.

And at the risk of embarrassing him, I want to state for the record that The Weather Channel will always be especially indebted to Dubby Wynne. Even when the outlook was darkest, Wynne continued to believe in The Weather Channel. During a period of terrible and tragic illness in his family, he put himself almost constantly on the road to meet with operators. We needed his personal determination to save our venture, and he willingly gave us that commitment. It was an enormous personal sacrifice, which I will never forget. Without Dubby Wynne, The Weather Channel could not have survived.

MANAGEMENT AND LABOR

With Coleman gone, Wynne took over as interim chief executive of The Weather Channel. He spent most of his time in Atlanta, with the initial goals of settling down a staff that was in turmoil and focusing the enterprise on a more hopeful future. The organization seethed with malignant divisions—between some people who were seen as Coleman's favorites, and others who had been brought in by Landmark—and these rifts were not bridged quickly. For many months, in fact, they impeded The Weather Channel's forward progress.

Wynne, who absolutely had to get back to his family in Virginia and, secondarily, his responsibilities at Landmark, hired an executive search firm to look for a new president for The Weather Channel. This search was tougher than it might sound. Cable programming was not yet seen as "the next big thing" in the media business, and The Weather Channel still was viewed as a shaky proposition. The consultants didn't find many prospects for our position, and those whom they did find tended to be out-of-work managers.

Under mounting pressure to sign a president promptly, we hired, in the spring of 1984, an Atlanta-based executive, John A. Janas, who had helpful contacts in the cable industry. During his short tenure as our president, Janas brought in a new head of affiliate sales and also made valuable contacts with some important cable operators. But after a little more than a year, he left. Counting Coleman, Wynne, and Janas, The Weather Channel now had

had three chiefs in less than two years—a depressing record, and not a prescription for healing an organization with some deep wounds.

Once again, Wynne had to go looking for someone to head up The Weather Channel. This time, fortunately, he found a first-rate candidate in-house: Michael J. Eckert. You'll recall that Mike Eckert was our first Chicago ad sales manager; he then succeeded Mike Ban in New York when Ban moved to Atlanta to head up our marketing efforts. Because of his distinguished work for us in Chicago and New York—both highly competitive media markets—in the summer of 1985, we named him the fourth president of The Weather Channel.

Eckert had his work cut out for him. That summer, we were faced with a union-organizing drive among our on-camera meteorologists, many of whom believed that, dating back to the beginning, work schedules were largely based on favoritism. If you were on the "ins," you got a desirable time slot; if you were on the "outs," you got the graveyard shift. And longstanding dissatisfaction with arbitrary salaries remained. I'm sorry to say that they did have ample grounds for complaints. I believe that, generally, unions flourish when management has allowed conditions to exist that breed grievances. And our management needed to address the root problems here. Wynne and I believed strongly that a union would hog-tie our fragile venture, and that any reduction in our flexibility might well do us in. He and our personnel head, Hugh Eaton, concentrated on rooting out and dealing with the in-equities, and in some cases, misperceptions, that had brought the union to town in the first place. Meanwhile, Ray Ban—one of our original band of on-camera meteorologists, who only recently had become the manager of that group—performed invaluable service in opening up avenues of communication with the staff. Eaton put in untold hours visiting almost all the on-camera staff at their homes. In August 1985 the union was voted down.

For many reasons, 1985 was a watershed year for The Weather Channel. As Ray Ban explains:

*We floundered until 1985, which was a big turning point. It was
then that we figured out in which direction we wanted to take
this thing. We were successful in the union campaign; we started
getting more distribution; sub fees had kicked in; and ratings
were beginning to increase.*

*Mike [Eckert] developed a sense of team, a sense of com-
mitment, of pride and a feeling of unity in the organization. His
strong leadership was what the company needed.*

This critical first year set the tone for Mike Eckert's long
tenure as The Weather Channel's president. Trained in the rough-
and-tumble world of ad sales, he was a strong, results-driven operator. He moved quickly to develop a spirit of teamwork and cooperation among his managers. In spite of months of chaos, a strong
core group in Atlanta still believed in The Weather Channel, and
they were committed to making it succeed. All they needed was a
leader with an equal level of commitment, and Eckert filled the bill.

NOT BUYING, NOT BEING BOUGHT

Word spread quickly that The Weather Channel had survived its near-death experience, saved by the support of cable
operators. This news was encouraging to would-be programmers
who were planning to launch new channels; some of these people
made their way to Norfolk to talk to us about possibly backing
their ideas.

One of these entrepreneurs, John Hendricks, called on us in
1984 while seeking support for a network he proposed to call the
Discovery Channel. His concept was to program documentaries
about nature, travel to unusual places, the environment, and similar "outdoorsy" themes. Hendricks struck us as a bright, creative,
forthright person—in other words, the kind of person we wanted
to do business with. We thought that his programming concept
could appeal to the growing number of viewers who were tired of

PREVIOUS PAGE: In the quiet before the storm, **JIM CANTORE**, on-camera meteorologist and member of the on-location coverage team, sets up to provide live coverage from Marathon, Florida during Hurricane Debbie in the summer of 2000. ABOVE: **MIKE SEIDEL**, on-camera meteorologist and member of the on-location coverage team, reports from Albany, New York during a severe winter storm.

On-camera meteorologist
VIVIAN BROWN presents a national
weather update in front of the
blue chroma-key screen.

OPPOSITE, TOP: JIM CANTORE reports from near the eye of the storm during Hurricane Bonnie in August 1998. OPPOSITE, BOTTOM: JOHN HOPE, tropical storm expert, showing the track of a hurricane. ABOVE: BILL KENEELY, on-camera meteorologist, reports from Dulles Airport in Washington, D.C. during a snowstorm in 1999.

BELOW: On-camera meteorologists **JENNIFER LOPEZ** and **PAUL GOODLOE** open the "Weather Center" program from the anchor desk. OPPOSITE, TOP: **VIVIAN BROWN** and **JIM CANTORE** discuss the top weather stories as they prepare for "Weather Center." OPPOSITE, BOTTOM: **HEATHER TESCH** and **MARSHALL SEESE**, co-hosts of "Your Weather Today."

ABOVE: **KRISTINA ABERNATHY**, on–camera
meteorologist. OPPOSITE: **JOHN SCALA**,
HEATHER TESCH, **MARSHALL SEESE**, and **DENNIS SMITH**,
the "Your Weather Today" team.

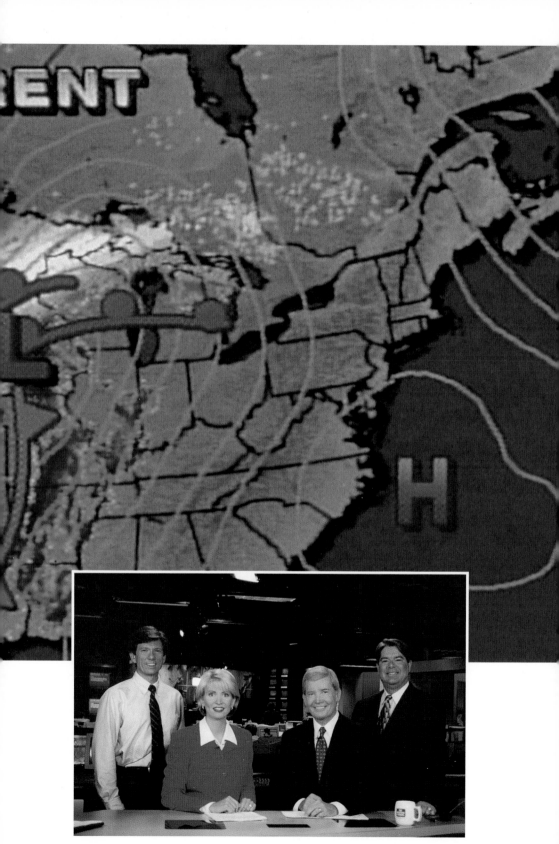

THE WEATHER CHANNEL

HURRICANE
SEASON '99

MIKE SEIDEL

ABOVE: **MIKE SEIDEL**, reporting from the field.
OPPOSITE, TOP: **MIKE SEIDEL** travels with The Weather Channel's "Storm Tracker" satellite truck and an on-location coverage team to present a live report on damage from an F5 tornado.
OPPOSITE, BOTTOM: **BILL KENEELY**, reporting from the field.

LIVE

SPECIAL REPORT
WRIGHTSVILLE BEACH, NC
HURRICANE BONNIE

THE WEATHER CHANNEL

ABOVE: **DR. STEVE LYONS**, hurricane expert at The Weather Channel, shows the path of a hurricane during a special update. OPPOSITE, TOP: **BOB STOKES** and **CHERYL LEMKE**, on-camera meteorologists. OPPOSITE, BOTTOM: **JIM CANTORE**, in the field.

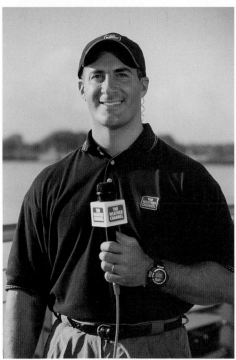

ABOVE: During Hurricane Bonnie in 1998, JIM CANTORE reports in the pelting rain. Parked between him and the "StormTracker" satellite truck is a station wagon, which provides coverage for the cameraman as he shoots Jim through the car window so the equipment will not get wet. OPPOSITE, TOP: JOHN HOPE and JIM CANTORE. OPPOSITE, BOTTOM: VIVIAN BROWN.

TOP: Briefings are held several times a day by meteorologists such as **DAVE MARGOLIN** (at monitor), shown here with on-camera meteorologists **NICK WALKER** and **KRISTINA ABERNATHY** as they prepare for their on-air presentations. ABOVE: **VIVIAN BROWN** and **JEFF MORROW** open "Weather Center" from the anchor desk.

the monotonous fare of sitcoms and soap operas served up by the three major broadcast networks. Hendricks expected that he could acquire many programs as reruns from foreign networks such as the BBC.

We worried aloud about whether enough of this kind of programming would be available at a reasonable cost. The main reason we passed on this appealing opportunity, however, was that we still were not entirely confident about the future of The Weather Channel. Even with subscriber fees, it was not yet clear whether we could attract enough advertising to cover our operating costs, and we still faced the large capital costs associated with installing WeatherSTARs in each new cable system. Did we really have the stomach needed to take on another labor of love right now?

In the end, we passed on the opportunity to own a large stake in what is now arguably the most successful of all cable networks. Hendricks—an effective salesperson for his good idea—was able to piece together enough capital to start his Discovery Channel. Interestingly enough, he soon faced a financial crisis similar to the one we had just lived through. Like The Weather Channel, Discovery was saved by support from some of the nation's largest cable operators, such as TCI, Cox, and Newhouse, who decided that they simply could not afford to lose its valuable programming. And also like The Weather Channel, Discovery was valued not only because it was popular with viewers, but also because franchising authorities viewed its programming as a public service.

Hendricks was a tiny fish then, and The Weather Channel was only slightly bigger: a very small fish. But both of us swam in a pond full of very big fish, some of which occasionally took notice of The Weather Channel. Our dramatic fight for survival earned us some attention from one of these leviathans, NBC. Like its rivals CBS and ABC, the National Broadcasting Company was then exploring prospects for entering the cable field. Somewhere in this period, just as things were starting to turn around, they approached us about a possible acquisition of, or major equity stake in, The Weather Channel.

At a time when our future was still in doubt, the prospect was tempting. A major investment by NBC would give the venture prestige and the support of a large sales organization. Most important, from our point of view, it could give us access to video of severe weather from local NBC affiliates, which would be more affordable than video from other sources.

After several exploratory meetings, though, both parties agreed to drop the idea. I know that some people in my own organization were disappointed, but the prospect of limiting our freedom by getting married to—or worse, acquired by—a partner with very different goals from our own was unappealing to me, and it still is.

TALES OF ADS AND GROWTH

During the period of litigation and deepest uncertainty about our survival, advertising sales efforts were severely handicapped, but they did produce some results. Surprisingly, nine contracts were signed in the last two months of 1983, including $613,000 in renewals and $306,000 in new contracts. Our largest advertisers, United Airlines and the Vick Chemical Co., stayed with us.

When Dubby Wynne announced that our subscriber fee plan had been successful, it gave the sales staff a much-needed boost in confidence. But it was not until Mike Eckert became president that advertising sales received the focus it needed. I believe that Mike's experience—and his powerful instincts for sales and advertising—made him the ideal leader for a business whose greatest need was to generate revenues, and in a hurry. As finance vice president Pat Clark recently put it:

He was a fantastic salesman. He believed so much in what we were selling. Whenever he ran into somebody who demonstrated

any interest in The Weather Channel, they got a sales pitch.
And it wasn't that he was really trying to sell them something;
he just felt so strongly about what we were doing.

I agree. But I have to add that we all did our part—up to and including the chairman. At some point during our nerve-racking season of uncertainty, I had an unlikely encounter that gave me bragging rights for many months. One day while out on the road, I was standing near the entrance of the United Red Carpet Room at O'Hare Airport, attentively watching The Weather Channel on a TV monitor suspended from the ceiling. After a few minutes, a man standing next to me spoke up:

"Do you watch this channel often?"

"Oh, every day," I replied, deadpan. "It's my favorite channel."

"Do you remember whose commercial we just saw?"

"Sure. Vicks Vapo-Rub. They advertise a lot on The Weather Channel."

"Well, that's very interesting," he said. "I'm the advertising director for Vick Chemical, and I like to ask that question whenever I get a chance." And with that, we left for our separate flights. Naturally, whenever Vick subsequently renewed one of our most prized contracts, I claimed the credit.

Selling ads for The Weather Channel was a tough business, for several reasons. One not so obvious one was that many advertising agencies and major corporations are based in New York City. If you think about it, an executive in the Big Apple can live pretty much sheltered from the elements: car to the suburban train station, train to subway, and subway to office. Norm Zeller, a sales manager who has been with The Weather Channel from its inception, tells how people in New York at first turned up their noses at the idea of buying time on a weather network. "They would look out of the windows of their fortieth-floor offices," he recalls, "and say, 'Nope, don't need weather.'"

Another early challenge was that some ad agencies didn't want to spend time dealing with such a small fish. It's far simpler for an agency to make a single big buy on behalf of a client—say, sponsorship of a major sports event—than to piece together a large schedule of relatively inexpensive spots on The Weather Channel and similar networks. And ad agencies, like the rest of us, are risk-averse. Why put a lot of time and effort into a campaign for a cable network that may not be around tomorrow? (The New York ad agencies, in particular, were sure that The Weather Channel would fail, partly because salespeople working for competing channels cautioned them not to make the mistake of sinking client dollars into a losing venture.) Even agencies that were willing to gamble on us tended to allocate only "test" dollars, which meant that ads would run for only four to six weeks.

For these reasons and others, we often found it necessary to run around the agencies and go directly to the client—to the irritation of the agencies, which naturally wanted to control these relationships.

A third challenge, already introduced in previous chapters, was that we had no ratings. Of course, we were conducting our own surveys to measure our viewing trends, and these surveys were showing continuing increases in our viewership. But until we reached the magic number of 15 million subscribers, Nielsen wouldn't bother tracking us. Without objective, third-party ratings, we couldn't prove that anybody was watching us, and we couldn't compete for "real" ad dollars.

This meant, of course, that we had to get our subscriber base up to the magic threshold. To some extent, we had only to survive to succeed at this game. Cable penetration of U.S. homes was soaring. Between 1982—when The Weather Channel went on the air—and 1986, the number of U.S. cable subscribers doubled from roughly 20 million to more than 40 million homes, almost 50 percent of U.S. households.

So far, I've focused on our challenges. But when it came to selling ads, we also had some distinct advantages. Some potential advertisers—tire companies, hotels, airlines, and pharmaceutical firms—sold products or services with a natural tie to the weather.

Working closely with the programming staff in Atlanta, the sales staff sold the sponsorship of various program segments to advertisers. "Winterize Your Pet," for example, was a natural for Ralston Purina, "Cold Wave Alert" for Quaker Oats, "Heat Wave Alert" for Gatorade, "Dress for the Weather" for DuPont, and so on. These tie-ins became the subject of wry jokes around the shop. At one point, some wit proposed that we pitch "Weather and Your Cheese" to Kraft.

Another advantage we had was that we were relatively inexpensive. Unlike entertainment and sports networks, we didn't have to pay exorbitant prices for programming rights. Thus we could sell ourselves as a cumulative medium. As Zeller explains, "At our prices, we could offer lots of spots to reach lots of different people—say, twenty-four spots on The Weather Channel versus four on ABC. The price was right, so advertisers could afford that kind of frequency."

And finally, we had the WeatherSTAR, which was the one selling advantage that no other network had, and which was responsible for much of the advertising we were getting. From early on, we were convinced that WeatherSTAR's localization capabilities would help us sell ads to companies that had nationwide dealership networks and whose products were in some way weather-related. Barry Roberts, a salesperson in our New York office, finally made a successful pitch to Michelin by arranging for airing of national tire ads, which would be followed by localized text delivered by the WeatherSTARs. One huge advantage to us—and presumably to Michelin—was that the localized campaign could be supported by "cooperative" dollars, kicked into a national kitty by the local dealerships. The ad agency didn't need to be involved, and we were able to close the deal on a handshake.

Michelin and its dealers were delighted with the results of this novel campaign. The company became our first year-round advertiser and remained our top account for the next fourteen years. Building on this highly successful model, we next targeted auto companies and their dealerships and automotive aftermarket advertisers and their dealerships. Success in these areas led to the opening of a new sales office in Detroit.

Because this is a book about The Weather Channel, I've focused mainly on the particulars of our little network's window on the world. But the real story in this period was the astounding growth of the larger cable industry. Cable operators accelerated their construction in large metropolitan areas and also found ways to make money putting cable into ever more remote rural areas. At the end of 1985, The Weather Channel was reaching only 18.7 million homes. By 1989, our subscribers had more than doubled, to some 40 million. Yes, we worked hard to get onto additional cable systems. But a huge tide was coming in, and we rode that tide.

Advertising on cable networks was exploding in parallel. In 1980, cable advertising in the United States totaled only $45 million. By 1986, it grew to almost $1 billion, and then it more than doubled again by 1989. As cable coverage became almost ubiquitous, cable became a serious competitor to the broadcast networks for advertising dollars. Cable advertising continued to grow exponentially—to $5 billion in 1995, and almost $13 billion in 2000—and the rules of the media game continued to be rewritten.

Finally, in the fourth quarter of 1984, our subscriber base was large enough to qualify us for Nielsen ratings. We just barely made the 15 million threshold, with 15.3 million households, or about 18 percent of TV-served households nationwide. For the first time, we would be able to give advertisers the kind of independent assurance they required about the size and demographics of our viewing audience.

Unfortunately, these long-awaited statistics, released in the spring of 1985, were disappointing. Although the demographics of our viewers were outstanding—they tended to be well educated, have relatively high incomes, and live in "higher discretionary income" counties—not enough of the overall subscriber base was tuning in to us. We were averaging about 54,000 households per minute in the morning and about 68,000 households at night.

Publicly, we said we were pleased with our numbers; privately, we admitted that we were not.

Part of the problem, we knew, was that The Weather Channel didn't have the resources to advertise for viewers. We counted on "channel surfers" discovering us on their dials, sampling us, and liking us enough to develop a regular viewing habit. The weak Nielsen ratings suggested that our relatively passive approach wasn't good enough, and that we would have to move aggressively to present a new face to our viewers. A massive advertising campaign was still beyond our means; therefore we had to make our product better. Many of us, including our new president, Mike Eckert, were determined to push hard in that direction.

ENHANCING OUR PROGRAMMING

The Weather Channel finally broke even in 1986, during our fifth year on the air. By that point, Landmark had invested something like $35 million in operating losses and capital expenditures in the venture—plus, of course, a wealth of priceless human capital.

What did we have to show for it? We had an organization of about 160 people who had weathered adversity together and survived. As a result of our budget woes, we knew how to stretch a buck. Meanwhile, we had created a "mecca of meteorology," a place where bright young weather experts wanted to work. We had a home-grown technology that gave us an enormous leg up in terms of ad sales. We had a product that America had begun to accept: We had made the difficult transition from being the butt of editorial jokes and cartoons to being perceived as a vital public service, and we were beginning to emerge as a strong brand.

But we also had those depressing Nielsen ratings to deal with. Determined to bring them up, we revisited our programming format. This began a process of revision and reinvention, both minor and major, that continues to this day.

For the three years since the network's inception, we left our original format mostly unchanged. Over the course of one hour, we would cover regional weather, national weather, the five-day forecast, and national radar, and intersperse those segments with local forecasts every five minutes. We repeated this same "one-hour clock," with its updated forecasts, twenty-four hours a day, seven days a week.

Clearly, this format was inadequate. One size didn't fit all. Surveys of viewers showed us that our audience demographics differed at different times of the day, and that viewers' interests differed at different times. We began adjusting our programming throughout the day to appeal to these different demographic groups and their differing interests—for example, by running longer segments during the "off-peak" viewing hours. This kind of variegated programming was more complicated to produce, of course, but we were rewarded in the next Nielsen report with ratings that were twice as high as in the previous round.

But the life of a programmer is a little more complicated than that. Yes, our ratings improved as our programming became somewhat more effectively targeted. But they also improved—and improved more dramatically—when the weather called attention to itself. Severe weather caused large spikes in our ratings, and quiet weather depressed our ratings. Hurricanes, blizzards, and tornadoes were seasonal occurrences, so The Weather Channel's ratings were likely to fluctuate seasonally, independent of our best efforts.

One lesson in all this was that we could help ourselves by improving our severe-weather coverage. This was our version of "fishing where the fish are." From the start, we had sought out meteorologists with special expertise in different kinds of severe weather. Take John Hope, for example. The National Weather Service's premier expert on hurricanes, Hope came to us when he retired from the National Hurricane Center in 1982. He has been a vital resource in our coverage of hurricanes ever since, explaining the behavior of hurricanes in interesting and understandable ways.

Because Hope approaches hurricane coverage responsibly, avoiding the hype that has become characteristic of too many television weather reports, he has developed a legion of loyal viewers.

John Hope literally personifies The Weather Channel to consumers, and he has been a pivotal person in our history. He is a role model to our staff and a symbol of what we stand for—integrity, expertise, reliability. Some call him the Walter Cronkite of weather.

And Hope is only one of our severe-weather experts, who include tropical-storm expert Dr. Steve Lyons, tornado and severe thunderstorm expert Dr. Gregory Forbes, and winter-weather expert Paul Kocin. Viewers have come to depend on these voices of authority for reasoned and accurate explanations of life-threatening weather.

In addition to adding to our in-house expertise, we also dramatically ramped up our live coverage of hurricanes, tornadoes, blizzards, and other severe weather. A major investment in this area in 1996, specifically in the realm of additional remote reports and purchased video footage, for example, contributed significantly to a 60 percent increase in viewership that year, as compared with 1995. Again, though, "pure" experiments are difficult to run, because the weather itself largely determines viewership. The weather in 1996 was generally more inclement than it was in 1995, and thus was surely responsible for some of the increase in our viewership.

The day-to-day work of producing The Weather Channel is mostly a story of endless attention to detail. Some of those details, as seen through the eyes of current staffers, are included at the end of this book. Another critical part of our story involves the remarkable technological developments that have made weather forecasting more accurate and have given us new ways to gather and present weather information. Those developments have spanned the better part of two decades and continue to this day. (Later we will look into these technological developments in more detail.)

Another way we could help ourselves was by learning even more about who watched us, and why. In 1994, we undertook our first in-depth analysis of how consumers of weather information feel about that information, and how they use it. Through the use of qualitative and quantitative information, we were able to segment the market into three kinds of weather consumers: "Weather Commodity," "Weather Planner," and "Weather Engaged."

In simple terms, the Commodity consumers tend to seek out weather information only infrequently, and then only for basic local forecasts. Weather Planners are heavy viewers of weather programs. They rely on weather information that can have an impact on their work, their recreation, and their children's welfare. The Weather Engaged are heavy viewers, too, but their interest in weather goes broader and deeper. They have a profound interest in—even a passion for—weather. They want to understand the causes of severe weather, as well as the ways it affects their family and friends.

Our research also showed an unexpected distribution of our user population across these three categories. Commodity consumers make up about one-third of the population, and Planners are about one-quarter. Surprisingly, slightly over 40 percent fall into the Weather Engaged category.

These findings gave us valuable insights into how to further adjust our programming to appeal to different constituencies. One key step was to shift our emphasis toward satisfying the Planners

Reprinted with special permission of King Features Syndicate.

and Weather Engaged viewers. For example, we embraced new technologies to make our forecasts and explanations clearer and more compelling graphically. Through several generations of re-engineering, the WeatherSTAR became more sophisticated, progressing from its original primitive, text-only local forecasts to vivid graphics and voice descriptions of local weather with current local radar. As predictive sciences improved, we complemented our traditional three-day forecasts with seven-day forecasts.

In retrospect, it's easy to see that we should have conducted this kind of deep customer-based research sooner. The return on that investment was clear: When we changed our programs to target our viewers, our ratings rose. We continue to update this information periodically, so that we are able to measure who watches, when, why, and what they need. And just as important, we can sift through proposed changes in programming with a much higher confidence level because we have a strong base of facts from which to work.

Partly because of our market research, we sought to improve our programming in one other important way: by changing the way our meteorologists presented information to the viewing audience. In the early days, our on-camera meteorologists delivered national and regional forecasts in an informal, down-home atmosphere, often with goofs, gaffes, and miscues. Sometimes someone would have a bright idea but not fully think it through before trying it out on air. Joe D'Aleo, who worked with John Coleman to develop our original programming and continued to play a key programming role until 1988, recalls one interesting moment in the annals of cablecasting:

> We were trying to cover a lunar eclipse at night. It was a cold night, and we had a camera up on the roof aimed at the moon. We went to commercial, came back, and Charlie Welsh and the other coanchor set the stage for what the viewer was about to see. But meanwhile, the moon had moved out of the camera view, and we just had a sea of black on screen.

159

So we yelled up to the fellow on the roof: "Hey—find the moon!" So he started looking for the moon through the camera—this is live, via satellite, to the entire country—and he focused in on a bright round object. Which turned out to be a Gulf station sign. So you might say we broke the news that there was a Gulf station on the moon.

In other cases, off-camera personnel would attempt to distract the on-camera staff and get them laughing. All kinds of practical joking went on just out of camera range. Scriptwriters would put together tongue twisters on purpose, just to see how certain people would field them on camera. Sometimes, especially during off-peak hours, things in the studio could get a little out of control. Cheryl Lemke, one of our first female on-camera meteorologists, recalls her reaction:

There were some practical jokers here. I recall very distinctly the first time I was on the air. I followed this other guy, and he was doing anything and everything to crack me up. He set up all these little roadblocks along the way. He thought it was funny. But for me, this was my first really big job in broadcasting. I was taking it very seriously. But for him, it was kind of like a frat-house atmosphere. It was a strange environment.

Some of these antics showed up on TV screens across the nation. To some extent, I suppose, they may even have helped us, by distinguishing us from the bland alternatives available on other stations. On the other hand, amateurism wears thin quickly. Meanwhile, more and more people were watching us. The stakes were getting higher.

So the inevitable push, over time, was in the direction of increased professionalism. This emphasis was reinforced beginning in the later 1990s with the introduction of a formal process for evaluating and improving the work of the on-camera meteorologists. A longtime outside consultant to The Weather Channel, Les

Davis, worked with our staff to develop a list of six primary characteristics that added up to the "perfect" weather presenter: professionalism, technical delivery, appearance, and so on. Multiple "subcharacteristics" were developed for each of the six major categories, fleshing out those larger topics.

We then asked panels of Weather Channel viewers to review clips of each of our on-camera staff and rate each presenter in each of the subcategories. In that way, we got an interesting and useful snapshot of each member of our on-air staff, ranging from the most seasoned veteran to the greenest recruit. Our managers then sat down with each on-camera meteorologist to review the results. The process soon became part of our routine. Lemke describes it thus:

> *I think after hearing all the feedback, you can always take away little snippets of things that you can use to make your performance that much better. So even though there may be things that you don't like to hear, you can still get some truth out of the process—some little nuance—and incorporate that to help improve your performance.*

Patrick Scott, current executive vice president and general manager of The Weather Channel, is responsible for improving our programming and presentation. He has used the evaluation process not only to improve individuals' skills but also to enhance our recruiting process. Beginning in the summer of 1998, moreover, Scott implemented a plan whereby compensation was linked to these objective measurements, and higher-scoring on-air personnel were moved to key slots in the programming day. "We want the best people in the best-performing day parts," he explains.

Not surprisingly, this emphasis on improved programming led us to look again at the question of "day parts"—insider jargon for distinctive time periods in the day or the week. Between 5 A.M. and 10 A.M., for example, The Weather Channel is the number one "news and information" cable-ratings entity. (If you include ESPN in the "news and information" category, we are number two. And a fast-breaking news story of major consequence can sometimes push CNN into the top slot in this day part.) For that time slot, we created two programs with slightly different emphases, reflecting what we know about the viewers who watch at that time of day. "First Outlook," which airs from 5 A.M. to 7 A.M., is "tilted" toward business and community leaders, executives, and business travelers. "Your Weather Today," in the 7 A.M. to 10 A.M. slot, tilts toward an audience that is predominantly female, affluent, and well educated. We have also made similar programming adjustments for additional day parts, including weekend, morning, and prime time (9 P.M. to 11 P.M.).

The goal of all these changes and tweaks, of course, is three-fold: to get more people to tune in, to get them to watch us more often, and to stay with us longer each time they watch us.

A CHANGING OF THE GUARD

Before moving on to some thematic chapters, let me carry one important part of our story—the leadership of The Weather Channel—up to the present.

Mike Eckert served as president of The Weather Channel for fourteen years: from 1985 to 1999. It was a period of extraordinary growth of the cable television business in general, and for The Weather Channel in particular. In March 1999, Eckert decided it was time to move on to fresh challenges, and he announced his retirement.

By that point, The Weather Channel was an old friend in 75 million homes. In addition, it was reaching millions of consumers of weather information through a variety of complementary media, including a Latin American cable network; a Canadian cable network in which we had a 50 percent stake; an Internet service (weather.com) that was serving up some 300 million page views each month; a radio network; newspaper syndication; an all-local digital cable service; and various kinds of wireless services. We'll look at the development of some of these successful ventures in the next chapter.

But it's not enough to measure a leader's contribution in quantitative terms like market share, growth, and number of products. Rather, a more telling measure of a leader is the caliber of the organization he builds. In Eckert's case, he built a remarkably strong organization. He had great instincts about the people he hired, all of whom have continued to flourish under his successor.

To replace Eckert, we went to an unexpected source. Decker Anstrom, president of the National Cable & Telecommunications Association, became president of The Weather Channel in August 1999. By this time, we knew Anstrom well. Dick Roberts, former president of TeleCable and a Landmark director, had been chairman of NCTA when Anstrom became its president. In the years when Dubby Wynne was a director of NCTA, he too had worked closely with Anstrom.

Both Roberts and Wynne admired Anstrom as a leader who demanded both integrity and outstanding performance. They also believed that he had the broad vision needed to lead The Weather Channel through its next stage of growth, and that his personal style—low-key, but forceful—would be an ideal fit with the larger Landmark culture.

CHAPTER SEVEN

BRAND BUILDING AND OTHER ADVENTURES

The brand has become a hot topic for scholars and practitioners of business alike. A great brand—achieved through a sometimes elusive process called "branding"—is a very valuable property and offers a powerful competitive advantage. And a company can use the power of a brand to launch extensions of its existing product lines, and sometimes even to venture into entirely new territories.

By general agreement, The Weather Channel is a great brand. In fact, several independent studies have concluded it is one of the two or three most recognized and trusted media brands in America.

So it may be surprising to advocates and aficionados of branding to learn that during The Weather Channel's first twelve years, we never gave a lot of thought to developing our brand. We had other things on our minds. At the outset, of course, we were fighting to survive. Then we were working hard to make our product better, to beat our competitors, and to run a more effective and motivated organization. All the while, the big blue square with "The Weather Channel" in blocky capital letters was just a thing in the background—a device used mainly to call our product to the attention of channel surfers with quick thumbs, and to lend some visual appeal to our letterheads and business cards.

How did our brand get built? I think it happened in three principal ways. First, and most important, we were *there*. We were offering millions of people quick and easy guidance for solving one of their most important daily challenges. Whenever they needed to know how their lives would be affected by one of the most changeable forces of nature, we were there to tell them.

Second, although our original product was rough and ready, people trusted it. Because we gave good information, and because we presented it in a low-key, nonflashy way, we earned our viewers' trust. Much of the credit for that goes to John Coleman, who insisted that we use real meteorologists on camera, and that we resolutely refrain from "hyping" the weather. Yes, ratings were important, but we refused to grab them by trying to make people laugh or scaring them to death. Whenever other weather-news sources—especially local TV outlets—worked themselves into a frenzy about a "storm of the century" that then failed to materialize, we looked good by comparison.

We consistently resisted proposals to add more information/entertainment programming ("infotainment"). These proposals generally came from people within the organization who thought the hard-weather news and the frequent local forecast insertions were "tune-out" factors for viewers. We heard and understood those analyses, sometimes wrung our hands over them, and nevertheless stuck with local forecasts every ten minutes. We believed that delivering solid weather news, *all* the time, was our main appeal to viewers.

Of course, we did do things to stimulate viewing, and some of those early promotional schemes probably worked against us. After some of our first primitive surveys of potential viewers were discouraging, for example, we decided to run contests to promote tune-in. The first few contests generated encouraging response levels: one, in fact, positively startled us by attracting 300,000 responses. In response, we stepped up the frequency of the contests, to the point where they became a joke to the weather anchors (who after all had to run these on-air contests). One day, an irreverent on-air meteorologist began a segment by announcing, "And now it's *weather* time here on the Contest Channel!" Belatedly, but not too late, we got back to our knitting.

Finally, our brand developed through extensions of our original cable "product line": through pushes into new geographic areas, new languages, and new media. Of course, the growing strength of our brand also made these line extensions possible. For example, our strong brand made our Web site possible, and our Web site ultimately made the "The Weather Channel" brand all that much stronger.

THE CANADIAN VENTURE

By 1987, a half-decade after The Weather Channel's debut, we had already started looking for ways to take advantage of our brand recognition to move into new ventures. That year, Lavalin Inc.—a prominent Canadian engineering company owned by the Lamar family, who was then looking to diversify out of the depressed oil business—came to us for advice and support in starting a weather channel in Canada. At that time, the Canadian Radio-television and Telecommunications Commission (CRTC) was actively awarding licenses for Canada's new and tightly regulated cable industry, and Lavalin, which had a longstanding interest in

167

meteorology as a result of its oil-drilling background, perceived an interesting opportunity. Our confidence in the future of The Weather Channel concept was quite strong by then, and we agreed to help and invest in a Canadian start-up.

The Canadian weather channel was a significant milestone in part because it was The Weather Channel's first significant diversification of any kind. We previously had started offering weather forecasts to radio stations as insertions—that is, short and "free-standing" weather updates—but we saw that activity primarily as a means of promoting viewership of our cable channel, rather than as a business opportunity. True, the insertions helped the brand by getting "The Weather Channel" into the ears of existing and potential consumers, but they were considered largely promotions. And to be candid, they weren't reaching too many ears, since only a handful of stations carried them.

Another reason why the Canadian weather channel was a milestone, from our point of view, was that this was the first business opportunity that came to The Weather Channel because we were *good*. It was the first time that somebody sought us out because we had a credible brand, relevant know-how, and a unique technology—that is, the WeatherSTAR system.

Canadian law prohibits foreign control of Canadian media and limits the amount of voting stock a foreign party may hold. Dubby Wynne worked out the parameters of a deal with Lavalin's principals, and Louis Ryan, our general counsel, negotiated an agreement that gave us 20 percent of the stock and a consulting agreement with substantial compensation for several years. We invested approximately $400,000, Canadian.

Aside from that investment, The Weather Channel's role in the Canadian venture was mainly advisory. Most of the meteorological, technical, marketing, and on-air presentation challenges the Canadians faced were similar to those we faced when we started in the United States. Mike Eckert (president, and an expert in sales and administration), Alan Galumbeck (technology), and Ray Ban and Chuck Herring (meteorology; no relation to Gordon Herring) spent many hours in Montreal consulting with our partners.

The Canadian venture was actually *two* networks: "Weather Now," aimed at the country's English-speaking majority, and the French-language MétéoMédia. (A few years later, "Weather Now" was renamed the "Weather Network," but for simplicity's sake I'll use the former name here.) The WeatherSTAR would be put to a new use in this bilingual setting, allowing Lavalin to direct French programming to French systems and English programming to English systems. The STAR enabled us to transmit both services using one transponder.

Another big difference came on the distribution side. The Canadian federal government, not cable operators, controlled most distribution decisions. The government regulators decided which cable networks were, in effect, "must carries"—in other words, part of the basic cable package. Our Canadian partners conducted a major lobbying effort to persuade their regulators that their two networks (French and English) should be "must carries." Dubby Wynne also testified in these licensing hearings. Weather Now's public-service role gave us a powerful argument for nationwide coverage in basic cable. Using real-life examples from our U.S. experience—for example, The Weather Channel's practice of relaying severe-weather alerts as soon as they were issued by the government—Wynne argued that a national weather network could save Canadian lives.

Fate intervened to strengthen our case. On the very day of our presentations before the CRTC—July 31, 1987—a devastating tornado ripped through Edmonton, the capital of Alberta. Killing twenty-seven people and causing $330 million in property damage, the Edmonton tornado was the worst natural disaster in that province's modern history.

Edmonton's tragedy almost certainly gave our proposal a new momentum. Lavalin soon got the licenses and the "must carry" designations it needed, and—with help from us—proceeded to organize its new networks. At the outset, the fledgling networks' financial foundations were different from The Weather Channel's, in both bad and good ways. On the negative side, the much smaller Canadian advertising market was not expected to be large enough to support the new service. The good news, though, was that federal regulators—who had the power to dictate the subscriber fees that cable operators paid to programmers—understood this fact. They established a relatively high fee structure, higher than fees the U.S. operators paid The Weather Channel. Because we could look forward to revenues from both cable operators and advertisers, the Canadian networks' prospects seemed bright.

Like our frenetic launch in 1982, the Canadian channels' launch—in September 1988—was full of drama and snafus. Chuck Herring, the manager and meteorologist who lived through both our launch and the Canadian launch, recalls that in Canada the launch was "far more frantic," because they had "nowhere near the operational resources needed to do it."

Former Lavalin meteorologist and current Weather Channel executive Ian Miller remembers that our WeatherSTAR technology was responsible for one of the scarier foul-ups:

> The night of the launch, the single biggest cable system that we were launching on in French—Videotron Montreal—had a STAR that was dead on arrival. I remember a staff member running out the door with another box, grabbing a cab, and rushing to Videotron to put the new box in. We got them up and launched within an hour of the scheduled launch time, even though the other box had died at birth.

But we had learned a lot from our mistakes in the States, and we set far more realistic goals for this new venture. After its rocky start, Weather Now soon began to gather strength. Its strong nationwide distribution worked in its favor, as did Canadian consumers' deep interest in the weather. Within a few years of its launch, Weather Now had evolved into a successful and profitable venture.

In the early 1990s, however, our partner Lavalin got into serious financial difficulties. By the spring of 1991, we were negotiating for our withdrawal from Canada. A Canadian company, Pelmorex, was interested in buying 100 percent of the venture, which necessitated a complex, three-way negotiation. We agreed to sell our share because we were not interested in Pelmorex's plans to start a radio network, and because they offered what seemed to be an attractive profit on our investment. However, Pelmorex would have to license our WeatherSTAR technology, which complicated things. We had never done that before, and the prospect of renting our crown jewels to another company made us understandably anxious.

The sale was completed in October 1992. We received $7.9 million, Canadian, for our stake. We licensed the WeatherSTAR to Pelmorex, with appropriate safeguards for our proprietary interests. Once again, The Weather Channel was a single-product, single-country operation—although, as it turned out, not for long.

A MISSTEP: THE TRAVEL CHANNEL

Even as our involvement in the Canadian venture was winding down, we were thinking hard about a new extension of our product line. For quite a while, Dubby Wynne had been pondering the close relationship between the travel and weather markets. It was no coincidence that some of our biggest advertisers were airlines and hotel chains. In the summer of 1991, he heard that the Travel Channel, a small, struggling cable network, might be available at a reasonable price. He turned his inquisitive eye toward this property.

Travel, founded four years earlier, was a creation of financier Carl Icahn, then head of Trans World Airlines (TWA), which was experiencing much-publicized financial woes. The network's programming—which consisted largely of talk shows and promotional videos from resorts, vacation destinations, and cruise lines—was generally dreary and boring. The network received no subscriber fees, and it reached only about 6.4 million households. Advertising was almost exclusively direct-response, which meant that the network ran commercial spots for free and then got a cut of any business they generated. Not surprisingly, the network carried many TWA "infomercials" aimed at selling plane tickets. Most cable programmers and operators assumed that Travel was deep in the red; few saw it as an interesting property.

Red ink or not, we looked at Travel differently. We believed there was a large and growing interest in travel among consumers and business people, many of whom were demographically attractive to a much larger group of advertisers than the network was then targeting. If we could invest in the programming to offer more original and live fare, that investment should be able to pay us back by delivering a larger and more valuable audience.

We also hoped that with the promise of more attractive programming, cable operators would be willing to pay fees to carry Travel. A survey of 308 cable operators showed that almost three out of five *would* pay fees. Only about a fifth recommended that the channel be kept free, with no improvement in programming. We would only get these fees, of course, if we could make the network's programming substantially more appealing. A small fix wasn't going to make the difference.

Dubby Wynne believed we might be able to cultivate a symbiotic relationship between travel and weather that could benefit both channels. Since we would be targeting the same consumer market that The Weather Channel was already serving, a strategy of cross-promotion might increase viewership on both networks. We also sensed an opportunity to package advertising sales. Again looking at the natural affinity between travel and weather, wouldn't sales packages on the two networks be appealing to prospective clients in the travel world and related businesses?

After doing this kind of analysis, Wynne called Carl Icahn in the fall of 1991 and expressed our interest in acquiring The Travel

Channel. He got an encouraging response and the two men met to begin negotiations. Although Icahn was indeed interested in selling, he wanted to hold onto four hours of programming time per day, so he could keep marketing TWA tickets. We considered this proposal seriously, but we ultimately decided that we weren't interested in any such arrangement. The Travel Network needed major surgery, and reserving a sixth of the available time for Icahn's marketing needs wasn't in our treatment plan. We told Icahn that it was all or nothing.

Early in 1992, we closed the deal. Landmark agreed to pay TWA $35 million plus $15 million for a noncompetition guarantee for Travel. We knew that we were paying a fancy price for a broken-down cable network, but we were convinced that we could turn it into a winner.

Whereas we had benefited from more than our share of luck with The Weather Channel, the gods of good fortune seemed to abandon us with the Travel Channel. We had jumped in and were hard at work fixing it—reprogramming it, at considerable expense, and persuading a number of our cable operator customers to pay us subscriber fees—when the Federal Communications Commission promulgated some crippling new regulations. The FCC decided to restrict cable operators' ability to pass along increased costs to consumers through rate increases. The immediate impact was that almost overnight, cable operators became a lot choosier before taking new programming that might involve a sub fee.

The FCC's new restrictions slowed our progress to a crawl. We began to suffer large operating losses, which hurt all the more because of our increased programming costs. We were facing much slower growth in distribution and subscriber fees than we expected. If we couldn't fix Travel's thin distribution, its advertiser appeal would be severely limited. As a result, the synergies between Travel and The Weather Channel did not develop as we had hoped.

By the spring of 1996, we began to talk about selling Travel. Shortly thereafter, we began several months of unfruitful negotiations with the Discovery Channel, which thought it could achieve economies of scale by adding Travel to its portfolio. When that deal fell through, we resolved to shrink Travel's operations and cut back on its expensive new programming—both to cut our losses and to make the network a more attractive candidate for acquisition. By early 1997, after taking one-time write-offs out of the equation, our U.S. Travel Channel was breaking even. This picture was deceptive, though, because we weren't making the necessary programming investments to make the network work over the long term.

Finally, in June 1997, we sold the network to Paxson Communications for $20 million in cash and Paxson stock, worth just under $60 million when we closed. Our chief financial officer, Al Ritter, handled this transaction quite skillfully. Counting about $20 million in profit from an investment we had made in Preview Travel because of our involvement in Travel, we escaped without serious losses. Curiously, several months after we closed with Paxson, they turned around and sold Travel to the Discovery Channel for a price that appeared to be less than what they had just paid us for the property.

In retrospect, it's hard for me to generate much enthusiasm for our departed family member. I have to admit that we once were very enthusiastic. But we hadn't anticipated that regulatory changes would derail our plans, and we had no alternative plans to offset this risk.

OFF TO EUROPE

When we left Canada, we did so with our heads held high. We had gone to another country—although admittedly, not very far away from our home base—and helped launch two new weather networks. And we had departed with a nice profit.

Now, by the middle 1990s, The Weather Channel in the United States was a resounding success, and we began looking for new worlds to conquer. We were extremely confident about our business concept, thinking, "If it worked in the United States, it will surely work in other countries." The department heads had developed a vision statement that spoke of The Weather Channel being the leading provider of value-added weather information *worldwide.* Throughout the corporation, many felt that same imperative: *First the U.S., then the world!*

It's not as if we had no warnings of the trouble we might be getting into. Back in 1988, for example, while talking about the prospects for weather channels in Europe at a Landmark board meeting, Dubby Wynne had offered us all a caution. "It's a convoluted market," he said, "with few cable households." I wish we had subjected our corporate ego to this kind of reality test when, seven years later, we plunged into Europe.

More than ego was involved, of course. If there was high ground to be seized, we wanted to seize it before somebody else did. And in Europe, somebody else was making way toward that big, undeveloped territory: Eckert learned that Pelmorex, our Canadian counterpart, was moving to set up weather channels in Europe. This development galvanized our newly expansive management into taking decisive action, both in the United Kingdom and on the continent.

Fully confident of success, we rushed to stake out our own European territory. We decided to start in Germany, and by extension, Austria. At the same time, we planned to gain a foothold in the United Kingdom, Ireland, Scandinavia, and the Netherlands, and we sent scouts to investigate prospects in France and Italy.

We chose Germany because it already had a strong head start on cable penetration—about 38 percent of German households, in 1996—with growth projected at about 88 percent over the next decade. Satellite TV was barely in the picture, so it wasn't a serious threat to subscription rates. The federal government—through Deutsche Telekom, a subsidiary of the government-owned Bundespost—controlled local cable companies. The regional systems decided which program services would be carried on cable. So far, so good.

On the down side, German regulations prohibited subscriber fees, so all our revenues would have to come from advertising. Here's where we started down the slippery slope of wishful thinking. The German advertising market was the largest in Europe. *If* we could get enough distribution and viewership, and *if* we could keep a tight rein on our costs, advertising revenues *ought* to be large enough to give us a fighting chance. And here's where somebody—namely, me—should have stood up and said, "Hey: Considering the fact that we couldn't make it on advertising alone in the States, with its far bigger advertising market, why do we imagine that we can make it on ad revenues alone in Germany?"

As in Canada, German regulations required that we have local partners with a controlling stake. We therefore took a minority position in the new network—called *Wetter und Reise* ("Weather and Travel")—allying ourselves with several German partners who had strong media and political connections. The deal was closed, and we made our investment in December 1995. We would provide the weather and programming expertise as well as the operating know-how. Our German partners would deliver the subscribers.

The situation in the United Kingdom was substantially different. There, the government had largely deregulated cable television. Cable was still in the early stages of development, with less than 20 percent household penetration, and industry analysts doubted that it would ever achieve strong penetration. That's because satellite television, supplied by Rupert Murdoch's BSkyB, was already in most multichannel households in the United Kingdom. Thus we would have to be distributed by BSkyB, in addition to cable, in order to get enough market coverage to be appealing to advertisers. (The situation in the United Kingdom wasn't exactly news to us. Landmark's cable subsidiary, TeleCable, previously had acquired several U.K. cable franchises. We sold them, at a handsome profit, when we concluded that U.K. cable companies probably could not overcome Murdoch's lead and would have to subsist largely on telephone rather than on cable revenues.)

Of course, we hired market research consultants in each country we investigated. They consistently told us that European consumers were every bit as interested in weather information as were viewers in the United States. We ran detailed financial models, which somehow always showed attractive returns and predicted profitable businesses.

Unfortunately, all the projections were based on a pyramid of assumptions, which is the shakiest kind of pyramid. If any of the fundamental assumptions are wrong, then every subsequent calculation has to be wrong. And when you stack a second bad assumption on top of that first one, things can go way wrong. As it happened, we misfired on most of our assumptions: distribution, full-time versus part-time carriage, pricing, audience, and advertising. The projections were more or less the mathematical sum of everything we wanted to have happen. Instead of earning attractive returns, we found out, we were soon incurring huge losses.

Meanwhile, we were experiencing all the usual surprises and difficulties associated with the launch of a new business, compounded by cultural complications. Chuck Herring made a half dozen visits to Germany in connection with the launch of Wetter und Reise. He recalls one specific example of cultural differences that caught him by surprise:

> *It's a very tight meteorological community in Europe. It's smaller, and they all know each other. So the head of one of the providers of data, a company in Europe, comes to visit on the day we're scheduled to launch in Germany—June 3, 1996, as I recall. An unbelievably fast-paced, difficult day. We've been working twenty-two-hour days for most of the preceding week.*
>
> *I walk into the forecast center, and everybody's gone. No one is there. It turns out that he took them all out for a beer. To me, it was bizarre that they would go out to a bar for an hour and half on the day of the launch. To them, it was very natural.*

Back in the United Kingdom, with cable penetration too low and showing no signs of gaining strength, we concentrated on getting distribution on Murdoch's satellite. Unfortunately, Pelmorex—our Canadian counterpart-turned-competitor—also was competing vigorously for carriage by BSkyB. The result was that neither of us got what we needed. Ultimately, our team won the competition, but it was a Pyrrhic victory. We got only four hours of coverage daily. Even then, we knew that wasn't going to be enough time to give us the audience we needed to attract sufficient advertising revenue. Nevertheless, we continued to move forward, betting that the coming of digital transmission would permit us to get full-time distribution on satellite TV.

Competition can be a healthy influence, but not always. In this case, we were so preoccupied by our competition with Pelmorex—I think some ego entered in here—that we failed to focus on the reality that *full-time* coverage on cable and BSkyB from the outset was essential to success. Round-the-clock availability is really the strength of our brand and a key contributor to viewership. If we had not insisted in the beginning on virtually universal full-time coverage in the United States, we would have failed in this country, too.

In the United Kingdom, we were getting part-time carriage from a number of the cable systems in addition to BSkyB. Here, too, we proceeded with the unlikely assumption that expansion of cable channel capacity would soon give us full-time coverage. But in fact we had no realistic hope of building an audience big enough to capture a sufficient share of a small advertising market. Nor could we make up for that with cable subscriber fees, since the race with Pelmorex for distribution had driven fees far below our assumptions.

In Germany, concurrently, we encountered many of the same circumstances. Scarce cable channel capacity and bureaucratic delays prevented us from getting even a reasonable fraction of the distribution we needed. Much of the distribution we got was part-time. With no hope for subscriber fees and not enough audience to attract advertising, our losses in Germany were high, too.

We had launched the U.K. and German ventures on the same day in June 1996, and our board voted to close them down in December 1997. During those eighteen months, we piled up the largest financial losses of my business career. And we couldn't do right by our people. When Landmark has had to shut down a business unit in the States, we have usually been able to offer people jobs somewhere within the larger company. Not so in Europe, and that made the shutdowns there even more painful.

I don't believe in scapegoating. And in fact, none of our fatal problems in Europe arose from the way the ventures were operated. They had able leadership, and by and large they were staffed by excellent people. The consumers who got our full service were happy with the product. "Consumer research [in Europe] was golden," recalls Patrick Scott, who helped set up our European operation. "I mean, the people loved it."

So finger-pointing didn't make sense, and we didn't do it. On the other hand, when things go wrong, it's important to figure out why they've gone wrong. In the wake of the European rout, I did a lot of thinking. The most damaging mistake we made was to presume that our American business model was so wonderful and powerful that we could export it and repot it almost anywhere. That initial bit of hubris led us to believe and protect, rather than test, our assumptions.

As a result, we neglected two key factors that have made us successful in the United States: twenty-four-hour coverage and the ability to tap into a large advertising market. Not only should we have realized that shorter broadcast times would hinder us, but we should have put more weight on the relatively small size of European advertising markets. Although we had investigated advertising thoroughly and intensively before starting the U.S. venture, by the time we got to Europe, we somehow ignored its importance. Either of these factors—the lack of 24-hour distribution or the lack of a very large advertising market—would have been as fatal in the United States as they were in Europe.

What else? Psychology helped us in the United States and hurt us in Europe. American cable penetration, as noted, was already higher and was growing much faster than in the United Kingdom and Germany. American cable companies were thriving and bullish, run for the most part by entrepreneurs who were willing to take calculated risks and bet on the future. German cable operators, by contrast, were more restricted by regulation. Their British counterparts faced the unpleasant challenge of beating Rupert Murdoch at his own game. It was hard for them to see how they would ever make decent money.

And that raises a related point: We took our American cost structure abroad with us. Maybe a much lower-cost weather service, using graphical presentations rather than video, could have succeeded in some of the European countries. In fact, we're now testing some of these ideas on the Web in foreign markets, something that wasn't even possible a half-decade ago. But my main point is that in 1995 we never seriously considered any other business model in Europe except our homegrown American model. Operating from that parochial, one-size-fits-all point of view proved to be a terribly expensive mistake.

When we finally acknowledged that our European ventures were hopeless, they had little or no residual value. In other words, nobody else could overcome the problems that caused us to fail. No one was going to come in and pay us back for even part of our investments.

Nevertheless, our European experience did have a bit of a silver lining. In the late summer of 1996, while we were still competing with Pelmorex for territory in Europe, Patrick Scott, the head of our U.K. venture, learned that Pelmorex was nearing a deal to sell a large equity interest to United Video, a U.S. media company with cable connections. Even though we had sold our interest in the Canadian networks only a few years earlier, Wynne mobilized us immediately and jumped in within hours to make a counteroffer for the Pelmorex interest.

As a result of a marathon weekend negotiation, Wynne, our counsel Louis Ryan, CFO Al Ritter, and Pierre Morrisette—the CEO and a major shareholder of Pelmorex—agreed that Landmark would acquire a 50 percent interest in Pelmorex for $30 million. We had gained considerable respect for Morrisette, and we had developed confidence in his organization and its prospects. And we also believed the purchase would rationalize our destructive battle in Europe. As it turned out, resolving that competition may have encouraged us to persist in our losing European calamity even longer.

Although Pelmorex and Landmark are now both out of the weather-channel business in Europe, we are optimistic about our reinvestment in the Canadian weather channel. I was proud of the speed and decisiveness with which Wynne, Ritter, and Ryan brought off a strategic acquisition in just a few hours. It gave a lift to everybody at The Weather Channel at a time when we needed such a lift.

A FOOTHOLD IN LATIN AMERICA

In keeping with our stated global "mission," we launched a second front in Latin America in November 1996—in other words, just six months after we started up in Europe. We entered the Latin American market fueled with the same presumption of success that moved us to try Europe. The woes of the European ventures had not yet become clear.

In Argentina we launched a bare-bones service. We bravely called it "The Weather Channel Latin America" (*El Canal del Tiempo*), but this channel was a far cry from our domestic U.S. product. Simply a text-and-graphics service, the network featured no on-camera meteorologists at all, either live or taped.

The Latin American staff was located in two offices: one in Atlanta and the other in Miami. To take advantage of our existing infrastructure in Atlanta, the new venture's master control, studios, and meteorology operations would be housed there. Sales and marketing would be located in Miami, which was reasonably close to Latin America and had a strong Latin/Hispanic business community. The alternative would have been to locate satellite operations in one or more Central or South American countries, but satellite technology—which could transmit Atlanta-based signals across the equator—allowed us to leverage our existing investments.

Miami proved to be an easy place to recruit capable Latin Americans to our staff. Atlanta, despite its growing reputation as a cosmopolitan city, proved to be more of a problem. But in this case we got lucky. NBC was then in the process of shutting a Spanish news service that was located in Charlotte, North Carolina. We rushed to Charlotte, interviewed about sixty Latin Americans from their staff, and hired about a third of them. Meanwhile, we did some methodical and selective recruiting for on-camera meteorologists in some of our key target nations: Mexico, Brazil, Argentina, and Chile. In a reasonably short period, we had staffs of about sixteen people in Miami and about sixty in Atlanta.

Initial planning had us aiming for three primary markets— Mexico, Brazil, and Argentina—with Peru and Chile as important secondary markets. Programming to these different markets was extremely complicated, particularly because we had access to only one satellite transponder. About a year after our 1996 launch in Argentina, we launched the Portuguese service in Brazil. At the same time, we introduced live on-camera meteorologists, who presented the forecasts throughout Latin America in both Spanish and Portuguese. In both cases, we relied on U.S. residents who spoke appropriate versions of these languages.

In 1997, we began conducting focus groups in Mexico City, Buenos Aires, and São Paulo, trying to get a better handle on what our target audiences wanted and needed from us. Initial responses were reasonably encouraging, suggesting that consumers were indeed interested in getting weather information. Only later did we learn that in many parts of Latin America, as in parts of California, people have a general perception that weather doesn't change much. As a result, consumers aren't necessarily in the habit of seeking weather information. Most television and radio newscasts did not have weather segments; in fact, many places had no television programming at all until 10 A.M. or noon. People watched little TV during the morning hours, which is when The Weather Channel in the United States usually has its largest audiences.

Television viewers in most of Latin America simply didn't know very much about weather. As Eddie Ruiz, president of The Weather Channel Latin America explains:

> *We soon realized that many people did not understand what we were talking about. They didn't understand what a cold front was, or what a high-pressure system was versus a low-pressure system. We said, "You know what? We're talking Chinese to these people, because they've never had this kind of information before." So we revamped our programming. Now it's about 50 percent weather information and 50 percent weather education.*

The programming task in Latin America is far more complex than it is in the United States. We have committed ourselves not only to working in two new languages—Spanish and Portuguese—but also to reflecting each of our target countries' distinctive characters and economies. To the untrained American ear, Spanish is Spanish. But across the vast stretches of Central and South America, each nation's accent and culture tends to be very different. Each country has its own character and economic peculiarities, as well as its own accents and conventions. Spanish idioms are different in Mexico and Argentina, and Brazilians speak Portuguese. Belinda Sym-Smith, vice president of programming and production for Latin America, elaborates:

183

*We feed three networks off of one transponder. We have the
Spanish network, the Brazilian network, and then we feed dual
language programming, as well. We're dealing with different cul-
tures across seventeen different countries and five time zones
simultaneously. In the U.S., you're dealing with one country
domestically—it may be large, but it's still one country. In Latin
America, we in essence are trying to give the appearance that we
are local on your street corner in seventeen different countries.
But, in reality, we are operating out of Atlanta, Georgia. And
because we cross the equator, we're dealing with summer and
winter at the same time. So I think in many ways, the challenges
are a lot greater.*

Our most urgent priority in Latin America was to gain distribution. Here we had two problems. First, we were late entering
the Latin American market. "We were three years behind the
curve," Sym-Smith says flatly. As a result, our challenge was, and is,
to gain distribution in places where channel capacity was almost
fully occupied. We have made progress and now serve more than
10 million households.

Our second problem was the lack of a WeatherSTAR capable of doing what we needed to do in Latin America. Our sales
staff had been promising potential advertisers, to whom we would
be able to offer localized advertising on a national basis. We had
counted on the arrival of a new generation of the WeatherSTAR,
the STAR XL, to make that possible. But the next-generation
STAR was far behind schedule. As the delays continued, we lost
credibility with advertisers.

As of this writing, our technical problems seem to have been
corrected. But only now are we beginning to reach enough eye-
balls to be appealing to advertisers, and—given our history of
technical woes—many advertisers are still looking at us skeptically.
As a result, Latin American advertising revenues are still far below
our expectations.

It's too early to render a verdict on the Latin American effort.
After five years of operations in Latin America, we had more than

$50 million invested in capital costs and operating losses. Ruiz is expecting to break even on our Central and South American operations by the end of 2003. Is that a good investment? Again, it's too early to say. Perhaps we'll be happy with our financial returns on this venture. Perhaps we'll find that we're settling for a lower rate of return than we expected, but that the long-term strategic advantages resulting from our presence in Latin America make up for shortcomings on the profit side.

IN OUR OWN BACK YARD

As the pros and cons of our various foreign ventures began to become clear, we started looking again for opportunity closer to home. Belatedly, we became more "brand conscious." We realized that we were missing an opportunity to focus more on developing and leveraging our brand. If our brand could become so strong without active attention, what would happen if we focused on developing it and using it? With encouragement from newly hired brand experts, both consultants and staff, we resolved to give high priority to investments in opportunities that would leverage and reinforce The Weather Channel brand.

Radio was one such opportunity. We had long been operating a fairly sleepy enterprise that supplied taped weather "inserts" to subscribing radio stations. We decided to push much harder on that button. With energetic leadership from our longtime ad sales manager Norm Zeller as well as Chuck Herring, who took over leadership of our radio business, our pieced-together "network" in the last few years has grown to more than 175 stations.

We have concentrated on serving stations that are the news/information leaders in major markets—for example, WCBS and WABC in New York and WGN in Chicago. Our revised business strategy is to provide our customized local weather service free to these stations in exchange for commercial segments that we turn around and sell to advertisers. Thus we have built a business that makes money as it promotes our brand. "The stations love The Weather Channel name," Zeller says. "The network is not a staggering success like the cable network, but we have been profitable for more than three years, and we're continuing to grow."

Radio is part of a bigger strategy as well. Our larger goal is to put The Weather Channel brand on whatever domestic outlet consumers turn to for their weather information. With the radio business now flourishing, the energetic and tenacious Zeller turned his attention to the newspaper business. Here we had a leg up, given Landmark's long track record and extensive connections in the industry. By 2001, we were providing locally oriented weather maps to fifty-six newspapers. Each paper gets a map customized for its particular market—for example, a Norfolk newspaper might get tide charts, and a Los Angeles newspaper might get a map with air-quality information.

Most recently, we have been providing interactive weather information to consumers via their personal digital assistants and cell phones. Now that users can access the World Wide Web through these wireless devices, they can readily obtain weather information for any city or region they specify. These services are very much in their infancy. Hoping to seize the "first-mover" advantage, we launched these ventures even before we had thought out business plans for them.

Why would we do such a seemingly unbusinesslike thing? Because sometimes you have to move quickly, and you have to enter murky areas that don't lend themselves to crisp estimates of revenues, costs, market shares, or returns on investment. Technological advances are clearly prompting the rapid development of various new media. We are betting that by providing interactive weather services through PDAs, cell phones, and similar devices today, we are positioning ourselves as well as we can to develop new, subscription-based revenue sources tomorrow.

We already have distribution agreements that make us the weather information source for all the wireless services—which builds our brand, and which may also build our future.

BABY STEPS INTO THE DOT-COM WORLD

By now, one medium may seem conspicuous by its absence from this branding story: the Internet. I can't claim that we were among the pioneers of the Internet, but I think we qualify as early homesteaders. In the early 1990s, Alan Galumbeck was becoming intrigued by e-mail. Using a small commercial Internet provider in Atlanta, Galumbeck began communicating by e-mail with a number of key technical vendors. This traffic grew steadily, and Galumbeck decided that The Weather Channel needed a full-time Internet connection. He learned about something called "domain names"—"addresses" for computer nodes on the Internet—and decided to reserve a few, just in case we ever wanted them. "Landmark.com" was already taken, so Galumbeck secured "landmark.net" for the corporate parent. Then he reserved "travel.com" for the Travel Channel, which was then still in our fold, and "weather.com." He makes no claim to being a visionary. "At the time that I got those domain names," he admits, "we had no plans to put up a Web site. I thought we might use them for e-mail, some time in the future."

It fell to a newcomer, who arrived several years, later to figure out what to do with "weather.com." Debora Wilson had worked for Bell Atlantic for nearly fifteen years, the last five developing marketing services for the Baby Bell's interactive and cable TV groups. She signed on in the summer of 1994 as The Weather Channel's senior vice president for "Enterprises." *Enterprises* was then a common term in the cable industry for new-business development groups, which tended to be a hodgepodge of going concerns, good ideas, and wishful thinking. And The Weather Channel's Enterprises group, as Wilson recalls, was no exception:

> *We had the radio network in there. We produced, distributed, and marketed weather videos, books, and calendars. We had 1-800-WEATHER, where you could call up and get weather*

information over the phone. We were dabbling in interactive tele-
vision, and we wanted to get a Web site up and running.

I think that to begin with, all these things were pretty
much of equal interest, because they were all small. It was just a
collection of start-up things that we were experimenting with,
to see which ones might become revenue-generators—and even-
tually, hopefully, net *income generators—for The Weather*
Channel and Landmark.

Perhaps highest on Wilson's priority list was the Internet. On
Groundhog Day 1995, The Weather Channel became the official
weather provider to the online service CompuServe. Within an
hour of this launch, The Weather Channel received literally
hundreds of e-mails from CompuServe aficionados, welcoming
TWC to cyberspace. Most came from CompuServe buffs who
were also fans of The Weather Channel. "We're so glad you're part
of CompuServe," as Wilson recalls a typical note. "Now we have
great weather information!"

An entirely new kind of conversation had begun—much
more personal and interactive than anyone at The Weather Channel had experienced up to that point. Wilson, in particular, was
struck by the very different nature of the e-mail messages we
received. They were intimate, immediate, and fresh. She printed
out the unexpected torrent of communications, tacked them up
on the wall in a conference room, and invited the entire company
to come experience this strange new phenomenon. It was hard to
imagine more convincing evidence of the strength and trustwor-
thiness of The Weather Channel brand.

Shortly afterward, Cathy Daly—a young product manager in
Wilson's area—approached Wilson with an informal proposal to
build The Weather Channel's own Web site. In a previous job,
Daly had put together a modest Web site for a client, and she was
convinced that weather.com could become something special.
Using borrowed resources—roughly a third of her own time, a

Reprinted with permission.

third of an editor's time, and a third of a technology person's time—Daly put together the first iteration of weather.com, which launched in April 1995.

Like almost all other Web sites at that time, weather.com began without any advertising—no revenue of any kind. The Internet had a strong anti-advertising culture at that point, although many sites were "ads" in their entirety for their sponsoring companies. But Web-based magazines began taking ads shortly thereafter and commanding (or at least asking) substantial sums for those ads. At a time when cable TV's cost per thousand viewers was in the $5 range, an electronic magazine like *HotWired* asked $150 per thousand. "I remember when *HotWired* made that announcement," says Wilson. "I photocopied and distributed it. Finally, an industry was starting to happen."

But our internal model, again, was borrowed resources. Rather than hire a separate sales force for weather.com, Wilson and her colleagues more or less begged the cable network's salespeople to sell Internet ads. Few buyers were interested in the

Internet at that time, however, and the sales force's incentive structure meant that the cable network would always get their best effort. Finally, the Chemical Bank bought an ad for a grand total of $1,000. "We were just thrilled," Wilson recalls. "We celebrated. It was just an incredible thing that somebody was buying weather.com."

When we launched weather.com, the Internet was still a clunky, unformed, poorly understood medium. Within a year, though, it had become a much more prominent subject of public discussion, particularly in media circles. We were getting a surprisingly large and enthusiastic response from users of weather.com even though we were operating it on a lean diet. We were providing largely warmed-over information and graphics from the cable network. This seemed right, because the site itself had almost no revenues and nobody had yet defined an appealing business model for it.

My son, Frank Batten, Jr., who was then heading up a new-ventures unit for Landmark, had become a frequent user and student of the Internet and was searching for Internet-related business opportunities for the company. He had been enlightening me on the potential of the Internet as a disruptive technology—in other words, a new technology that threatened to upset existing ways of doing business—for most of our media properties, particularly for The Weather Channel. He thought we should make a major commitment to develop weather.com, and do it promptly while we had a large head start in the weather venue. Dubby Wynne agreed and asked Mike Eckert to bring Debora Wilson and Cathy Daly to meet with us in Norfolk to discuss their recommendations for developing the Web site.

According to Wilson, that meeting was a defining moment for weather.com:

> *Cathy and I presented our resource requirements, and we thought we were being rather aggressive in that context. I don't know who said what, but collectively, the two Franks and Dubby*

said to us, "We don't think you are thinking aggressively enough about what this could be. Who knows what weather.com could be? But it's clear that it at least has the potential to become something very important. You really need more than this, and you need to run like heck."

Wilson was taken aback. She had expected to be challenged, and to have to defend their resource proposal. "Instead," she recalls, "we got the opportunity to go back to them within weeks with a much stronger plan, which set us off on a growth curve that was substantially different from what it would have been otherwise."

The Web site hit many bumps in the road. For example, it took a while for Wilson and her colleagues to educate the rest of The Weather Channel organization about the purpose and potential of weather.com. An intuitive "brander," Wilson began talking about cross-promoting—The Weather Channel steering viewers to weather.com, and vice versa—but she encountered either indifference or resistance. As Alan Galumbeck explains:

When the Web site was launched, Debora couldn't get The Weather Channel programming people to put the URL, www.weather.com, on the cable network's IDs. They kept saying, "But people won't know what it is." My response was, "Those who can use it will know what it is." But it was months and months before Debora was finally able to persuade the TV people to put the URL on all of our network promotion material.

Sometimes internal staff complained that weather.com enjoyed favorite-child status. And in, say, 1997, it was indeed easier for weather.com to add another programmer or sales person than it was for the cable network to add another master controller. But the Web site was in the building phase of its existence and needed to call upon a disproportionate share of our development resources. When people asked me about our investment priorities, I had a ready answer. I pointed out that in the early 1980s our fledgling cable network "stole" resources from our existing media properties—just as, in an earlier day, our construction of cable systems was funded by our newspaper businesses. Investing for the future—even when you can't really see the future clearly—is the essence of a growing business.

The fact that weather.com was almost totally integrated into the fabric of The Weather Channel offset most such jealousies. Something like two-thirds of the people who made weather.com go also had important responsibilities with the cable network, so "us versus them" attitudes were relatively rare.

By mid-1998, only three years after its launch, weather.com was logging 90 million page views per month, which made it one of the top thirty Web sites in the world. By September of that year, the page view count had exceeded 150 million—a 67 percent increase in just three months. We had projected revenues of $6 million for 1998, and we were pleasantly surprised to find that we would exceed that goal. By the end of the year, we were nineteenth in Relevant Knowledge's world rankings of Web sites.

For these reasons and more, 1998 became known internally as the "Wonder Year" at weather.com. And more good news came early in 1999, when we signed a three-year deal with America Online. Under the terms of the agreement, The Weather Channel became the exclusive branded weather content for three key Internet portals: AOL, CompuServe, and Netscape. All three listed prominent links to weather.com, which promised to drive still more traffic to our own site.

As of this writing, weather.com delivers 3.5 billion page views per year to an average of 10 million unique (different) viewers per month. This count includes only viewers who go directly to weather.com. If you add viewers who enter through AOL, the number rises to 14 million. Our partnership with AOL is a powerful one, and may serve as a model for future partnerships. We are continuing to add more depth by adding content in topics such as gardening, travel, driving, and recreation, which are important in people's daily lives and which are tangentially related to weather. This kind of depth is possible only on the Web. As Wilson explains,

> *Of course, we always look through the lens of weather. But we have added things like airport delays, climatology databases, hour-by-hour forecasts, ten-day forecasts, and thousands of current conditions and forecasts for international cities. These are things that could not be presented on The Weather Channel, because there's not enough time and space.*

Perhaps as a result of this depth of content, our personal relationship with users is remarkable. We receive between 7,000 and 10,000 e-mails a week from weather.com users, and we try hard to answer all of them within a reasonable time. (Most inquiries are frequently asked questions, and we use interactive tools that allow us to respond to many of them automatically.) The staff at weather .com value this steady flow of communication because it tells them what their consumers want from the Web site. More generally, we believe that these personal contacts go a long way toward creating the kind of identity relationship with our consumers that Steve Schiffman—The Weather Channel's executive vice president for marketing, and an expert in branding—tells us is at the heart of brand development.

From its inception, weather.com was closely tied into the infrastructure of The Weather Channel. This closeness had countless advantages at the outset. By using The Weather Channel's meteorological, marketing, sales, and back-office resources, the new Web site was able to get up and running quickly with a useful service.

It gradually became apparent, however, that before weather.com could achieve its full potential, it had to be freed from the arms of its parent. This reflected my own belief, based on long experience at Landmark, that potentially competitive units or products usually need substantially separate organizations. And so, a half-decade after weather.com first took to the wires, we made it a separate division of The Weather Channel. Debora Wilson became its president, reporting to The Weather Channel's CEO. The new division would continue to share certain staff functions with The Weather Channel, but all other functions—especially those with potentially competitive goals and demands, such as sales—were made independent of each other.

As I recall the relevant discussions that led up to this change, all the key players agreed *intellectually* that we would not hogtie the new venture. We wouldn't be driven by concerns that it might compete with The Weather Channel, or cannibalize its audience, or do some other bad thing to the parent. I recall reiterating that the Big Three networks made a huge mistake when they decided initially to stay out of cable programming for fear of cannibalization. Everyone seemed to understand and agree.

But intellectual agreements only go so far. The "liberation" of the Web site made this point very clearly. When it came to cutting the ties and actually setting weather.com free, we saw considerable internal resistance, and from many more sources than we expected. Business is sometimes about logic and calculation, but it is just as often about emotion and gut instinct.

THE LAST WORD ON BRANDS

In 1992, ten years after The Weather Channel's launch, an independent industry survey ranked us second in recognition, ahead of all other cable networks except CNN. This was only one of a number of published surveys of brand strength that various marketers, advertising agencies, and researchers have conducted. All these surveys ranked The Weather Channel near the top of media brands in satisfaction and importance to consumers.

We were consistently surprised by these results, surprised that consumers ranked what was then our relatively small venture above the brands of all the broadcasting networks, and above almost all cable networks.

Of course, we weren't complete innocents, nor did we develop our brand through blind luck. We realized, early in our efforts to broaden our business base and create new opportunities, that there were two basic ways to exploit our brand. One was to serve different consumer markets, like foreign markets. The other was to serve the *same* consumers in new ways, such as we did with our expanded radio network, our newspaper venture, our ventures into wireless, and our Web site.

We devoted most of our early efforts to serving different markets. In those markets, though, we realized that The Weather Channel brand did not have enough consumer recognition to be of much value. Only later did we realize how much more valuable our brand was when we extended it to serve the same consumers—and we adjusted our strategies accordingly. We certainly didn't stop trying to make new friends, as The Weather Channel Latin America story illustrates. But we reordered our priorities. And of course our current and future leaders will probably reorder those priorities yet again when the landscape of opportunity changes.

Throughout its almost twenty years, The Weather Channel's brand has continued to gain strength and market share. In 2001, the most recent independent survey, *Myers Media Brand Tracker,* reported that The Weather Channel has "established itself as the strongest electronic-media brand among all 24-hour news and information channels, and extends that leadership as the dominant online brand among 22 news and information Web sites." The Weather Channel ranked first, by wide margins, in all eight attributes: "frequency of viewing, different, relevant, fulfills expectations, quality, indispensable, informative and trustworthy." For example, 51 percent ranked The Weather Channel first in the "indispensable" category, whereas 28 percent chose Fox News, the second-ranked network. Weather.com also ranked first among news and information Web sites in all eight attributes.

So although the branding story has a "happy ending"— at least for the moment—I feel obliged to underscore again that

Networks   The Weather Channel ranks first among news and information channels for key brand attributes

Percentage of respondents rating each network 5, 6, or 7 on a 7-point scale

Trustworthy

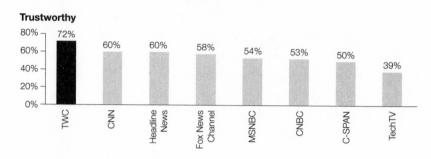

Relevant

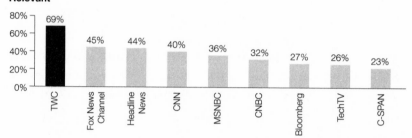

Fulfills Expectations

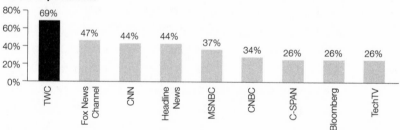

Indispensable

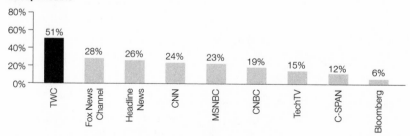

2001 Myers Media Brand Tracker: 24-Hour News & Information Channels

Web Sites   Weather.com ranks first among news and information Web sites for key brand attributes

Percentage of respondents rating each Web site 5, 6, or 7 on a 7-point scale

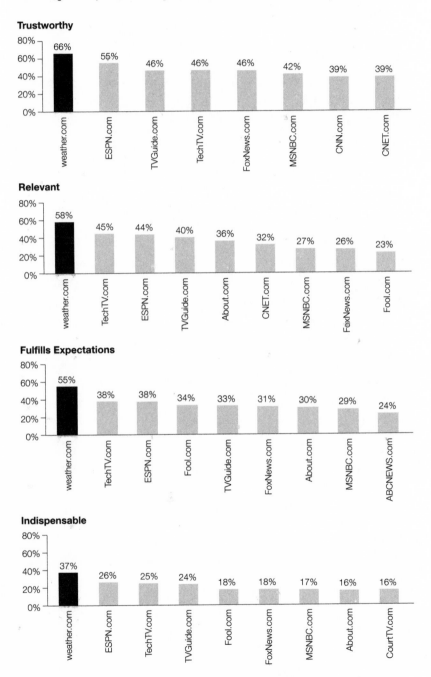

Trustworthy

weather.com	ESPN.com	TVGuide.com	TechTV.com	FoxNews.com	MSNBC.com	CNN.com	CNET.com
66%	55%	46%	46%	46%	42%	39%	39%

Relevant

weather.com	TechTV.com	ESPN.com	TVGuide.com	About.com	CNET.com	MSNBC.com	FoxNews.com	Fool.com
58%	45%	44%	40%	36%	32%	27%	26%	23%

Fulfills Expectations

weather.com	TechTV.com	ESPN.com	Fool.com	TVGuide.com	FoxNews.com	About.com	MSNBC.com	ABCNEWS.com
55%	38%	38%	34%	33%	31%	30%	29%	24%

Indispensable

weather.com	ESPN.com	TechTV.com	TVGuide.com	Fool.com	FoxNews.com	MSNBC.com	About.com	CourtTV.com
37%	26%	25%	24%	18%	18%	17%	16%	16%

2001 Myers Media Brand Tracker: 24-Hour News & Information Channels

we were lucky, more than we were brilliant. Luck carries you a long way.

In addition, we have usually had enough good instincts about "branding" to overcome our occasional bad instincts. Sometimes we haven't known what to do, but we always seem to know what *not* to do. When our survival was still in doubt and we worried about whether we could get enough audience, some said, in effect, "We have this valuable connection into millions of homes. We should start offering other kinds of information, too, to attract more viewers." Some suggested that we offer sports results, because people want them, they change every day, and they lend themselves to localization.

At first blush, it was an alluring suggestion, especially since back in the mid-1980s, when the proposal was first floated, The Weather Channel was starving. Ultimately, though, we decided not to be wooed away from our singular focus on weather. We concluded that any drift away from weather would fuzz up our identity and probably drive away viewers.

In hindsight, that was the right decision. If we had gone any other way, it would have set back the creation of our strong brand. It would have made it much harder when, in the late 1990s, we finally mounted our first serious efforts to reinforce a powerful brand that had more or less created itself.

CHAPTER EIGHT

DISRUPTIVE TECHNOLOGIES

The late 1980s and early 1990s were a time of accelerating change at The Weather Channel. Under increasing competitive pressures from the marketplace, we also struggled to improve the quality and distinctiveness of our product. Among other things, this effort again required technical interventions. It also pushed us to make formal alliances with some technically oriented companies and to make a major acquisition.

And finally, we had to begin placing bets on a host of new technologies, in an effort to serve our customers in other "weather spaces" and stay ahead of our new legions of competitors.

I'm anything but a technologist myself. I wasn't the first in my company to embrace word processing, or e-mail, or the Internet. Part of what this chapter is about is how someone schooled in older media—newspapers, cable television, broadcasting—begins to understand the real threats and opportunities inherent in disruptive technologies.

PUSHING THE STAR

The invention of the WeatherSTAR (Satellite Transponder Addressable Receiver) began with Gordon Herring, Alan Galumbeck, and their collaborators in Salt Lake City. And although the STAR's technology proved to be remarkably durable, we needed to change its design because of changes in the marketplace and also because of regulatory changes.

Our technical legacy was complicated. The STAR technology was conceived in an era before there were any generally accepted protocols. Galumbeck and his colleagues had both the luxury and the burden of working in an industry in which standards had only begun to emerge.

Gradually those industry standards did emerge, and The Weather Channel had to keep developing proprietary solutions so that its key technologies could keep functioning in the new digital age. Of course, it was good to have proprietary, patentable processes. But our uniqueness meant that we had to be very sharp operationally. If something broke, most likely we were the only ones who could fix it. And our rapid growth increased this challenge significantly.

Between 1982, when we introduced the first STAR, and the mid-1990s, the STAR underwent incremental improvements, suffered from technical conservatism, and sparked mounting frustration. We had a good horse, and we rode it with increasing success. But a changing regulatory context, as well as new opportunities, pushed us to push the STAR through a series of generations, some of which challenged us enormously.

200

When we discovered that our first WeatherSTARs were radiating energy in a way that interfered with the antenna's reception of Channel 2, we developed a way to eliminate the radiation leakage. And thus was invented STAR 2. Then, in 1985, the FCC decided to reduce the spacing between geosynchronous satellites to make room for more satellites. I'll skip the technical aspects of what this entailed for us—suffice it to say they were complicated. We enlisted the help of Wegener Communications in Atlanta and, at the cost of about $2 million, figured out how to adjust the STAR so that it transmitted our localized weather data differently. And thus was invented STAR 3.

The STAR 4—soon dubbed the STAR 4000—was a different story. We conceived the STAR 4000 as a major leap forward technologically. As Dubby Wynne explained at our July 1988 Landmark directors' meeting, there were two main pushes behind the STAR 4000. The first was our desire to upgrade the system's graphic capability substantially. Specifically, we wanted better color and animation, and we wanted to display radar imagery, all of which were beyond the capabilities of the STAR 3.

The second push arose from our desire to support an interesting new application of the STAR technology. John Sie, programming chief of TeleCommunications Inc., came to us with an idea for a program-previewing service for cable networks. Sie called his idea *Prime Time Tonight*. Cable viewers could see previews of programs that their cable network was carrying, along with the local air time and channel number. We liked the idea, and soon we launched a joint venture with Sie, on the assumption that our new and more capable STAR 4000 would be available to this venture.

Unfortunately, we had a terrible time delivering the STAR 4000. It was all the more frustrating because we desperately needed a more capable STAR to support the two-language commitments of our Canadian weather channels. In fact, the plan was to develop the STAR 4000 in tandem with Lavalin—our Canadian partner in Weather Now—and their Halifax-based subcontractor. But the difficulties of making a major technical leap forward across two countries and three companies proved insurmountable.

Meanwhile, *Prime Time Tonight* had signed contracts to deliver the units by a certain date. To hit that deadline, we essentially had to write special software to make the STAR 3 act like a STAR 4000 was supposed to act, so that the STAR 3s could deliver *Prime Time Tonight*. It was not a good solution.

The *Prime Time Tonight* experiment was short-lived. The cost of producing the segments was too high for the operators to sustain. For our part, we eventually got the improved graphics capabilities we had been looking for. We reclaimed the old STAR 3s when our larger customers took the 4000s. Our second-tier customers were still generating plenty of demand for the third-generation STARs, and we happily sent the refurbished 3s out into the marketplace—thereby saving ourselves substantial capital investments.

In the fall of 1989, we began planning to offer an economy weather service for small cable systems. By that point, we had achieved a relatively high rate of penetration among the larger multisystem cable operators) and we were looking for new markets to enter.

Two such markets, completely different in every characteristic except size, were in plain sight. One was the vast stretch of thinly populated rural areas of the United States, mainly west of the Mississippi River. At the other end of the lifestyle spectrum was the world of "satellite master antenna television," or SMATV: apartment buildings, coops, and condominium complexes, almost exclusively in densely populated urban areas, that had their own satellite dishes. All told, thousands of such rural and urban systems were out there—either in existence, or on the drawing boards—each serving fewer than 1,000 subscribers.

Neither The Weather Channel nor the local cable operator could afford to install a full-fledged STAR 4000 system in either of these settings. STAR 4000s, when they were finally available, cost about $3,800, which was a big price for a small cable company or apartment complex to pay to add The Weather Channel to its system. And we didn't have the capacity to manufacture and service thousands of new high-powered STAR systems. As a result, these potential customers simply did without our services. But if we could develop a smaller and cheaper version of the STAR—easier to build, easier to maintain—we might be able to serve these markets cost-effectively.

By 1989, we didn't have the in-house technical capabilities to build a stripped-down STAR system. Reflecting the "team" approach to innovation and quality improvement that was then in vogue in many American businesses, we decided to take a team approach to developing the new system. Several types of teams were involved. One was a cross-functional team within the company, headed by Peter Ill, whose job it was to ensure that all groups got their say in the design of the new system. This group set some basic requirements for the new system, including a price tag: under $1,000.

A second team crossed company boundaries. It included not only our employees but also a cadre of technical people from Wegener Communications, the subcontractor that had already helped us enormously with previous generations of the STAR.

Landmark and The Weather Channel had used team-based management in the past—mainly to support the larger goal of continuous improvement—but we had never attempted anything quite like this, especially in a technical realm and involving an outside partner. The process required both up-front planning and many mid-course corrections.

Although teams didn't always serve us well at The Weather Channel, these particular teams did. The smaller STAR, dubbed "STAR Jr.," was completed on time and on budget, which was highly unusual for us. In fact, we introduced it into the marketplace at $750, which was about our cost. It enabled us to add nearly 4,000 cable systems nationwide.

The STAR Jr. today serves some of our most loyal viewers. Many live in isolated rural areas that, coincidentally, suffer through tornadoes and other kinds of severe weather. For these people, The Weather Channel is a valuable public service.

The next generation of the STAR, the STAR XL, fared less well. We conceived of the STAR XL in the mid-1990s as the opportunity for The Weather Channel to begin a transition to the digital realm. We knew that at some point in the future, the country's traditional analog broadcasting system would be complemented, and eventually replaced, by a digital system, and it made sense to begin investing in that technology sooner rather than later. We signed an agreement with California-based Silicon Graphics to provide the platform for the XL.

We wanted to make the programming improvements associated with digital broadcasting available to our largest customers, so we decided that we would offer the XL as a free upgrade to our larger multisystem operators, which numbered some 2,600. At about $6,500 per unit, this was a significant capital investment on our part—something like $17 million, not counting development costs.

But the STAR XL fell victim to a serious case of what might be called Reverse NIH ("not invented here") Syndrome. Faced with the daunting challenge of reinventing the STAR, someone decided to make a clean break with the past—in short, to reinvent the wheel, and to outsource the task. One casualty of this approach was Alan Galumbeck, the technologist who was indispensable in developing the STAR in the first place. In 1996, when the outside firm began developing the STAR XL, the project manager told Galumbeck that he wasn't going to be consulted because he was "too anchored in the past," as Galumbeck recalls. Accordingly, Galumbeck—a proud and highly employable individual—immediately submitted his resignation and retired from the company. This was a tremendous loss for us. And as events soon demonstrated, Galumbeck wasn't the problem.

In July 1997, Mike Eckert had to report to the Landmark board that we were experiencing "significant problems" with the STAR XL technology, which by then was nine months late. He acknowledged that the continuing delays were hurting the company but asserted that solutions were forthcoming.

Part of the problem was that although we had turned away from our internal experts, The Weather Channel was not particularly skilled at using outside technical help. We didn't outsource the development work effectively. Simply put, we took our hands off the technical reins, with results that seem predictable in hindsight. As one Weather Channel technical expert explains:

> *Software engineers are much closer to artists than they are to engineers. Imagine trying to round up forty artists to paint some elaborate painting. Each of them has his or her own ideas about the right medium—watercolors, pastels, oils, or whatever—and how to work in that medium. Trying to coordinate that many independently minded, spirited people is literally an impossibility when they are not in your organization. Can't be done.*

So we had outsourced a function that didn't lend itself to outsourcing, and then we had taken our eye off the ball. At the same time, we weren't using our own technical personnel effectively, either on the STAR XL or other engineering projects. "People didn't have clear direction," recalls Pat Clark, currently The Weather Channel's executive vice president for finance and administration. "There wasn't necessarily a clear owner for some of these projects." Our technical ranks were becoming dispirited.

And to be fair, part of the problem was of my own making. Dating back to my newspaper days, I had always made it clear that I would frown on the emergence of a high-tech empire within our company's newspapers. Data processing (as it was called back in those days) wasn't our business; it was a function that supported our business. Budgets for high-tech pursuits—data processing, information systems, MIS, or whatever —had a hard time growing under my skeptical eye.

Finally, The Weather Channel (and by extension, Landmark as a whole) shared a problem with a lot of companies that had in-house technical people: We didn't really know how to reward technical competence. We knew how to reward our managers, but when a highly skilled technician chose to stay off the managerial track, he or she became something of a lost soul in our organization. This hampered our ability to hire and retain the best people.

Both in Atlanta and Norfolk, we were becoming increasingly concerned about our ability to seize upon and deliver new technologies. The world was changing rapidly. We knew we had to respond to the convergence of cable and telecommunications technologies, the move to digital video compression, the emergence of interactive television, and a host of related issues—but we really didn't know how to respond.

UPGRADING TECHNOLOGY

The STAR XL project was to be The Weather Channel's great leap forward into the digital age. But by the summer of 1997, the XL was in deep trouble. Moreover, it was only one of several stalled products that we had already promised, but not delivered, to our customers.

Then, in January 1998, The Weather Channel took a small but significant step into its future. With a nudge from Howard Stevenson, one of Landmark's directors, we hired a chief information officer, Rob Strickland, who initiated a serious and successful push into the digital age.

Strickland had left Continental Cablevision when U.S. West acquired it, and he was looking for a new challenge. At The Weather Channel, he found one. Sizing up the situation in Atlanta, he was very concerned about what he found. The company lacked basic project management skills in the technical realm. Deadlines were rarely met. One software project had been in process for almost ten years without a deliverable. The Weather Channel rarely initiated technical projects based on user requirements. We had shown little skill at building strong relationships with suppliers—a critical capacity, in a company that had to draw on specialized skill sets in unusual ways. Outside contractors were writing the company's code, creating potential ownership problems for the company. As Strickland recalls:

In general, we had a very unsophisticated approach to things. My strong sense was that sooner or later, our approach was going to get us into real trouble. We could no longer ignore the fact that our product was a very sophisticated one, which had to be delivered in a very sophisticated way, by sophisticated people, who played according to a clear set of rules.

One example of the company's relative lack of sophistication was its approach to data security. Strickland noticed that The Weather Channel's headquarters was very security-conscious, but only when it came to people. Guests had to sign in at the front desk, wear ID badges, and have an escort while in the building. But the company's computer network had almost no security, nor did its Web site. "The network was totally open," he recalls. "It took me five months to get approval for a firewall, and the request had to go up to Norfolk." This wasn't bureaucracy run amok, says Strickland; it was a case of "an organization not really understanding the game in which it was playing."

I've been focusing on our technical problems, which were increasingly troubling in the later 1990s. But just so you don't think all was chaos at The Weather Channel, let me put these problems in context. By 1998, the cable network's performance in the marketplace was exceptionally strong. It was distributed by 98 percent of the country's cable systems, thus reaching over 70 million subscribers. Advertising revenues were growing, and many advertisers were using our unique, proprietary STAR technology to deliver commercials with localized messages. The Weather Channel brand was powerful and still gaining strength, and we had strong relationships with our cable operator customers. But clearly, we needed to work out a better way to handle technology, to enable us to build on what we had. With telecommunications changing over from analog to digital, we needed a top-notch technical organization to help us make the transition.

A major subplot here is the challenge of "bandwidth." Again, I'm not going into great technical depth here. But our analog TV signal—in other words, the cable network's transmitted signal—provided us with almost unlimited space for transmitted information, or bandwidth. This allowed us, and inclined us, to put a lot of energy into the package *around* the content. But moving to the digital realm, and toward technologies (like wireless devices) that had much less bandwidth available, generally meant that we had less room for the packaging. (The exception was the new realm of digital TV, into which we were making an initial foray with our 24/7 "Weather Scan" local forecast product.) In fact, in this realm, especially in the world of personal digital assistants and cell phones, the packaging more or less had to disappear. The *content* had to come to the fore.

U.S. vs. The Weather Channel Cable and Satellite Subscribers

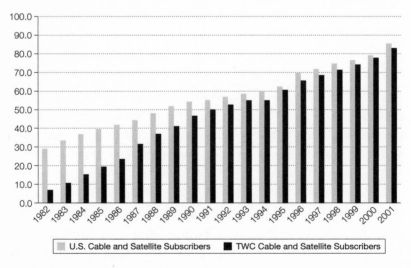

Source: Nielsen Media Research, Kagan World Media

In this new world, rewards would go to the competitor who could move quickly—making good decisions in a hurry, and bringing new, information-rich products of modest bandwidth to market quickly. Our technology staff was not prepared for this challenge. The four dozen or so technical people then on the payroll were mainly experienced in servicing the analog cable network. They were very bright, capable analog engineers who knew how to make the studio operate, and knew how to get product out to the satellites, but they weren't prepared to lead the charge into the digital realm.

In the summer of 1998, Strickland joined Landmark's corporate staff in Norfolk. Mike Eckert began looking for a chief technical officer for The Weather Channel, and he knew we needed a new kind of help, someone who had lots of experience with the fast-changing technical world. Eckert hired Brian Shield, who previously had been CTO at Scudder Funds. The new CTO, who started work in Atlanta in September 1998, immediately began signing on digitally oriented engineers to complement the existing analog cadre. Some cultural difficulties ensued, as Shield recalls:

> One of the major challenges I found here was bringing the existing engineering department into the new fold. Some didn't have an appreciation for the kinds of issues that technology departments elsewhere had been wrestling with for the previous ten years. They still saw the "core network"—and that was the phrase you'd hear—as basically being central to everything we would ever need to do.
>
> Technology is doable. You can see it, you can visualize it, and you can achieve it. The hardest part, the most stressful part, is the cultural impact on the existing people. That's hard.

At the same time, Shield began trying to grapple with the company's disparate technology base. "You name it," he says, "we had it: DEC, IBM, Sun, SGI, Apple, and everything else you can think of." He realized that to some extent, this hodgepodge reflected the company's traditional "lean and mean" approach to hardware. People were more inclined to make do with cobbled-together equipment than to fight for a bigger equipment line in the budget. Shield argued that we were making false economies. Multiple operating systems meant that The Weather Channel either had to have more technicians on the payroll, or had to hire those rare—and very expensive—people who understood multiple operating systems. Shield opted instead for standardization, choosing Oracle as the company's database standard, and Sun Microsystems as its primary server environment.

Meanwhile, the stalled STAR XL project needed to be revitalized. In early November 1998 the first STAR XLs (built by Silicon Graphics) went into beta testing. The hope then was that the XLs could be deployed to cable systems beginning in January 1999.

Concurrent with these investments, with urging first from Rob Strickland and then from Brian Shield, The Weather Channel's technology core consciously adopted a business discipline, which cut in two directions at once. On the one hand, things no longer got done simply because they were technically possible. If someone proposed to roll out an improvement across ten thousand head ends, for example, that proposal was now subjected to a rigorous return-on-investment review process.

At the same time, as a result of the company's new business discipline, other technical decisions went toward the expensive end of the spectrum. Particularly in software engineering, the company no longer automatically defaulted to "most efficient"—in other words, "cheapest." Now we began insisting on "most effective."

All of this meant more money, and The Weather Channel's technology budget experienced a dramatic spike. In 1998, it was approximately $8.5 million. In 1999, it climbed to $15.9 million. And in the following year, it reached $22.5 million.

I've already described the development of the STAR Jr., and how cross-functional and intercompany teams brought in a new

STAR generation on time and under budget. Unfortunately, we discovered that this success was the exception to the rule. Like many U.S. companies in the 1990s, we embraced "team management" wholeheartedly. For example, Brian Shield recalls that when he arrived in Atlanta, he was responsible for a total of 32 people, who were on a grand total of 144 teams! But when everybody is responsible for everything, there is no accountability. And when nontechnical people begin making technical calls, trouble is sure to ensue.

On balance, I'd say we got our technological wake-up call a few years late. We certainly would have benefited from doing some things better and sooner. But as Dubby Wynne never hesitates to point out, an earlier large-scale plunge into technology would have given us an expensive infrastructure that would have needed replacing almost immediately.

So we had dodged a bullet before our problems damaged us in the marketplace.

BACK TO THE WEB SITE

Somewhere off to the side of this maelstrom of technological change sat weather.com, our much-visited Web site. The ever-increasing traffic at weather.com was beginning to throw a harsh spotlight on the site's inadequacies. Some of these inadequacies arose from the shortcomings of the larger organization's technical infrastructure; others had more to do with the particular ways in which weather.com had come together. As Debora Wilson, head of the original Web site development project, explains:

> We borrowed a guy part-time from the network's IT group. Let's call him Tom. And he had his own language, which I'll call "Tom Talk." Tom wrote in a way that nobody else would ever be able to decipher, and we soon learned that this was a very risky thing for us.

But the fundamental problem for us was that we were working off an infrastructure that had been optimized for a broadcast network. We started out simply by leveraging—by taking the product that was developed for The Weather Channel, all the maps, the graphics, the text—and just putting that stuff up on the Internet. So we were inextricably linked to that infrastructure, and that product base. It was a combination of not knowing what we didn't know, and not necessarily having the resources to manage the thing.

CTO Brian Shield began poking around the shop. He didn't like what he learned about weather.com:

When I arrived here, a lot of people talked about the lack of commitment to making weather.com a success, from a technical point of view. The technology ranks within The Weather Channel saw it as a poor stepchild to the cable network. I think some people thought, "What the hell is that? We're going to lose money on that thing for years to come. It's a money pit!" And if you're given a choice between a money pit and a cash cow, most people have a tendency to start making mooing noises.

Internally, the staff used another barnyard metaphor to describe weather.com: "pig with lipstick." The site's front end was appealing, but it was "band-aids and bubblegum."

"The latency of data was completely unacceptable," says Shield, meaning that content tended to sit on the site past its useful life. "And supportability—heading off problems and fixing problems that emerged—was a disaster."

In October 1999, we hired a CTO just for weather.com: Mark Ryan, previously the CTO at the online auction house eBay. His new job was to figure out what to do about weather.com. It turned out to be an enormous task.

One problem grew out of the differences between a Web site and a 24/7 cable network. The cable product was, of necessity, updated constantly. The Web site, by contrast, was updated less systematically—especially the less visited pages. Thus the Web site might give a different outlook than the television channel—say, "sunny and 70," versus "65 and cloudy."

At the same time, users naturally expected the Web site to be more localized and more specific to their needs. Thus—at least in theory—the site needed to have many thousands of pages of information, all of which would require constant updating. Chuck Herring, currently in charge of our weather-related radio and newspaper businesses, was involved in the early days of weather.com. He offers an interesting statistic:

> *A couple of years ago, when I was responsible for meteorology operations, we did an analysis of how many graphic products our systems produced on a daily basis. Say we had a temperature map that was updated hourly; that would count as twenty-four products. We found that we were generating between 115,000 and 120,000 graphic products* per day.

Even if only a small subset of those graphics wound up on weather.com, that was a huge amount of graphics to update. These vast numbers argued for a centralized database and forecast "engine," from which all of our various platforms would draw their information. (More about that a bit later.)

Meanwhile, there was plenty to work on at weather.com. The site had been developed by a small group of freewheeling webmasters, who were skilled at things like setting up servers, building code, cranking out HTML pages, and building graphics. This group responded to requests for new functionalities by sticking on a patch here and a bandage there. Changes required a lot of trial and error: Make the change, see if anything bad happened as a result, and see if you could add a patch to fix the new problems.

Because of the relatively high turnover among Web developers, no one seemed to know who had done what, or why. In fact, no one had a clear sense of how the Web site actually worked, and there was very little documentation to fall back on. The Web site was something like a giant rubber-band ball, with layer upon layer of code, but providing no clear sense of the underlying architecture. Meanwhile, it resided on a whole variety of different servers, some of which turned out to be in development areas of the shop. In other words, there was always a chance that someone working on an obscure corner of the site "off-line" wasn't off-line at all, and could bring down the whole site unwittingly. "Half the time," recalls developer Brad Bacon, "we wouldn't know where something was actually running."

Many of the Web site's pages were of a seasonal nature—for example, pollen counts, ski reports, and air quality. When the pollen season began, the Web site team had to go looking for last year's version of that product, which might have resided on a server that no longer existed, or which no longer tied into the network in the right ways.

Meanwhile, the demand for the Web site was increasing steadily. If the staff didn't expand the system's capabilities, the site inevitably would become slower and less functional. They couldn't even determine the system's limits, though, because the lack of a consistent architecture—a consistent code base, consistent servers—meant that load testing was impractical, and that scaling up was impossible. "Here's this successful URL that made it into the Top 25 most visited sites in the world," Mark Ryan recalls. "But it was built so indiscriminately, there was a risk that it could bog down."

Accordingly, early in 2000, Ryan's team set out to rebuild the weather.com architecture from scratch. They aimed to create a scalable and transparent architecture, meaning that it would be able to grow as necessary, and would be comprehensible to those charged with maintaining and growing it. They were determined to rely heavily on user testing, and to maintain a constant presence on the Web—in other words, there would be no down time when the new site was "swapped in" for the old one. The informal goal was to rebuild the site in time for the heavy traffic that traditionally accompanies hurricane season in the late summer.

The team actively solicited responses from users in the field. Once a partial beta site was up and running, developers put a live button on the existing Web site, inviting users to explore the new site and make comments and suggestions. Thousands of e-mailed comments poured in, leading to literally hundreds of changes in the site.

The revised site was launched in mid-August 2000, just in time for the arrival of Hurricane Debby. Among insiders, this was considered to be the acid test: Traffic at weather.com was sure to spike as Debby approached the mainland. And, in fact, on August 23, the site took 15 million page views—double the total in an average day—and barely even slowed down. Debby fizzled, but weather.com did not.

(A few months earlier, in April, weather.com had celebrated its five-year anniversary. Appropriately, Debora Wilson invited Alan Galumbeck—our departed technology guru—to join in the celebration, even though he had never actually worked on the Web site and few people in attendance knew who he was. "We had around 200 people there," Wilson recalls. "I called him up to the podium, and thanked him for the contribution he had made to weather.com—even though it took us a couple of years to figure out exactly how much we owed him.")

Today, weather.com is living up to its potential, and then some. Traffic is enormous: more than 300 million page views in an average-weather month. (That's right: more than 3 *billion* page views annually.) We are successfully aggregating an audience that is of increasing interest to advertisers. In the future, as the quality of our weather information continues to increase, it is likely that some version, or some areas, of weather.com can move to a sub-scription basis.

Meanwhile, the interactivity of the current site continues to increase. Visitors can "chat" with their favorite on-camera mete-orologist from The Weather Channel, participate in contests, or use new features—climatology databases, ten-day forecasts, and so on—to plan their business trips and vacations.

To me, one of the most interesting indicators of user engagement with weather.com is the popularity of Photo Gallery. Web site fans have sent us literally thousands of photographs to post on the site; many are accompanied by very personal annotations. Most of these photographs, almost all taken by amateurs, have at least a tenuous connection to the weather. But others seem to be mostly about sharing something personal, and thereby connecting with a virtual community: a picture of a beautiful flower in a garden, a view from the Ponte Vecchio in Florence, a day at the beach in Maine.

There is a gentle paradox in all this. By calling on deep databases, extensive automation, and other high-tech tools, weather.com provides to millions of users a personalized, warm, and even intimate experience.

INTENSIFYING METEOROLOGY

In 1994, our senior vice president of meteorology, Ray Ban, started making an interesting argument in the offices of The Weather Channel and Landmark. Ban had enormous stature—he had been with us since the cable network's founding, and probably had done more than anyone else since John Coleman to shape The Weather Channel's product. So we listened carefully to him.

The Weather Channel, Ban was saying, had enjoyed a remarkable fifteen-year run, in large part because we had moved first into the all-weather-all-the-time space, and because we had perfected a way of presenting the national and local weather to a mass market that none could rival. But our content, Ban reminded us, was not what distinguished us. In fact, most of our content came directly from the National Weather Service. Of course, WSI, our data intermediary in Massachusetts, also intervened to process and format that content to our specifications. But anybody else who had the resources and the inclination to tap the NWS's data stream could do so, and present on the Internet more or less the same content as The Weather Channel.

That's exactly what was beginning to happen in the mid-1990s, Ban was telling us with increasing urgency. Suddenly, literally hundreds of Web sites were offering NWS-derived weather data. Ban recalls his increasing sense of disquiet:

> *It seemed to me that the content available on the Internet might put The Weather Channel at a serious disadvantage. It might begin to give consumers the perception that we were great packagers, but that the guts of the information being presented were pretty shallow.*
>
> *So what were we going to do—what plans were we going to lay—that would enable us not only to come to grips with our content challenge, but also to go beyond where the market was at that time? How could we leapfrog into a new zone? How could we skate to where the puck was going to be?*
>
> *"Somebody is going to do it," I kept saying. "Somebody is going to make that commitment, and that investment. Why shouldn't it be us?"*

Ban began making allies. In 1997, Mike Eckert told our board that The Weather Channel simply had to have the best proprietary weather information available. This meant developing or buying a "weather engine" system that would be superior to anything that was out there in the market. Our two choices, Eckert continued, were to buy an existing system or to develop a system in partnership with someone else. We decided to pursue both tracks more or less simultaneously.

First we looked for a new way to apply computing power to the challenge of forecasting. There was a period, in the late 1970s and early 1980s, when chess Grand Masters could still beat the most powerful computers of that era. Eventually, that period ended. Electronic computers became powerful enough to overwhelm even the most astounding human computer.

The same is true of weather, although we are several decades behind the chess parable. Today the computer generally can out-perform the human meteorologist for forecasts beyond the first day. There are simply too many variables—fronts, currents, jet streams, anomalies—for the human brain to keep track of.

Forecasting can get only better if you can somehow compare what was forecasted with what actually happened. So it isn't simply a case of hiring the hundreds of additional meteorologists. We would also have to hire many more people—possibly hundreds—to carry through the post-forecast phase. Meanwhile, we'd be under increasing pressure to add more countries, more regions, more cities, with more frequent updates everywhere.

Another relevant issue, raised earlier in the context of weather.com, was consistency across our growing number of plat-forms. If we could come up with an increasingly automated fore-cast system and then point all our platforms toward that system, we could entirely sidestep the problem of having different forecasts on, say, The Weather Channel and weather.com.

I should also emphasize the more positive side of these argu-ments. By its nature as a 24/7 cable network, there is only so much content that The Weather Channel can present. There is only so much time on the clock. Increased international coverage, for example, necessarily implies decreased domestic coverage. Deeper local coverage would necessarily mean less frequent regional and national coverage.

But a centralized database of weather information, processed by a high-powered weather engine, could effectively and effi-ciently answer questions at almost any level of specificity, and meet a user's needs in real time, via the Internet.

All these lines of thought, and others, led, in December 1997, to a relationship with the National Center for Atmospheric Research, or NCAR. Based in Boulder, Colorado, NCAR is the research arm of the University Corporation for Atmospheric Research (UCAR), a unique entity that accepts both federal dollars and private money to conduct atmospheric science research and development.

NCAR had its own "weather engine" system, which in its early generations was known as the Weather Window. Basically, this system involved the use of "fuzzy logic." The fuzzy logic model draws on multiple weather-information databases and interprets those inputs to make forecasts. Equally important, it compares predictions with subsequent outcomes, and gets progressively better over time. For this reason, the system is referred to as an "intelligent integrator."

We retained NCAR's services to develop a later-generation derivative of their system for our proprietary use. This product became known as "DiCast" (short for "Digital Intelligent Forecast System"). As Ray Ban explains it, DiCast is essentially saying, "OK, I've got all these inputs—weather data, climatology data, numerical weather prediction models, and so on. And I know what the weather pattern is in general right now. So what would I do with all that, if I were a human?"

Ian Miller, The Weather Channel's vice president for weather systems, elaborates on the "intelligent integrator" concept: "The secret ingredient in DiCast is that it's the *arbiter*. It looks at various inputs, and decides the proper weighting for each to create the best forecast."

We brought DiCast online initially to serve weather.com. Today, all the information on weather.com—forecasts for 20,000 U.S. sites, hourly forecasts out to forty-eight hours, and three-hourly forecasts out to ten days—originates from DiCast. All 200-plus cable operator customers of Weather Scan (our digital television 24/7 local forecast product) get DiCast products. In the summer of 2001, we began the complex process of tying DiCast's products into the cable network.

Even as we sought to improve our *content,* we also knew that we had to keep working on our *packaging*—our ability to process and present data in compelling ways. We knew it would be difficult to build a new front-end packaging system on our own. We were determined, therefore, to buy a skilled partner. We saw only three credible candidates in this fairly arcane field. One was WSI Corporation, which had helped us think through the data–acquisition part of the first STAR system, and from the outset had been The Weather Channel's data intermediary with the National Weather Service. In addition to building truly high-end graphics systems, WSI had enormous expertise at ingesting weather data and fashioning it toward specific product ends. WSI President Mark Gildersleeve says,

> *You don't know our name, but you see us every day. There is probably a 70 percent chance that if you're looking at TV weather, that weather is coming from us, and the graphics were generated by our systems. There is an 80 percent chance that if you've taken a flight in the last month, flight dispatchers were looking at our data to plan your flight. So we're part of your everyday life; you just don't know it.*

And as we knew from experience, WSI was a "high-touch" service provider. They went out of their way to provide outstanding service to their customers, who included The Weather Channel, 350 television stations in North America, and twelve of the fifteen largest air carriers. These customers absolutely depended on their data and their presentation systems being reliable. As a result, WSI was able to charge a premium for its services. A good part of this premium was plowed back into the company, which traditionally has spent more than 10 percent of its revenue dollars on research and development.

At regular intervals dating back to just after our launch in the early 1980s, we had considered trying to purchase WSI, but mostly through accidents of timing, that company was never quite available when we were in a position to make an offer for it. By the mid-1990s, WSI had changed hands several times and was now owned by Litton Industries, which had acquired it as part of a larger package. As a defense contractor, Litton didn't know exactly what to do with its high-end weather forecasting and presentation division. We were concerned that if we didn't acquire WSI, someone else would.

So Dubby Wynne contacted Litton's CEO and, through a straightforward negotiation, reached an agreement for Landmark to pay Litton $120 million in cash to acquire WSI.

The deal was closed March 10, 2000, and WSI formally came into Landmark's corporate fold. As anticipated, WSI's Weather Pro system—with something like a million and a half lines of proprietary code behind it—provided a new foundation for the "weather engine" that The Weather Channel had been seeking. But The Weather Channel was not simply a passive purchaser of a canned solution. The two companies immediately began working together to improve forecasting and presentation tools.

Brian Shield soon organized the "Weather Systems" group at The Weather Channel, populated mainly by meteorologists who have gravitated into technology during the course of their careers. This group today serves as the operational arm of the forecasting process. They monitor DiCast and serve as the in-house liaison with WSI.

Mark Gildersleeve adds that his company has long had a focus on "automating the generation of information products"—in other words, shifting the burden of weather-data interpretation from people to machines:

> The Weather Channel was always more people-intensive, and more hand-crafted, than WSI. Now they're making a transition to using products on multiple channels—in other words, taking products from the Web site and using them on air, or vice versa, or taking radio products and using them on interactive TV. And we can help a lot with that.

As WSI's new owner, we now have a new kind of influence with our key supplier. But we are also WSI's biggest customer, by far—as we have been for many years—and WSI remains intensely customer-focused. For all these reasons, I'm optimistic that we can bring WSI's special skills to bear on The Weather Channel's unique challenges.

BETTING ON THE FUTURE

As I look into the future, let me say first what I think is not going to happen in the near future: Analog TV broadcasting and cablecasting are not going to go away. Although the FCC is systematically setting the stage for the digital broadcasting era—assigning bandwidth, requiring hardware changes, and so on—analog TV is likely to stay alive and kicking for many years. We are committed to protecting our analog "shelf space" all across the United States.

At the same time, the future is clearly digital. Our challenge in the broadcast realm is to create a digital "footprint," just as creating an analog footprint was the key challenge back in the early 1980s. Our Weather Scan channels on the "digital dial" are only one step in this direction.

The future is also about converging technologies. The Internet and television are becoming more similar to each other. Before long, full-motion video will be routine on the Internet. We have to imagine all the platforms and spaces where people may go in the future for weather information and get there as quickly and as effectively as possible.

Our redesigned Web site, combined with DiCast, began this transition. It combined the *centralization* of all of The Weather Channel's product content with the *personalization* of that content, as well as *localization* of advertising. This set us up to jump onto any number of new platforms—a process that is well underway.

One of our early forays into this market was providing a weather product for personal digital assistants. The user asks for a weather report for a particular location—where he or she is today or will be tomorrow—and the device accesses our database, which passes back a five-day forecast.

One challenge for us, in all this, is who builds the strong relationship with the customer? The manufacturer of the wireless device might argue that since it's their device that permits one-stop shopping, they should "own" the relationship. At the same time, the telecom company would argue that it's their network that's connecting everybody, so they should control the relationship.

We have our own view of the world, of course. *We* want that relationship. To get there, we need to have our customers to see us on every platform. When they look at their morning newspaper, they should see a Weather Channel map. Their car radio should bring them our weather inserts. They should see The Weather Channel on cable TV, of course, along with the local version of Weather Scan. We want their pager to go to weather.com, and we want them to make it their home page on their home and business computers. We want their PDA and their cell phone to default to us.

Say our customer's name is Hank, and say that by his own accounting, Hank is really interested in golf. Well, we want to provide Hank with every kind of golf-related weather information. We want Hank to check with us before he makes his weekend plans. If those clouds above the fifteenth tee look ominous, we want Hank to be able to pull out his wireless device, call up the local radar in real time, and drag his stylus across the screen to see just where this storm is in relation to him. If the storm is moving rapidly, we want to be able to send Hank a real-time lightning alert through his pager or cell phone. And we want to be able to dial Hank at home, through the Internet, if there's a tornado heading in his direction in the middle of the night.

And suppose Hank's a weather buff in his (nongolfing) spare time. The visualization of weather is only going to get more striking and powerful as relevant technologies continue to improve. Ray Ban paints a picture of what tomorrow's weather buff will be savoring:

> *Imagine geostationary satellites generating full-motion color video with one-kilometer resolution. Imagine drawing on a network like that to watch a hurricane come over a major U.S. city at night. You're seeing the lightning flashing around the eye. Then you're seeing the lights of the city peeking through, as the*

eye passes over. And this is almost real—in fact, it's just around the corner.

Weather for planning, weather for safety, weather for inspiration, and weather for fun: All this weather makes us extremely valuable to Hank. And, of course, it helps us earn more revenue from advertisers or a subscription fee from Hank for parts of the service.

The DiCast integrator also holds potential for a range of interesting products. Where do people go for information today if—for example—they want to take a vacation in the third week of March in the continental United States, and they want to know where the smallest chance of precipitation might be? The *Farmer's Almanac* makes long-range forecasts, but not very reliably. If someone wants to schedule a wedding in June in Bangor, what's the weather likely to be? In other words, we are learning that weather is not necessarily a perishable commodity. When good longitudinal data are run through powerful models, very useful products can result.

Meanwhile, we have to keep in mind that an intelligent integrator like DiCast may turn out to be only an intermediate step along the way to a truly great weather-predicting machine. Every day, the cost of observing weather—the cost of collecting the data that may allow us to look hours or days into the future—is going down. Satellites, remote sensors, and other technologies may make it possible to gather and interpret all these data and create the "perfect" numerical weather model. Just plug in all these observations—including information from the most remote parts of the ocean and every level of the atmosphere, and generated by both public-sector and private-sector entities—and out pops a highly reliable forecast.

Such a model won't arrive next year, or the year after. But it might arrive within a decade. If it does, The Weather Channel needs to be there. We need to be participating, and we need to help make it happen.

CHAPTER NINE

THE WEATHER CHANNEL
IN CONTEXT

This book arrives more or less on the twentieth anniversary of the founding of The Weather Channel. I can say safely that it has been an interesting, and sometimes even intense, two decades. Writing this book has given me an opportunity not only to reflect on that experience, but also to put it in a larger context. What have we learned from our twenty-year adventure in meteorology, marketing, and entrepreneurship? What *should* we learn?

Growing The Weather Channel has been a little bit like raising a child to young adulthood. When you parent teenagers, you try every way you can think of to develop their savvy and independence, and yet you have mixed emotions when they actually learn to live without your constant advice. That's how I feel about The Weather Channel. Anyone who has ever been through the parenting experience will understand me when I say that rearing The Weather Channel to young adulthood seems to have taken forever—and at the same time, it has all gone by far too quickly.

WHO IN THE WORLD IS LANDMARK?

Before summing up some general thoughts about The Weather Channel, I'd like to put the network within the context of its parent company, Landmark Communications, Inc. In the preceding pages, I've talked about Landmark only to the extent that it's been helpful in conveying The Weather Channel's own story. As a result, I've probably given a skewed impression of what happens day to day at corporate headquarters in Norfolk. A privately held company, Landmark is the parent of a wide range of media-related enterprises, including newspapers and television stations. Most of these ventures exemplify our strategy of investing in start-ups and acquiring underdeveloped businesses. I'll mention a few of them here.

You've read in these pages about TeleCable, our cable television subsidiary. In 1984 we spun it off to stockholders. Then, in January 1995, as the cable industry was undergoing rapid consolidation, we merged TeleCable with TeleCommunications, Inc., then the nation's largest cable company.

Landmark also has two other important businesses that are fifty-fifty ventures with partners: Trader Publishing Company and Capitol-Gazette Communications. Trader, jointly owned with Cox Enterprises, is the larger of the two. It is a nationwide network of classified advertising publications, principally focused on employment, automobiles, boats, apartments, and homes. It publishes 678 different publications—most of them weeklies—which have a combined weekly circulation of 9.4 million.

Capitol-Gazette Communications, owned jointly with Philip Merrill, the CEO of the company, publishes several newspapers in and around Annapolis, Maryland, as well as *Washingtonian* magazine.

In addition, Landmark still owns KLAS-TV in Las Vegas, as well as NewsChannel 5 Network in Nashville. And it still owns newspapers, including Sam Slover's flagship newspaper, the Nor-folk-based *Virginian-Pilot*.

All told, Landmark's total revenues were $790 million in 2000. The Weather Channel, once only a small piece of Land-mark's net worth, now accounts for a sizable portion of it. Of that $790 million, The Weather Channel contributed $302 million.

THE POWER OF THE WEATHER CHANNEL CONCEPT

The Weather Channel was far more than just an interesting start-up. It was our first incursion into cable programming. It was our first nationally oriented business, brimming over with poten-tial and visibility and pitfalls. It became our pride and joy. It was our *baby*.

Looking back to the troubled birth and infancy of our baby, it's natural to wonder how The Weather Channel became such a robust young adult. I think the most important factor—especially at the outset—was the *power of the business concept*.

John Coleman recognized a compelling human need that was overlooked and unfulfilled. Now that weather information is instantly available and routinely used by millions, the need for something like The Weather Channel seems obvious. And yet venture capitalists and big media companies alike, even the savvy Dow Jones, rejected Coleman's idea. Even working journalists, who presumably should be in reasonably close touch with con-sumers' interests and needs, expressed their disdain when we at Landmark announced that we would back the weather-channel concept. "You've got to be kidding," they hooted. "Weather, twenty-four hours a day, seven days a week? What in the world are you going to talk about all that time? And who's going to listen?"

Well, the answer is that millions of people will listen. They want the latest weather information every day, at all hours, and they want it available on demand. After the public gets hooked on this kind of thing, lots of people ask, "Why didn't I think of that?" So the question wasn't, "Why a twenty-four-hour weather channel?" It was, "Why *not* a twenty-four-hour weather channel?"

Once we heard Coleman's pitch, we almost immediately warmed to his concept. I had been a sailor for much of my life, and I liked Coleman's idea because of my personal need for the service he was promoting. Our cable company's experience with primitive weather channels convinced us that others needed it, too. We didn't do any consumer surveys or other research. We depended on our personal experiences and gut instincts.

I believe that in the case of many start-ups, personal experiences and instincts can be more reliable than market research. My gut reactions can often lead me to commit to a business concept much more easily than can statistical summaries of the reactions of faceless focus groups. And this point is important, because when you're faced with adversity, "gut" commitment can give you more strength to get through it than just the knowledge that the concept, or the project, looks good on paper.

From the beginning, therefore, both Coleman and Landmark, the inventor and the operator/money partner, were unified in their commitment to the business concept. To paraphrase a line from *Field of Dreams,* we simply believed, "If we build it, they will come." Thus our due diligence focused on whether we could acquire the technology and distribution to execute the concept and whether the market was large enough to *support* the concept. As I've already explained, our judgments on technology and distribution turned out to be reliable, but we greatly underestimated costs and overestimated advertising revenues. We relied on a brilliant performer with no relevant management experience to estimate the cost structure. And we misjudged how long it would take for advertisers to take this new cable TV medium seriously.

Not surprisingly, when we began losing large sums of money the first year, we began second-guessing ourselves—even though that's almost never a useful exercise. We should have realized that these kinds of misjudgments are common with start-up ventures. And at the same time, we should have developed an alternative strategy—a fallback plan—in case our estimates were seriously flawed.

As it turned out, the power of the business concept rescued us. Even as we were planning to shut down The Weather Channel, our cable operators came to us and told us how to save our venture. "The service is so valuable to us," they said, "we'll pay you to carry it."

A CASE OF CORPORATE ENTREPRENEURSHIP

The Weather Channel story illustrates some large differences between *individual* entrepreneurship and *corporate* entrepreneurship, and it makes a strong case for the importance of the latter. Many of the factors that helped The Weather Channel succeed grew out of its family relationship with Landmark. These advantages would not have been available to an individual entrepreneur.

Landmark and its divisions had made innovative changes and had started up new products before, but most had been line extensions of our newspapers and cable systems. No prior Landmark venture had exposed us to high financial risk. True, we entered the cable television field while it was a new medium in its entrepreneurial stage. But our start-ups of cable systems were spread over a decade or more, so no single cable investment created high exposure for the company.

All our pre-1982 media properties served local or regional markets. The Weather Channel, by contrast, was conceived as a national network. In spite of Landmark's lack of experience and established resources for serving national markets, we did have certain competencies that were invaluable to this kind of venture:

- Through TeleCable, we understood the cable TV marketplace intimately. We could make realistic judgments about the overall demand for cable service and how cable operators would react to various kinds of programming under specific conditions.

- We had valuable relationships with many of the cable operators who would become essential customers of The Weather Channel. TeleCable and its managers were respected in the cable industry for integrity and quality operations. Much of this goodwill was transferred to The Weather Channel.

- Through our television stations, we understood the television advertising marketplace, and we had experience in television production. We knew the value of weather on our newscasts.

- With the WeatherSTAR, we invented an indispensable USP ("unique selling proposition") for advertisers. The invention would not have been possible without the know-how and creative talent of Landmark people. And without that invention, The Weather Channel's audience in the early years would have been far too small for most advertisers to consider, and we could not have survived. With it, The Weather Channel became the only television network able to localize national commercials, which offered a unique benefit to advertisers with either regional emphases or local distributorships or franchisees.

And, of course, the STAR gave The Weather Channel another critical advantage: It enabled us to deliver current *local* weather information to viewers continuously—something no other network could do. The large capital investment in this patented technology gave The Weather

Channel a sustainable competitive edge that helped solid-
ify our first-mover advantage.

• Landmark had a pool of management talent that could be
moved to The Weather Channel for temporary or per-
manent assignments on short notice. Lacking the stability
of a large organization, an individual entrepreneur would
have been hard pressed to attract the kind of talent that
we could. He or she certainly wouldn't have had the luxury of moving someone like Dubby Wynne, for example,
in and out of the operation as needed.

• Most important, Landmark enjoyed a climate of trust that
encouraged managers to stick their necks out. Our managers were willing to take on new assignments in which
they lacked experience. They were willing to plunge into
another business without fear of being left behind or left
out in the cold if, after an honest effort, the business did
not succeed.

At Landmark, we often quote a joke about the five stages of
a new venture: "from wild enthusiasm . . . to dawning disillusion-
ment . . . to mad panic . . . to the search for the guilty . . . to the
promotion of the nonparticipants." In the case of The Weather
Channel—and I hope in all other cases—Landmark studiously
avoided these last two stages. In fact, we often promoted the participants. Patrick Scott, the head of our failed European weather
venture, is now executive vice president and general manager of
The Weather Channel.

Does this mean that Landmark "rewards failure"? Of course
not. In Europe, our trials and tribulations did not reflect poor
management on the ground. Our mistake was to start the channel
to begin with. But the experience that Patrick Scott got in launching a new venture was among the best possible business seasoning
one can get. This is true whether the business succeeds or fails.

My point, again, is that we enjoyed all these advantages because we were a corporate entrepreneur. An individual, even with

ample financial backing, would not have enjoyed most of them. Business historian Alfred P. Chandler has observed that while there are certain things that only small companies can do well, there are other things that only companies of a certain scale and scope can pull off. The Weather Channel was a success achieved by a medium-sized company, with adequate financial resources and without bureaucratic obstructions—the kind of company, in other words, that Peter Drucker argues is most likely to succeed at entrepreneurship.

Ownership structure, as well as size, makes a difference. A private company like Landmark often finds it easier than a public company to swallow large book losses until a new enterprise breaks even. Obviously, this makes it easier for the parent company to adopt, and stick with, a long-term investment horizon.

I don't want to overstate the value of these advantages. In and of themselves, they are very helpful. In combination with a powerful business concept, they can be extremely powerful.

WHAT WE DIDN'T HAVE, DIDN'T WANT, AND DIDN'T NEED

What was *not* essential to The Weather Channel experience? The first thing that comes to my mind is stock options. Landmark has never had stock options. Rather, we have a stock purchase plan for managers. In some divisions, we also have long-term incentive plans that provide attractive rewards to people in high-demand positions. Valuations of both plans are based on long-term operating performance—that is, over periods of years—rather than on performance in the stock market.

In 2000, we dodged a bullet. At that time, we faced strong internal pressure to make an initial public offering and offer stock options to members of our weather.com unit. At the height of the dot-com frenzy in the stock market, weather.com's managers were finding it difficult to recruit and retain excellent people. We were experiencing extraordinarily high turnover, which was disrupting operations and hurting sales. Many of our good people were lured away with promises of stock options and the prospect of "getting rich quick" through a subsequent IPO.

We debated this issue very seriously, and we ultimately decided against an IPO and options. Instead, we installed a long-term performance incentive plan for weather.com staffers. A few months later, that decision was validated when the dot-com market came tumbling down.

I've been asked why I objected to an IPO when the dot-com market was crazy-high. Why not take the cash in at a fantastic price? Actually, we might have made an extraordinary return if we could have pulled off a stunt like that. But I had two problems with the idea—one practical and the other a question of ethics and fairness.

The practical problem was that the odds of pulling it off would have been low. That's clear in the wake of the NASDAQ meltdown, but it seemed to me to be a big problem even before the crash. Let's assume the "market value," on paper, of weather.com had been bid up into the billions after an IPO. Securities and Exchange Commission rules would have locked up the equity positions of Landmark and its employees for some months. After the lock-up period, *if* the value had still been high, Landmark would still have been limited to dribbling stock sales into the market in small lots. The market for those stocks would have been so thin that any sizable sale would have killed the price. So Landmark could have cashed in a big bundle only if the stock had stayed drastically overpriced for a long time.

The ethical problem was that it didn't feel right to engage in the equivalent of "tulip mania." Some dot-com prices had no relationship to any return most of these companies could make in decades. Companies like Amazon and Yahoo! were wildly over-priced, let alone what I call the "smoke.coms" (smoke, mirrors, and little else). I could not justify selling a new stock knowing that, in all probability, a few Wall Street insiders would make a small killing on the IPO while many "widows and orphans" would get ripped off. A business strategy of making investments with the goal of making quick bucks in crazy markets would be akin to shooting craps at Las Vegas. Over the long term, the odds might be better at the craps table.

And finally, there was one telling question to which I never got a satisfactory answer: "What does the *next* generation of good people at weather.com get, after the value of the company has been handed out to this generation?" As long as I lacked a good answer to that question, I felt an IPO would be hard to justify.

When the stock market crash came, we still had a problem with our performance incentive plan, and we had a new decision to make. In the wake of the dot-com collapse, and particularly the dot-com advertising market collapse, we had to think hard about the performance incentives we had established for weather.com employees. Dubby Wynne and my son, Frank Batten, Jr.—by then the chairman of Landmark—agreed they should adjust the targets so that people who had been offered this incentive plan still had realistic performance incentives. They reasoned that the people who had elected to stick with us should not be punished for the bursting of the dot-com advertising bubble.

For many newer employees, this decision turned out to be another demonstration of Landmark's corporate culture and values. I believe that it's these kinds of actions that in the long run help us recruit and retain outstanding people, without resorting to what for us are the double-edged swords of IPOs and stock options.

Some interpret my aversion to stock options and IPOs for Landmark to mean that I have a general hostility to these methods. Not at all. I simply believe that they are incompatible with the rewards and incentives systems we have at Landmark. I have sought to build a company whose aims are to create long-term growth in value, and to do it with products and services we can be proud of. Options almost inevitably focus managers on short-term goals and measurements of results by stock markets. They can and do work just fine in companies with different aims from ours.

We have had enough experience with our "Executive Stock Plan," created in 1967, to know how important a role that plan has played in aligning our key managers with Landmark's aims. As a result of the plan and its rewards, which are based on long-term growth in profits, most of the participants think and act like owners. Today, 227 active and retired managers, not counting my family and me, own 32 percent of Landmark's stock. For many of these managers, the stock constitutes large portions of their net worth. I believe it would greatly diminish the motivational value of our stock plan if we were to refocus most of the ownership rewards on *some* of our businesses on short-term stock market performance rather than on long-term operating performance. There is nothing wrong with short-term rewards. We have them in the form of cash bonus plans, but they are not incompatible with the incentives of ownership. *In Landmark's case,* I believe options and IPOs would risk damaging a long-term reward system and compromising a set of values that we know work for us.

Because values are established by what a company *does,* rather than by what it *says,* it takes years for values to become ingrained in a company. And even though a positive corporate culture never shows up on a balance sheet, it can be an enormous asset. When ad salesman Norm Zeller was trying to figure out in the early 1980s whether to take a job with Landmark and The Weather Channel, he sought out and spoke with a number of Landmark old-timers. More than once while conducting these informal interviews, Zeller heard the story about how my uncle went to great lengths to avoid layoffs during the Great Depression. Now, as I calculate it, none of the people with whom Zeller was speaking were old enough to have personal knowledge of events that had taken place fifty or sixty years earlier. They were retelling stories that had been told to them in the lunchroom or around the water cooler. They were living, and reinforcing, a culture. That's an asset I wouldn't trade for most others.

And this brings me back to my earlier theme of corporate entrepreneurship. When facing a life-or-death crisis, a precarious venture like The Weather Channel has a better chance of survival when it is backed by an established company with values that inspire confidence. I will never forget the confidence of so many people who stuck with us when it looked like The Weather Channel would not make it. It is rare for individual entrepreneurs or venture capitalists to be able to generate and sustain that kind of confidence.

DOUBTS AND FOCUS

In my time at Landmark, we have entered a variety of media ventures. Some have been start-ups. Others were going concerns, usually underdeveloped or in the early stages of development. A few have been successes—extraordinary successes. More have been losers. Fortunately, the gains from the successes have dwarfed the losses from our losers.

I cannot remember any venture of any size we have undertaken that didn't elicit expressions of doubt from some of the ablest people in Landmark. And I suspect that many more doubts went unexpressed. Usually, the misgivings centered on the wisdom of our investing time and money in businesses that were new to us, rather than concentrating our resources on our already successful businesses. These kinds of doubts still crop up today, as we continue to invest in new businesses.

Some Landmark people make the case that the company should "stick to its knitting." Retrospectively, they argue that we might have gotten even better results from our investments and our organization if we had concentrated entirely on growing in the newspaper and broadcasting businesses and their spin-offs and related ventures. That would have made the most focused use of our knowledge and experience—and, of course, would have avoided some of the substantial investment losses we have incurred.

We will never know the result of such a concentrated investment strategy. But what I'd say in response is that the same argument was made against our initial forays into the cable television business. And that by being selectively entrepreneurial, we ventured into three extraordinarily successful businesses whose enterprise values and cash flows grew much faster and higher than comparable investments in newspapers and TV stations could ever have grown. They were cable television (which we entered in 1964), The Weather Channel (1982), and Trader Publishing Company (1989).

These three ventures grew out of newly developing trends in technology and marketing. Each had internal critics at the outset. They were only three out of more than a score of Landmark ventures—some successes and others failures—spread over almost a forty-year period. So there it is: We had only three big hits in about forty years, which is not exactly a great batting average. On the other hand, the total result of these ventures was an extraordinarily high financial rate of return. We also wound up with a legacy media company that had some real competence in managing new ventures. Young people looking at Landmark as a potential employer could find evidence that we were forward-looking and selectively adventurous.

To arrive at these good results, we had to be patient. We had to resist the temptation to cut and run, abandoning an entrepreneurial strategy in the face of a series of disappointments. Failures are an inevitable result of risk taking and entrepreneurship. The trick is to face up to a failing venture quickly, and cut off the bleeding before it becomes a hemorrhage. The next step is to probe the failure for its lessons—and then continue to search for the next opportunity.

EATING OUR OWN

I have long believed that Landmark should have the audacity to undertake attractive new ventures without pulling its punches—even when it means invading the territories of our own highly profitable established businesses. Why? Because if we don't do it, someone else will. In some of these cases, particularly with The Weather Channel, our experience, resources, and brand recognition give us the best prospects for exploiting the new venture. That's a competitive edge that we should celebrate and exploit.

The Internet has been a disruptive technology for many media businesses. In our case, it would seem to be most disruptive to The Weather Channel. It's easy to imagine broadband technologies and developments in meteorology making weather.com an even more appealing and functional source of weather information than The Weather Channel—for many people, under many circumstances. Our Web site has the capability to interact with viewers, and to tailor their weather information to their individual needs. It can give them weather information, on demand, for almost anywhere on the globe. Eventually, it will accommodate full-motion video, and plenty of consumers will have a broad enough digital pipeline to take advantage of full-motion, real-time, streaming video. In fact, weather.com has an unlimited capacity to present information. As its president, Debora Wilson, says, "It is only limited by what we choose to put on and what customers will use."

In addition, we have the ideal Internet URL—weather.com— thanks to the foresight of our longtime technology guru, Alan Galumbeck. And we are investing heavily to develop the preeminent presentation and meteorological capabilities for delivering weather information to consumers and businesses.

Meanwhile, our flagship cable network continues to grow. Yes, it has clear limitations on available air time—even 24/7 only goes so far—which means that it can cover only a circumscribed number of cities and regions. Does that mean that weather.com will bury The Weather Channel? I doubt it. I think we're placing the right bet: that investing in both platforms will increase the consumption of weather information and enlarge our overall audience. In any case, we have no choice but to make these parallel investments. *If we don't do it, someone else will.*

With weather.com, our main challenge is to develop a more profitable business model for it. If it continued to depend on banner advertising only and began to "steal" viewers from The Weather Channel, we would lose. So weather.com will require additional revenue sources.

Interactive direct marketing is one source. A unique advantage of the Internet as an advertising medium is its ability to deliver highly targeted messages and communicate with individual users. Web sites with valuable direct-marketing capabilities can tap into an advertiser's sales and marketing budget, which usually comes out of a different pot than the advertising budget. In a sense, this is exactly how The Weather Channel made its first big advertising breakthrough, when the STAR enabled it to tap the dollars of local Michelin dealers rather than depending on Michelin's national ad budget. We are depending on the ingenuity of creative people inside and outside The Weather Channel to develop weather.com's potential as a direct marketer.

Fees will also be important. Just as The Weather Channel needed subscriber fees to supplement its ad revenues, the Web site will probably have to charge fees for high-value-added, customized services, which we will supply directly to customers who subscribe to them. But because there is widespread aversion to fees in the Internet world, our services will have to be outstanding to justify charging for them.

All this points toward how we think about our newest child. We have to think creatively and opportunistically, if we hope to find really good new solutions. We first operated weather.com as a line extension of The Weather Channel, rather than as an entirely different medium. It was not until we split off weather.com as an independent unit that it received the kind of focus and freedom to compete that was needed to reach its full potential. Whether or not it eventually cannibalizes The Weather Channel, we are developing weather.com with the same energy and determination that we put into The Weather Channel.

So we embrace cannibalism. Well, maybe "embrace" is too strong a word. But we engage in it willingly, in all directions. For years, we have offered branded Weather Channel information to radio stations. More recently, we began distributing it to newspapers and to an array of new distributors using wireless technologies. Through our newly acquired subsidiary, WSI, we deliver weather information to commercial users such as TV stations, airlines, private pilots, and energy companies. Don't these hurt The Weather Channel, too?

On balance, no. Our strategy is to make our brand ubiquitous, so our customers can find it in some form wherever they go. At the same time, we are determined to prevent anyone from sneaking up and flanking us.

CI AND VISION

In 1991, we inaugurated a "continuous improvement" effort throughout Landmark. The aim of this management initiative was to make Landmark a "world-class" competitor and build quality into our efforts. Of course, many companies went through similar exercises in the late 1980s and early 1990s. Our version of "CI," as we came to call it, embraced many of the quality improvement techniques first made popular by W. Edwards Deming. It was intended to have a long-term influence on the way Landmark works and competes.

We embarked on CI because the media business, like many other industries, is in the midst of a competitive revolution largely spawned by technological change. During much of my nearly fifty years at the head of Landmark, our newspapers and TV stations operated in protected markets. The newspapers were local monopolies, and nobody seriously challenged their dominance of local advertising. The TV stations were protected from strong TV competition by the federal government's licensing process. They were nearly perfect monopolies and oligopolies because we faced no serious competition and our prices were not regulated.

Beginning in the 1970s, the situation changed. A floodtide of new media, enabled by new technologies, began rewriting all the rules. Several dozen cable networks began eating into the audience and advertising base of television stations and their networks. Classified advertising publications—like our *Auto Traders*—were starting to attack newspapers' largest advertising source. Even a new medium like The Weather Channel was facing challenges, as fiber-optic and digital transmission enabled scores of new cable services to target our advertisers and viewers. Last but not least, the Internet was on the horizon, with its huge potential to challenge *all* existing media for their consumers and advertisers.

One important element of Landmark's CI program was to train staffers at all levels how to work in teams to enhance quality and productivity. We asked these teams to identify opportunities for improving customer service and productivity, and to eliminate unproductive effort and resources. We hired consultants to train our organizations from top to bottom in the tools of process improvement and team management.

During the first years of the program, our teams uncovered and eliminated a significant amount of waste. And many parts of the company continue to rely on team management processes, which have improved decision making and cooperation and have resulted in better performance for customers. But by the latter part of the 1990s, during a booming economy, the focus on productivity improvement diminished.

Another focus of CI is to engage corporate managers and managers of each unit in articulating their organization's purposes and goals. Using CI techniques, they develop statements of the organization's mission and vision. These efforts seek to help managers focus their organizations on common goals and also elevate their sights.

I have no doubt that developing these statements has led to better communication and cooperation among diverse parts of our organizations, and also to a deeper understanding of what we are seeking to accomplish. But at times the process has also led us astray. One case where it did so was at The Weather Channel. In a commendable effort to think boldly, the drafters of The Weather Channel's mission and vision statement wrote that our vision was to become "the preeminent provider of value-added weather worldwide."

I'm not sure how the word *worldwide* survived our reviews of this statement, but it did, and it clearly helped justify some extraordinarily expensive miscalculations of the prospects of our foreign ventures. With a vision statement that simply *asserted* a worldwide hegemony for The Weather Channel, we jumped ahead without rigorously analyzing whether market conditions in Europe were favorable for starting an American-style weather channel. My point is simply that *words are powerful,* especially in the context of an organization that prides itself on doing what it says it's going to do. Yes, mission and vision statements can help focus an organization on the right goals. But they have to be carefully drafted. After all, we have to live by them.

DAVID AND GOLIATH

In the 1990s, we saw a wave of consolidation in the cable industry and among its programmers. The Weather Channel is among only a handful of "virgins" left among cable programmers. By no means is The Weather Channel a lonely wallflower. We have been approached by all the logical suitors, some of whom arrived in Norfolk with very lucrative marriage proposals. I have resisted all such proposals.

I have been asked more than once why I am so stubborn in this regard. In fact, there are several reasons. Most important, I believe we can operate The Weather Channel better than any of the large consolidators. Some may be able to make a few more bucks in the short run. Over the long haul, however, I believe we will give The Weather Channel more care and attention—and more love—than anyone else can. And that attention and love will continue to provide more value for shareholders and more value for our customers.

Think about it: We live and breathe weather. For most of our suitors, by contrast, The Weather Channel is just another advertising medium, albeit a first-rate one. Would you rather get your weather information from somebody who has a passion for it—and can also calculate return on investment, by the way—or from a conglomerate that approaches news, sports, weather, and whatnot with exactly the same attitude?

Some argue that we are playing David in a land of Goliaths. In other words, can't one of the big operators just squash us? I'm willing to take that risk because, like David, we have powerful competitive advantages. (David won, by the way.) Landmark has deep enough pockets to afford to fight almost any competitive battle. We know more about weather programming. We have developed superb proprietary forecasting capabilities, and through WSI we have superior presentation resources. We have unique technologies that give us valuable distribution advantages. We have incredibly loyal viewers, many of whom "live by" The Weather Channel. As a result, we have a powerful brand. And just as we were the "first mover" with weather on cable, we intend to be first and best in providing weather information to consumers through other new distribution venues.

Last but not least, most of the consolidators are already making good money from The Weather Channel in *our* hands. If it's money they're after, they're already doing fine simply by "going steady" with our network.

But let me emphasize that, strangely enough, I *like* the threat of potential competition. Intel founder Andy Grove was right when he said, "Only the paranoid survive." If we are paranoid about competition from any source, it can only make us better and more attentive to our customers. Meanwhile, we are having too much fun running The Weather Channel—and deriving too much satisfaction from providing a genuine public service—to turn it over to others.

WHAT'S IN A LEADER?

Lurking behind many of the issues in this book is the question of leadership. A great deal has been written on the subject, and I'm not sure I have a great deal to add. But let me tease out a few themes, which seem to present themselves in two categories: the "unqualified" and "qualified" dimensions of leadership.

By "unqualified," I mean those things that don't have to be accompanied by a statement that begins with a phrase like "on the other hand." For example, effective leaders *must* be willing to accept and lead change. Since my days as an economics major in college, I've embraced economist Joseph Schumpeter's idea that "creative destruction" energizes and drives the capitalist system.

The tougher aspects of leadership are the ones that come with qualifications attached. Yes, leaders have to be forceful and decisive. *On the other hand,* they have to be great listeners. They have to be both tough-minded and empathetic. They have to delegate, but they also have to grab up the reins when circumstances demand swift action. They have to learn how and when to let go of responsibilities, making way for others to grow—but they can't take the easy way out.

When I hold myself up to these tough standards, I give myself mixed grades. My lowest grades with The Weather Channel come out of our failed European expedition, which lost us many millions of dollars. Even though I had reservations about our prospects for success in Europe from the outset, I didn't express them strongly enough (which is uncharacteristic of me). My rationale was that I was trying to prepare the organization for life after my retirement. I had relinquished the CEO title. I also had accepted the job as chairman of The Associated Press, an organization that was confronting large strategic issues and which would occupy much of my time for the next five years.

So we moved forward in Europe, in what I thought would be an exploratory incursion. It soon became a full-scale invasion, to which we were committing extraordinary sums of money. Quickly, it became clear that my worst fears were coming true, along with a lot of other bad outcomes I hadn't even thought of. Europe was now a certified train wreck in the making. Again, I expressed my view, but again, not strongly enough to stop the train.

I *could* have stopped the train, and I didn't. Since that time. I have brooded more than a little bit over why I didn't act decisively. I'm afraid I rationalized that if I pulled the plug on Europe while all those involved were convinced they could succeed, it would have sent a signal to the organization that we had become risk-averse. And for sure, it would have been interpreted as a strong signal that I had lost confidence in the individuals involved (which I hadn't).

In hindsight, I should have acted much sooner and much more decisively. If ever there was a time for top-down leadership, this was it. I should have grabbed the reins and then depended on time to heal any wounds that resulted. When I noticed that no one was rigorously addressing critical issues, as the ultimate one responsible, I should have taken the role of Tough Questioner much more seriously.

That's what I give myself the worst mark for, I think. I suspected that the European venture was a mistake from the beginning. I didn't stop it. So I own the mistake, as well as the millions that it cost to make that mistake. My best excuse for these short-comings? When you get out onto the "qualified" ground of leadership—where one good impulse tugs in exactly the opposite direction from another good impulse—it's very easy to get it wrong.

Now that I have confessed to one of my worst failure of leadership, I feel free to mention one of the things that has *worked* for me and for Landmark.

I had the good fortune to become CEO of our much smaller company at a very young age, so I could take a long-range approach to reaching my goals. The organization I inherited had declined and become flabby, self-satisfied, and resistant to change. By necessity, I had to focus my main effort on rebuilding it. Thus I had to concentrate most of my time on developing an organization with the kinds of talents, customs, and goals I set my sights on. In the process, I learned by trial and error about building a vibrant, committed, entrepreneurial organization. In fact, this long-term organization building is the most valuable work I ever did for Landmark. Forty-seven years later, Landmark has a well-established set of values that has been a polestar for the company and our people. Those values have been a source of pride and inspiration for employees. They have given us the zeal to dare, the pride to be builders, and the courage to persist.

OWNERSHIP AND PRIDE

Throughout this book, I have referred to the virtues of private companies. I should qualify that. I am biased toward companies whose control is in the hands of one person or a small group whose mission is to perpetuate a vibrant company with high standards. This ideal is easiest to accomplish when the ownership is concentrated. That happens most often in private companies, but not always. I'm thinking of examples in my own industry, like The New York Times Company and The Washington Post Company, which have maintained concentrated control in companies with public stockholders.

Concentrated control makes it easier to preserve values and standards from decade to decade and from generation to generation. Of course, there is a downside to concentration when control is passed to people who are not competent to oversee a vigorous business, or to people who have mainly selfish motives, or to people with irreconcilable differences. I've certainly seen companies that have lost their vitality when the owners' motives and values become divided. But I've also seen others, including Landmark, that have successfully passed control and values from generation to generation.

My uncle convinced me that the surest way to preserve standards is to concentrate control in the hands of one person. Throughout his career, he had various money partners, but he always arranged to keep absolute control. When he wanted to retire, though, he sold a lot of his stock—and with it, control of the Norfolk newspapers—to a group of his managers. He soon regretted the effects of the diffused control, when the papers became inflexible and antiquated in their management structures.

When I came into the business, we managed to reacquire control, which he then turned over to me. In turn, I have passed control of Landmark to my son, Frank Batten, Jr., who is now CEO of Landmark. He and I share similar values and ambitions for Landmark. Fortunately, he also has a passion for the kinds of new technologies that are so critical in today's business—and which I don't even begin to understand. We don't claim to have found any sort of Eternal Way, but I believe we have a good chance of sustaining a high standard of performance and service for at least three generations.

And The Weather Channel embodies our ambitions. A business we started in the face of almost universal skepticism—even ridicule. A business that weathered a nearly fatal crisis. A business whose services now are welcomed in the homes and offices of millions of people every day. A business whose services enrich lives, and save lives. A business that continues to grow and enlarge its service. And most important, a business of which we are deeply proud.

CRAIG HENRY AND THE
MILLION-DOLLAR TRUCK

All by itself, in a service lot alongside a nondescript eight-story office building tucked away on the northern suburban outskirts of Atlanta, sits a gleaming white truck.

The truck, thirty-one feet long with a state-of-the-art aluminum satellite dish mounted on its roof, looks very much like a surveillance vehicle from a high-end spy thriller. The impression is heightened by the fact that the signs on both sides of the truck—which read "The Weather Channel"—are removable. Take them off, and you'd have a generic, slightly ominous-looking machine, clearly designed for nothing but data gathering and transmittal.

Inside the truck's windowless cargo area, senior satellite uplink engineer Craig Henry is organizing his tape library. For Henry, staying organized is important, partly because the truck's edit bay is equipped to edit six different types of videotape, and there are lots of cartridges and cassettes to keep track of. But it's also important because the working space inside the truck is cramped. In this tiny space—The Weather Channel's mobile studio—a little mess would go a long way.

Whether at the truck's wheel or amid the densely packed studio equipment, Henry is king of all that he surveys. He drives this million-dollar piece of hardware into storm country so that front-line on-camera meteorologists can get close—but not too close—to the weather. He maintains the truck and stays in close touch with its vital signs. This, too, is important. If the truck were to break down in the path of a tornado, Henry would have to get it going again, and fast. Most important, Craig Henry gathers on-the-scene live pictures, processes them down to a digital format, and uploads them to a satellite for broadcast on The Weather Channel.

The mobile studio is a little bit like an aircraft carrier in wartime: too valuable to expose to foreseeable dangers. And like a carrier, its job is to advance the battle, but not get in the middle of the battle. As Henry explains:

> This truck is my responsibility. The buck stops with me. I'm the one who's supposed to pull it out of harm's way. But I have lots of help, too. During hurricane season, I'm constantly on the phone with our hurricane experts, John Hope and Steve Lyons. They'll figure which areas are safe and unsafe, how much of a surge a particular area is supposed to get, and so on. And of course, I talk all the time with Patrick Walsh, our assignment manager, who ultimately controls where this truck goes. They're all talking back and forth, and we follow their lead. But if I see something like a tornado, we're out of there.

Tornadoes are astoundingly destructive, but the chances of getting picked up and tossed around by one are relatively small. The real threat that Henry keeps his eyes out for is hail, which tends to crop up all over Tornado Alley. The satellite dish atop the truck—a $30,000 item—was recently reinforced to withstand baseball-sized hail. Bigger than that, though, and Henry would be in trouble. The Weather Channel's live remotes from where the weather is happening might well be knocked off the air. So, too, would live storm feeds for ABC News and CONUS Communications, both of which have reciprocal arrangements with The Weather Channel.

Reprinted with permission.

So Henry has a strong aversion to hailstones. Having grown up in southern Louisiana, however, he admits to liking nothing better than a good hurricane. He began working for The Weather Channel the day the truck arrived in 1997 from Florida-based BAF Satellite & Technology Corporation, which outfitted the vehicle with both its external and internal dishes. The internal tracking DSS (digital satellite system) dish enables Henry to watch The Weather Channel as he heads into a storm. An accomplished photographer, he happily displays his fat portfolio of dramatic, weather-dominated prints. "That's Hurricane Bonnie," he says, pointing to one striking image. "And of course, that's Jim Cantore standing in the rain."

Henry spends a lot of time with Cantore and the other Weather Channel anchors who volunteer for on-the-scene live remotes. In less than four years, he has racked up 130,000 miles in the truck. During one five-day storm-chasing stretch in the summer of 2000, he traveled 4,200 miles: from Kansas into

Texas, through New Mexico and Colorado, then up to Nebraska and South Dakota, back down to Texas, and back up to Denver.

That trip involved one harrowing episode, which Henry narrates by talking his way through another spectacular print, this one featuring a green-black Midwestern sky that might have been lifted from the frames of Twister:

> The storm came out of Colorado towards us in Kansas, going about 70 miles per hour. We could see the whole supercell, probably around 60,000 feet tall. Spectacular! Here's the wall cloud that came over us. Here's the "hook," which is usually the signature that you get at the base of a supercell, where your fiercest weather is going to be, and where your tornado will usually drop out of.
>
> See this blurry spot? That's called "inflow"—it's actually dirt being sucked up into the cloud. Well, as soon as Jim and I started seeing that, we decided to pack it up. As we were leaving, that's when the pea-sized hail started to drop.
>
> Well, that storm got bigger and bigger, and all of a sudden, the worst part was passing right over us. We got hit with pea-sized hail. A little further down the road, it dropped baseball-sized hail. And another two miles away, it dropped an F-3 tornado. So. Safety's the first thing I think about. I take all kinds of precautions—and still, there are close calls.

Henry's wanderings are carefully tracked not only by his supervisors in Atlanta, but also by The Weather Channel's competitors. After all, The Weather Channel has a reputation for being in the right place at the right time and usually not in the wrong place at the wrong time. So one simple way to get great live footage is to go where Henry goes, and to break out the cameras when Henry does. Oftentimes, Henry and his on-camera meteorologist manage to get off one or two live shots in weather-lashed solitude before the competitors' trucks arrive. Competitors use The Weather Channel's cablecast images—and presumably some obliging local residents—to figure out exactly where Henry has parked the truck. They then rush to that spot in their own mobile studios and set up shop. When Henry decamps, he often finds the competitors trailing along behind him.

This creates the opportunity for a cat-and-mouse game, even though the "mouse" weighs northward of 28,000 pounds and is just over thirteen feet tall. When Hurricane Bonnie smashed into the southern coast of North Carolina on August 26, 1998, Henry and Cantore were looking for a likely spot to set up shop. Six competitors' trucks were already in position at the Hampton Inn in Atlantic Beach, and The Weather Channel's crew was reluctant to join them there.

At that point, a local resident and Weather Channel fan turned up. He had a house on the inlet side of the barrier beach, he told Henry, and he was planning to ride out the storm there. The Weather Channel was welcome to camp out at his house, he said. Henry was skeptical at first—do we really want to be out on a sandbar in a category 3 hurricane?—but eventually drove out to the beach to check out the location. The house turned out to be a two-story, L-shaped frame structure that was well built and reasonably sheltered, and provided great visual backdrops. Henry was able to back the mobile studio almost all the way into the house's garage. The onshore winds, already blowing at gale force, rushed over the top of the house, lofting flying debris well out into the yard and away from the truck.

It was practically indoor work. While Craig Henry watched from the relative comfort of the garage, Jim Cantore—wired for sound, and decked out in his trademark rain gear—would dash out into the yard, make his windblown report, and then duck back to safety.

Meanwhile, over at the Hampton Inn, no one could figure out exactly where The Weather Channel was broadcasting from. Gradually, though, answering that question became a secondary concern. By the luck of the draw, Bonnie had chosen to lash the Hampton Inn and its surroundings with a special fury. Flying debris knocked first one mobile unit off the air, and then another. One by one, The Weather Channel's competitors were being picked off by Mother Nature.

"We got real lucky that day," Henry concludes. "And that day, they didn't."

BEHIND THE BLUE WALL WITH PATRICK WALSH

"I went storm chasing once as a producer, and got caught in a tornado," recalls Patrick Walsh. He is smiling broadly, although with a hint of guilt. "And if I didn't have a wife and three children, I'd go out every single time."

Walsh, assignment manager in The Weather Channel's Production Department, works inside the suburban Atlanta office building alongside which Craig Henry parks his mobile studio. The building is The Weather Channel's headquarters, and it is Walsh who schedules Henry's jaunts in the network's million-dollar truck.

In many companies, the most interesting things happen on the upper floors. Not so at The Weather Channel. All things being equal, TV studios do better without windows. So most of the exciting activity that takes place in this building—the high-energy, trapeze-without-a-net stuff—takes place underground.

Walsh's desk is tucked into the semidarkness of the main control room. For most of his waking hours, Walsh is surrounded by banks of electronic machinery—fans whirring, lights winking. Through a large, thick-glassed window he can see the main set of The Weather Channel, familiar to millions of viewers.

Most striking about the set is the "blue wall"—the electric blue backdrop around which the on-camera meteorologists hover as they make their reports. It is a wall of illusion. To the viewer at home, it appears that the meteorologist is working with a series of maps and other images that are magically being projected on the wall. "In the Rockies," the weather anchor might be saying, gesturing toward a stunning graphic of the Continental Divide that seems to be behind her, "we're expecting unseasonably warm weather, and as a result, we may be looking at some substantial early snow melt." With a hand-held clicker—little more than a souped-up garage door opener, technologically speaking—she keeps the images coming at a steady pace, moving eastward across the country with details of local weather conditions.

Through it all, despite all the gestures, clicks, and enthusiastic narration, the wall stays resolutely blue in the eyes of everyone in the studio. How can this be? It's an old television trick, invented decades ago as a way of pumping better graphics out to viewers. Elsewhere in the building, in the bowels of the studio's powerful computers, the images of the meteorologist and the Rockies are merged electronically and in real time. The meteorologist participates in this sleight-of-hand by keeping an eye on one of two monitors just off-screen. That monitor shows the live signal—the merged images—that will be beamed out by satellite a split second later. With a little practice, the meteorologist can use the monitor's image to orient herself, and to point with reasonable precision at a "Denver" that doesn't actually show up anywhere on the wall.

Patrick Walsh, a meteorologist by training, has never stood in front of the blue wall. He spent a year at CNN in production before coming to The Weather Channel in 1989. He worked as one of dozens of off-camera meteorologists, doing all the kinds of number-crunching, image generation, and analysis that are needed to keep meteorologists on the air twenty-four hours a day, seven days a week. The on-camera personalities are only the visible part of a team of people—including meteorologists, graphic artists, producers, and executive producers—who generate the unending flow of The Weather Channel's product.

Part of that product is video footage, including the kinds of dramatic storm-related material that Craig Henry and his roving meteorologists beam back to Atlanta. When John Coleman was setting up his all-weather cable network in the early 1980s, he laid down an iron-clad policy: no remote feeds—that is, no live broadcasts from the field. He had good reason to formulate the policy. Although potentially dramatic, remote feeds sometimes failed to deliver the goods, and they were almost always expensive. The wisdom of Coleman's edict was borne out by CNN's experience in the spring of 1982, when Argentina and Great Britain became embroiled in an undeclared war over the remote Falkland Islands. CNN won kudos for its extensive on-the-scene coverage—and nearly broke the bank doing so.

Gradually, though, as a result of competitive pressures, The Weather Channel moved away from the no-remote-feed policy. As professional video equipment became cheaper and more portable—and as consumer camcorders became ubiquitous—viewers came to expect great visuals of severe weather on The Weather Channel. If they didn't find these scenes there, they would look for them somewhere else.

By the mid-1990s, The Weather Channel was scrambling to keep up with these expectations, although with no specific budget or equipment allocated to the task. Then, in 1996, a variety of severe-weather conditions taxed the network's limited resources to the maximum. That experience led to the purchase of the mobile studio, soon to be piloted by Craig Henry. It also led to the creation of a formal budget and a new "assignment manager" position within the production department. Based on the 1996 experience, seventy "crew days" were allocated to live coverage.

Patrick Walsh was named assignment manager. In some ways, Walsh was an odd choice, given that he had no news experience. But in recent years he had spent time informally helping the executive producers in the program department decide how and when to put crews in the field. And perhaps more important, Walsh was an experienced meteorologist, and that was what The Weather Channel needed in that job. As he explains:

The challenge is to assess the meteorological importance of a given situation, put it in a news context, and decide whether or not we cover it. Well, if you had only news experience, you'd have to listen to whoever was talking to you, and here, you might have between five and ten meteorologists giving you their opinions. What I'm able to do is listen to all these opinions, assess the computer models, and make the call as to whether or not something is worth covering.

Since that time, the live-coverage budget has grown to three hundred crew days per year. Competition from both cable and broadcast networks has continued to intensify. For example, on May 3, 1999, eight supercell thunderstorms generated at least fifty-nine tornadoes in central Oklahoma. By coincidence, Walsh had sent a field producer and photographer to Oklahoma City to do some prep work for the kickoff of the tornado season. They happened to land two hours before a devastating tornado struck, and they were able to shoot some terrifying and awe-inspiring footage.

Walsh recalls what happened next:

They fed the video back to us, and—unbeknownst to any of us—one of our competitors was looking in, and took the live feed without checking with anyone.

Well, I happened to see this on the bank of monitors behind me, and I realized it was our video, showing up on our competitor's broadcast. I happened to be on the phone with our field producer, so I asked him to stop and recue. So they stopped, and sure enough, the video stopped on our competitor's station, and started up again as soon as ours did.

I blew a gasket. I got on the phone with these characters, and demanded that they get our stuff off their network. Somehow, it took them forty-five minutes to get around to it. Well, the next time they called and asked for a favor—it was the Saturday morning when Hurricane Bret made landfall, as I recall very well, and they wanted some of our pictures—I said, "Gee, guys; I wish we could help you with that!"

Hurricane Bret hit Mexico and Texas in late August 1999. Although Bret eventually missed major population centers and petered out in the Texas ranch country, it at first appeared to be a killer storm, and people on both ends of The Weather Channel link—Atlanta and the Gulf Coast—were keyed up. At one point, watching a live feed, Walsh and his colleagues in Atlanta were horrified to see six waterspouts touching down just offshore from The Weather Channel's field crew. "We told 'em to hit cover," Walsh recalls.

But even without threats to life and limb, having live crews in the field during what Walsh calls a "weather situation" can be extremely taxing. The Weather Channel broadcasts live continuously—not just at 5, 6, and 11 P.M.—and live reports from the field must be worked into the programming on a real-time basis. Meanwhile, the next day's activities have to be blocked out, based on the latest computer models. Where should the crews head next? How should they get there? Where should they stay? ("In a weather situation," says Walsh, "the Internet is my best friend.") Every six hours, a new run of the computer models comes up, and previous plans may hold up—or they may wind up in the scrap basket. "It gets really crazy," Walsh says with evident understatement.

Other parts of Walsh's job are less competitive and less dramatic, but no less important to The Weather Channel's cablecast product. Fans of the network appreciate front-line images of severe weather. Ratings go up all over the country whenever a hurricane hits the Southeast, or a tornado ravages the Midwest, or a snowstorm buries the Northeast. At the same time, viewers want to see their own weather on The Weather Channel, severe or not. They want reassurance that The Weather Channel is in touch with their local situation. Is dense fog blanketing half of Delaware, their home state? That ought to show up on The

Weather Channel. Is Minneapolis enjoying its fifteenth day in a row of spectacular spring weather? There ought to be some footage of the daffodils that are blooming this morning at the Walker Arts Center.

As recently as the mid-1990s, the network used a video service to procure noncritical footage—say, of that fog in Delaware, or that sunny day in Minneapolis. But the video-procurement budget was small, and usually no more than one piece of video was purchased per day. As a result, a given video clip might run for two or three days. Only one staffer was assigned the job of "bringing up the video"—that is, patching video clips into live broadcasts—and that person worked only from 9 A.M. to 6 P.M., Monday through Friday. During off-hours and weekends, the use of video footage tailed off dramatically.

Beginning in 1997, concurrent with the upgrading of the live-remote activity, The Weather Channel began investing heavily in the purchase or licensing of third-party video. Walsh got a big budget increase for this purpose, and he soon entered into an agreement with ABC to purchase a half-dozen clips daily. The "feed bay" went from that lone individual to three full-time and three part-time people, who collectively staff the desks from 4 A.M. to 11 P.M., Monday through Sunday.

All this licensed and purchased footage is now being procured with an eye toward other products and platforms. When The Weather Channel de-emphasized long-format productions in the late 1980s, the network's video library was allowed to atrophy. Recently, though, programmers have reversed course and have made a renewed commitment to long-format pieces. Today, two people work full-time securing rights to prime footage—not only for use in close-to-real-time, but also for subsequent uses. "It's extremely important to us," Walsh explains, "that this stuff is documented, and saved, and repurposed—not only for our new documentary programs, but also for the Web platform.

"All of what we do," he says, "is part of a bigger picture."

THE 4:00 P.M. SHOW

Fifty feet away from the desk from which Walsh makes his calls
and dispatches his troops, a woman is seated at a desk in a
cramped bullpen area of the studio. She is intently scrolling
through a document on an oversized computer monitor. A
middle-aged man is seated in the adjacent cubicle, talking with
a visitor. Both are dressed and coifed like television personalities,
which is in fact what they are: Weather Channel on-camera
meteorologists.

In this corner of the studio, the light level is about halfway
between the extremes of Walsh's dark lair and the bright lights
of the main set. Here the meteorologists who are working a shift
talk with their producers, run through the scripts for the upcoming hour, and rest briefly between on-air stints.

Jeff Morrow is resting. His teammate and cubicle neighbor,
Vivian Brown, is prepping for the 4:00 P.M. show.

Morrow has been an on-camera meteorologist since 1986.
He politely fields questions about his professional life. Like most
Weather Channel on-air talent, he is eager to talk about the
weather, but beyond bare biographical details, not particularly
interested in talking about himself. Every once in a while during
the interview process, he casts a casual eye toward a nearby digital readout, which is clicking down the seconds to when he's due
back on the air.

Even among The Weather Channel's seasoned pros, Morrow
is considered a cool character. "Excuse me just a sec," he says. He
stands up, plugs in his wireless mike, puts his suit coat back on,
and walks directly on camera—live to mid-afternoon viewers—
and begins his segment without missing a beat.

Vivian Brown takes up the slack with Morrow's visitor.
Brown also came to The Weather Channel in 1986, but originally
had no intention of going under the bright lights. She studied
meteorology at Jackson State University, in a program that
emphasized the *science* of the weather, as opposed to its presenta-

tion. She came to The Weather Channel as an off-camera meteorologist, a role that she performed for about two and a half
years.

In her second year in Atlanta, she became interested in trying her hand at the on-air side of the shop. She talked informally
with several of the on-camera staff, who encouraged her in her
newfound ambition. She applied for the "OCM" apprenticeship
program, in which experienced on-camera meteorologists work
with younger people to develop their presentation skills. Very
soon thereafter, she found herself presenting the nation's weather
to millions. "My personal story," she says, "is one of positive
inroads, as far as diversity at The Weather Channel goes."

Right now, she explains, she is reviewing the proposed elements of the 4:00 P.M. show. This particular day, everyone around
the shop seems to have agreed, is one of the most boring
weather days of the year. Across the vast stretches of North
America, literally nothing is happening. There's some chance that
a thunderstorm off the Gulf Coast of the Florida will come
ashore. There's also a chance that it won't. Absent any current
weather situations, the producers and weather anchors have to
lean heavily on the aftermath of recent weather (floods in the
Northeast) or the consequences of no weather (droughts and
fires in the Southeast).

Another youngish women approaches Brown's cubicle. This
is Valerie Butler, a producer, who has produced the "rundown"
(or script) for the 4:00 show, and who now seeks Brown's reactions and—she hopes—her concurrence. This is a delicate balance, something like the Joint Chiefs of Staff approaching the
president.

History might seem to work against an easy collaboration.
For most of The Weather Channel's history, on-camera meteorologists were their own producers. They followed their own
instincts, spec'd and stacked their own slides in the computers,
and usually worked without partners, producers, or directors. The
results were often good but sometimes less than good. Gradually,

producers and later executive producers and directors were brought in to help create a more professional and consistent product.

Over time, conventions were established. Except on the deep graveyard shift, for example, everyone got a partner. Based on longstanding broadcast-television wisdom, these teams were almost always of mixed gender. The "two-shot"—the opening shot of two weather anchors, one female and one male—became standard. The dialogue for the opening two-shot and eventually also for the closing shot was scripted and put up on a TelePrompTer. The "rundown" script was introduced, showing time allotments for each segment down to the second. Two clocks were added to the monitors that the meteorologists used to orient themselves to the blue wall: one on the left side displaying how far the program was past the top of the hour, and the other on the right side showing how much time remained before the next commercial break.

As a result of all these changes, the free-form, sometimes amateurish presentations of The Weather Channel's early days became less commonplace. An undisciplined on-camera meteorologist soon learned that running overtime cut into the time that was available to his or her partner for the next segment. Gradually, discipline was embraced.

Today, producers put together segments in their entirety. Three producers work each shift, each doing a ninety-minute increment on a rotating basis. The exception is the window between 1 A.M. to 5 A.M., during which the on-camera meteorologists act as their own producers. The producers—under the direction of an executive producer—get a ten-minute briefing from the off-camera meteorologists (the "mets"), who bring them up to speed on the continuing and emerging weather stories that are likely to be featured in the upcoming hours.

Following the briefing, each producer sits down at a computer and generates the rundown, using a sequence of events that is by now very much standardized. Each event has a name—

the "tease one," the "bump," the commercial break time—and normally comes at about the same point in each sequence. The producer checks to see if any live reports are coming in from the field, and also finds out what other video may be available.

So the producer has enormous clout. Nevertheless, when the producer approaches the weather anchor—who is the one who actually has to get up there in front of the blue wall, and the one who will have to wing it when something unexpected happens—tact and courtesy are in order.

"Here's what we're thinking," producer Butler says to meteorologist Brown. "We're starting with the Northeast and Midwest, and Jeff Morrow is going to do those together. Since we don't have a lot going on today, our main thrust is going to be the Connecticut flooding. We're going to try to get in this animation explaining how the Connecticut River is rising, and we're going to talk about Hartford and when they're going to see the crest.

"Jeff's going to talk a little bit about the Midwest flooding, too, because that's still an issue. You'll take the south, and for now, you have Atlanta video. At 4:30, we're probably going to get some video of fires. We think we've found some fire footage from Florida. You can talk about how the rain helped yesterday in Miami—"

"But we had that earlier," Brown interjects.

"Yes, but that was yesterday's video," Butler continues. "We're trying to get some new stuff. I'm writing that up for you now. We're focusing on Interstate 1, which was closed down due to the fires. It's now open, so we're trying to work that video in, and get out the news about the road re-opening."

"Would that be in addition to the Atlanta footage?"

"No, we'll swap that out, since we've been using that all day. Then you've got the forecast, and you'll have to toss back early to Jeff so he can do his Storm Week tease. Then we tease and we're out. So it's an easy kind of day." Brown nods slowly, fixing in her mind these minor adjustments, and making a mental note that it may not be until the last minute that she learns whether her next segment will include balmy weather in Georgia or smoky interstates in Florida.

"So I have only one more item up here to be loaded," adds Butler, "and that's current U.S. temps. Obviously, that's your opportunity to talk about how nice it is, just about everywhere. So if that sounds good, we'll go ahead and get that in."

Again, Brown nods her agreement, and Butler heads off to make her last-minute adjustments and track down the Florida fire footage. The clip is not yet in hand, but it's scheduled to air within the hour. Before she is out of sight, another young woman approaches Brown's cubicle. Tanya Lieberman, a director who works in Master Control, wants to know when Brown wants to use the "Atlanta nice" footage in her upcoming segment. Brown picks a slot, and Lieberman heads off to arrange for the insertion.

INDEX